The Rebuttal

A Biblical Response
Exposing The Deceptive Logic
Of Anti-Gay Theology

The Rebuttal

A Biblical Response
Exposing The Deceptive Logic
Of Anti-Gay Theology

Pastor Romell D. Weekly

F
Judah First Publishing
JudahFirst.org

This book is dedicated to the members of New Revelation Christian Church, who have taken the difficult journey from legalism to liberty and have become a better community of believers as a result. Your pastor loves you more than words can say!

Contents

Section Three
Comprehending And Dealing With Sexuality

Appendices

Introduction

Turn the other cheek... I've seen and heard that phrase used on countless occasions as a plea for Christians to allow themselves to be abused. Some in the extreme-rightwing of the Church have used it to convince wives to remain with their physically abusive husbands, thereby facilitating that abuse and reinforcing the husbands' authority as the heads of their respective houses. On the other philosophical extreme, it's been used to compel Christians to live pacifist lives—to never fight back when attacked, whether individually or as a nation.

Personally, I have a problem with both of these extremes. They're born of a literalistic approach to Christ's words that ultimately miss the actual point He was making. We are not to be people who are always on the "mark", just itching for someone to push our "go" button, giving us an excuse to fight. We're to be patient, kind, forgiving, and full of care and concern, even for those who wrong us.

But are we to sit back and allow people to lob unrelenting barrages of physical or verbal assaults on us, all without response? I'd say no. While love compels us to the virtues mentioned above, it also must necessarily challenge us to take defensive action when other means of diffusing destructive situations have failed. No one should feel obliged to allow him/herself to be assaulted, except when there is a greater purpose at work (e.g. the arrest and crucifixion of Jesus).

Think of the parable of the Good Samaritan. Must we wonder how the story would have progressed had this Samaritan happened upon the scene while the assault was still taking place? Should we think that such a man—a *good* man—would stand there and wait for the assaulters to finish the deed before demonstrating his "goodness" by nursing wounds he could have prevented in the first place?

Surely, the same love that breeds mercy and compassion must also compel good people to take action when injustices occur. Let's remember that the same Jesus who taught His followers to turn the other cheek, and even allowed Himself to be abused by His Jewish and Roman captors, violently cleansed the Temple of the injustices taking place there. The same God who said that vengeance was His alone also commanded the Israelites to take up arms and fight when the situation called for it. Ultimately then, Jesus' teaching was not a treatise against defending oneself or others against various forms of abuse; rather, it was a warning against taking personal revenge, and against reflexive responses to mistreatment.

This is why it's important for us to be students of Scripture. One can take a seemingly obvious statement like "turn the other cheek" and produce disastrous results, all through misinterpretation. We must, consequently, be people of balance—never sold to one extreme or the other, but always committed to a reasoned, sober approach to the teachings of Scripture.

This is why I wrote *The Rebuttal.* I don't consider myself "good" in the truest sense of the word; but in my quest to *be* good, I can't sit back and allow to go unanswered the misinterpretations of God's word in the abuse and condemnation of gay people. How could I ever hear the words, "Well done, good and faithful servant," if I passively allowed such devastating rhetoric to go unopposed?

But, fighting back is not a matter of emotionalism. It's not a matter of responding in kind. It's a matter of presenting the *true* teachings of Scripture, and allowing God's word to fight on our behalf. So, while some may choose to fight this war in the courts or in the social sphere, my burden is to fight it in the Church, using the sword of the Spirit—the word of God.

While I wanted to produce a much shorter work, the number of pages that follow are an unavoidable consequence of my desire to offer thorough responses to some of the more common arguments used to condemn homosexuality. But, rather than respond in general, I felt it important to deal with specific points raised by those who have put themselves on the frontline of this theological conflict.

In particular, this rebuttal responds to arguments raised in five books, each of which presents the traditional perspective against homosexuality.

II

1. Dallas, Joe. *The Gay Gospel?*. Harvest House Publishers, 1996/2007.

2. Dobson, Dr. James. *Marriage Under Fire*. Multnomah Publishers, 2004.

3. Gagnon, Robert A. J. *The Bible and Homosexual Practice*. Abingdon Press, 2001.

4. Schmidt, Thomas E. *Straight and Narrow?*. InterVarsity Press, 1995.

5. White, James R. & Jeffrey D. Niell, *The Same-Sex Controversy*. Bethany House Publishers, 2002.

Most arguments levied by traditionalists were addressed in one or more of these books. It is, therefore, my hope that you find in the pages that follow a shield against every misinterpretation of Scripture that will ever be presented to you in opposition to homosexuality.

Perhaps you still operate under the misconception that Scripture condemns homosexuality, as I did only a few years ago. I pray that this humble addition to other affirming works that have preceded it will help to free you and those you converse with in the days to come from traditionalism and legalistic approaches to God's word. May you come to know it as it was always intended to be—a source of life and liberty, rather than judgment and condemnation.

I encourage you to read with an open mind and a sincere heart. If it is the case that my arguments do not reasonably refute the anti-gay positions presented, so be it; but you are charged to consider the words objectively and follow the evidence wherever it leads. In the end, we should all want to *be* right, rather than simply have our existing beliefs vindicated.

And finally, please don't approach this as just another book. Consider it a study guide. Have a pen, paper, highlighter, and, most importantly, a Bible on hand whenever the pages fall open. Challenge the claims referenced in the profiled books, as well as those I make in rebuttal. Pray and ask the Spirit to guide you into the truth, not at the suspension of logic and reason, but in conjunction with it.

I look forward to sharing the self-defeating arguments offered by those who consider themselves authorities on what the Bible says about homosexuality. May you see through the veneer of religiosity and face-value legalism they so incessantly rely on, and let the rightly divided word of truth make you free!

Section

1

Where The Problems Lie

1
Homosexuality 101
Relearning What It Means To Be Gay

As a gay man, I've had a vested interest in consuming tons of information on homosexuality, particularly from a biblical perspective. I've read many affirming and non-affirming material, and have found one fact that characterizes the non-affirming material above all others—the writers do not have a solid grasp of the nature of sexual orientation. So, before we get our hands dirty in the arguments and counter-arguments surrounding this controversial issue, it's important that we establish precisely what it is we're talking about when referring to homosexuality, or to being gay.

I remember conversations with family members just after I came out. I'd mistakenly taken it as a foregone conclusion that they understood what it meant to be gay, even though they still didn't agree with it theologically. I learned from those conversations that it's better to not assume anything when it comes to a subject as engrained in people's spiritual and social psyche as homosexuality.

The problem is that most people don't form their opinions on personal observations. If such were the case, it would be easy to change their hearts and minds by simply introducing them to one or more gay people. Their new experiences would compel at least some degree of shifting in their worldview.

Unfortunately, religious and conservative leaders have fed Christians on a healthy diet of misinformation for so long that it will take a lot more than personally knowing a few gay people to break through all of the propaganda. And propaganda is exactly what it is because what gay people are really about is worlds apart from what people are told on talk radio, in books, and particularly, in their local churches.

The first step in relearning is to *un*learn the misleading dogma. This is, without a doubt, the most difficult step. I remember my days as a choir teacher and director. One of the worst things I could do was teach the wrong lyric or vocal part to the choir, only to have to correct it at the following rehearsal. It always took longer for the correction to work its way through the choir members' minds than when they first learned the song.

So, if you're straight and have preconceptions about what it is to be gay, I want to begin by stating that I understand the difficulty in washing your mind of your existing beliefs, and allowing yourself to look at this issue afresh. I can only challenge you for the sake of truth, for the sake of love for your neighbor (which is commanded by Christ), and just for the sake of our common humanity to get a picture of gay people *from* gay people. Reading this chapter with an open mind is a great first step.

What is it about being gay that we need to relearn, exactly? Unfortunately, we have to begin at square one. Anti-gay Christians grossly misunderstand and misrepresent even the most fundamental aspect of being gay.

We begin with the definition. When people say that they are gay, what exactly are they saying? How much of their story is contained in those three short words, *I am gay?*

Contrary to what some people claim, "gay" (more precisely, "homosexual") describes a single thing—same-sex attractions, be they emotional or sexual. These attractions aren't chosen, as though people decide one day the type of person they find attractive. They are an inherent part of our internal makeup, just as opposite-sex attractions are in the case of heterosexuals. This is why they're referred to as an orientation. People are naturally *oriented* toward one sex or the other (or, in some cases, both). The morality of such attractions is another issue altogether. Before we broach that subject, we must understand that *being* gay only describes the attractions themselves.

Think about how people are naturally oriented to either right or left-handedness, while a few are ambidextrous. The same can be said about sexual orientation. Ironically, there was a time when Christians believed right-handedness was somehow morally superior to left-handedness, even to the point that they believed left-handed people were of the devil. Reason changed the nonsense surrounding hand orientation. By God's grace, it'll change the modern nonsense surrounding sexual orientation.

Personally, I came to the realization that I liked boys in "that way" fairly young. Note that I came to *realize* my attractions. I didn't choose them. Anyway, I remember an incident when I was in the fourth or fifth grade (somewhere between ages 9-11). A group of us kids built a makeshift clubhouse near the school grounds, which happened to be around the corner from my house. One day, one of the boys brought his older brother's dirty magazine to the clubhouse. They drooled over the pictures, but I was completely uninterested. Of course, I feigned excitement; but as soon as I felt it was okay, I told the guys I had to go home. It turns out that was a pretty good call because they were caught later on by a school official and were in serious trouble. Unfortunately, they ratted me out as a member of the club. So, I, too, was called into the principal's office. I lied and told Principal Davis that I'd left because I knew it wasn't right to look at the pictures. She said that because I did the right thing, she wouldn't get my mother involved. But, the other parents were called, and they had to attend a counseling session on sexuality with their boys. Little did Mrs. Davis know that the sexual content wasn't what I objected to, but rather, the sex of the models.

This is my earliest memory of liking other boys, which means that my same-sex attractions predate this event by any number of months or years. I share this anecdote to point out how young some gay people are when we begin to experience our attractions.

At the time, I didn't fully understand what it meant to be gay, but I was still too embarrassed to tell my friends that I didn't like the images they were gawking over. I knew from overheard discussions and television that I did *not* want to like boys. Besides, the clubhouse incident made me the odd boy out, and I certainly didn't like that.

I wish people understood that we didn't choose to develop the attractions we have. For my part, I fought these desires with everything within me for two decades. I convinced myself that having a girlfriend would change things, but it didn't. I then began thinking that having sex with a girl would make the difference. But, I came to find that that, too, was a misplaced hope.

It's easy for people who don't understand what being gay is like to say that I simply didn't try hard enough to be delivered; but I know the tears I cried. I know the rituals of baptism I went through both publicly and privately, attempting to wash the gay away. I've blessed myself with anointed oil, prayed in English and in tongues, fasted, made promises to God and to myself… all in my attempt to be what I thought He wanted me to be—straight. So, it betrays an arrogant assumption on the part of some in telling us that we must not have wanted deliverance badly enough because if we did, we'd have it. If sexual orientation were a choice, I guarantee you that I would be straight today, for I chose heterosexuality time and again, but to no avail. Only within the past few years have I learned to be thankful for my orientation, but I certainly wasn't thankful for my first 28 years.

While we're defining what it is to be gay, it's important to note a difference between how we, as gay people, describe ourselves, and the rhetoric people are fed in ex-gay ministries and the like. For us, gay is generally the same as saying "homosexual." The words are often used interchangeably to refer to one's attractions; although because "homosexual" sounds so clinical, being used often by anti-gay Christians to describe us, most of us prefer the term "gay".

It's important that you don't assume that people embrace their orientation simply because they identify as gay. The term is a personal acknowledgement of existent attractions, whether those attractions are welcome or not. In other words, some gay people don't *want* to be gay, yet acknowledge that they are, nonetheless.

I'm homosexual. I'm gay. I'm same-gender loving. I have same-sex attractions. I struggle with same-sex attractions. I'm tempted with same-sex attractions… Each of these statements conveys precisely the same reality. The latter two simply dance around the controversy of orientation, making it more palatable to our "ex-gay" brethren.

Gay people exist in every walk of life. We're in every nation, religion, financial bracket, and every other conceivable people-group. Politically, there are gay liberals and gay conservatives; gay Democrats *and* gay Republicans. Religiously, there are gay laity and gay leaders. There are promiscuous gay people and gay virgins. Gay people are all over the spectrum—*every* spectrum. Some affirm homosexuality, while others don't. Heck, there are even gay people who are also straight! They're called bisexuals.

How is all of this possible? It's simple really. Being gay does not dictate a person's social worldview, political persuasion, religious beliefs, sexual activities, personal tastes, eye color, or handedness. It only describes a person's existent (rather than desired) attractions.

Consequently, a ridiculous myth that must be debunked is the so-called "gay lifestyle." There is no such thing! How can there be, when "lifestyle" is indicative of a manner of living, whereas "gay" says nothing whatsoever about how a person lives, or even how a person *believes* he/she should or should not live?

One can speak of a *Christian* lifestyle because the Bible offers principles surrounding how Christians should live. No such standard exists for gay people; so the term "gay lifestyle" is nothing more than a way of rousing antipathy toward the gay community.

Among the anti-gay rhetoric that irritates me the most, the "gay lifestyle" falls within the top 3. Another phrase that makes my blood boil is "gay agenda." Once again, there's no such thing. No gay people are sitting around a conference table somewhere discussing strategies to take over the world. There is no agenda that gay people are advancing, with the sole exception of opposing discrimination based on sexual orientation (and oftentimes, gender identity). If that qualifies as an agenda—with its patently negative connotation—we've got a long way to go as a society.

But, I guess if there was a Black agenda during the 50's and 60's, maybe there *is* a gay agenda today. We may not be getting hit with water cannons, harassed by the police as the normal course, or have a cultural history that includes slavery in the relatively recent past, but that does not subtract from the fact that we are, in fact, discriminated against in many aspects of social and religious life. Many of the benefits associated with marriage are out of reach, we're denied housing and jobs, and we're ridiculed in the public square with slurs like "fag"—the "nigger" of the gay community.

Ultimately, the only thing most gay people want from society is to be treated with the same respect as others. We're not asking people to affirm us, only to respect us as their neighbors, co-workers, and fellow citizens. Is that really asking too much?

Another misconception that needs to be dispelled is that gay people are out to "convert" others. I'll deal with the notion of orientational conversion in Chapter 9; but I think it's important to state here and now that while people choose the sexual activity they engage in (behavior), sexual attraction (orientation) is not something that can be opted for, or planted into someone. So, I can assure you that gay people are not out trying to recruit your children.

Having said that, let me also state that although I'm openly gay, straight women have flirted with me, knowing full well that I'm not straight. They did this not to convert me, but simply in good-natured fun. I say this to acknowledge that it's very possible that gay people hit on straight people. I did in my younger days. But, that doesn't betray some conspiratorial plot to change people's orientation. It betrays human nature, and the often-flirtatious social climate that exists today.

This isn't to say that I believe the flirtatious nature of our culture is a good thing. In fact, I believe it plays a role in some of the poor sexual choices people make, be it premarital or extramarital sex (neither of which I believe are moral acts). I only say this to acknowledge reality, and to point out that this does not indicate intent on the part of gay people to convert straight people. To make such a case isn't fair, and is just a scare tactic.

For the sake of clarity, I should also mention that "gay" has both narrow, and wide meanings, depending on the context. It can refer to homosexual males, as in the case of the acronym GLBT (Gay, Lesbian, Bisexual, Transgender); however, it can also refer to both male and female homosexuals. In its broadest sense, it can refer to anyone who is not solely attracted to people of the same-sex—a reference that also includes bisexuals. In the pages that follow, I use the term to refer to both male and female homosexuals.

I hope that if any of the stereotypes or misinformation I've pointed out describes things you believe about gay people, you'll take a moment and reflect on what I've said before reading on. This is important because until you see gay people simply as people who happen to have same-sex attractions, it will be too easy to lump us all together and demonize us, as so many have done and continue to do.

Jesus commanded us to love our neighbor as ourselves. In fact, that command is second only to loving God. So, when I say, "For the love of Pete, stop stereotyping us," I really mean it. Pete is gay, and he's tired of being viewed as a particular type of person based on that single aspect of who he is. There's so much about him that's worthy of being known. Don't minimize him to a sexual orientation. Get to know him as a person—as a multifaceted human being who adds his uniqueness to the vast diversity of the human community.

Let love for your gay neighbors compel you to get to know us as people who just happen to be gay, rather than as gay people. It's not as though the word describes anything about us beyond our attractions.

2

Gay Christians
An Oxymoron Or The Gospel Truth?

Although I came out of the closet only a few years ago, I'd already come to acknowledge the fact that I was gay at about the age of 12. I knew I liked boys before then, but I didn't understand it to mean that I was gay until later. Now, don't confuse acknowledge with accept. Although I had my share of boyfriends, I didn't want to be gay. In fact, most of my relationships ended precisely because I was trying to be straight... again!

During all of that time, though, one thing I never doubted was the fact that I was a born again Christian who was totally in love with Jesus Christ. I knew He lived in me. I could feel His presence, challenging me to draw closer and closer, compelling me to study His word, and ultimately filling me with His Spirit.

Now, fast forward to age 28/29. I undertook what was, ironically, my first in-depth Bible study on homosexuality. Although I knew where the passages were, could quote each one, and could even deliver a convincing message on them based on what I believed at the time, I hadn't *studied* the passages in all those previous years. During my examination, I began consuming as much information as possible by purchasing books on both sides of the issue, critically thinking through everything I read.

During my quest, I was presented with a particular argument from the non-affirming side over and over again—that it wasn't possible for someone to be truly saved and gay at the same time... that while it was possible for a person to be gay and *then* become a Christian, the two states couldn't co-exist. I knew that this couldn't be further from the truth. Not only did my own relationship with God dictate the falsehood of this claim, but also, everything I've ever read in the Bible concerning salvation left that argument utterly impotent.

The anti-gay crowd seemed either unwilling or unable to believe that a person could actually be both a Christian and a homosexual simultaneously. Here are but a few of the many examples of this line of reasoning.

> "Most conservative Christians—myself included—believe homosexuality in any form is a violation of biblical standards. And for that reason we don't feel that 'gay' and 'Christian' are compatible."[1]

> "The term 'Christian homosexual'... is an oxymoron, just as using 'Christian inventor of evil' (Ro. 1:30) or 'Christian who practices regular wickedness' (Ro. 1:29) would violate all canons of logic."[2]

The problem with this line of thinking goes way beyond the issue of homosexuality. It pierces the heart of the most fundamental and important doctrine in Christianity. It's the doctrine that defines our faith, setting it apart from every other religion on the face of the earth, including the other two great religions, Judaism and Islam. This doctrine is soteriology—the doctrine of salvation.

As I continued to read about how gay people couldn't be Christian until they became straight, what vexed me was not personal offense at the notion that they didn't think I was a Christian. I knew I was, and that was the bottom line. What weighed so heavily on my heart was that either 1) these Christian leaders had a horrifically skewed understanding of the very basis of the Christian faith—the free gift of salvation, or 2) these leaders understood salvation just fine, but their negative feelings about homosexuality rose to such a level that they didn't think Jesus' blood powerful enough to endure the "sin" of homosexuality. Either way, I had a major problem with the trend I was seeing.

---

[1] *The Gay Gospel?*, 62.
[2] *The Same-Sex Controversy*, 137.

This issue has nothing to do with whether homosexuality is or is not a sin. For the sake of discussion, let's assume for the remainder of this chapter that it *is* a sin. Regardless, the belief that someone cannot be gay and saved simultaneously is contrary to what Christ accomplished in the shedding of His blood on the cross—as though one of the qualifications for receiving salvation is being straight. We qualified for a savior precisely because of the presence of sin in our lives, and as sin continues to linger, we continue to qualify for His saving grace—a grace that we must all depend on until the day this corruptible has put on incorruption (1Co. 15:53-54).

When considering such a proposition, one is left to wonder if there are certain sins that cannot co-exist with salvation. Are there certain sins that have more power in their evil than the blood of Jesus has in its good? Do certain sins diminish the efficacy of Calvary? According to some, the answer is yes; yet if you ask this same question outside of a context of homosexuality, they'd likely answer in the negative. Regardless, Scripture teaches nothing of the sort!

"For by grace you have been saved through faith; and that not of yourselves, it is the gift of God; [9] not as a result of works, so that no one may boast."
Ephesians 2:8-9

"My little children, I am writing these things to you so that you may not sin. And if anyone sins, we have an Advocate with the Father, Jesus Christ the righteous; [2] and He Himself is the propitiation [atonement] for our sins; and not for ours only, but also for those of the whole world."
1 John 2:1-2

"He saved us, not on the basis of deeds which we have done in righteousness, but according to His mercy, by the washing of regeneration and renewing by the Holy Spirit, [6] whom He poured out upon us richly through Jesus Christ our Savior, [7] so that being justified by His grace we would be made heirs according to the hope of eternal life."
Titus 3:5-7

The very essence of soteriology is that not a single human being ever to have lived—save God in the flesh—deserves or has earned salvation. Isaiah 64:6 says that all of our righteous deeds are as filthy rags before God. In effect, our best isn't much better than our worst in comparison to the high standard that our holy God requires of us. So powerless are we to meet this standard that God had to come to earth and exist as a human being in order to meet it for us!

Now, because we so desperately cling to the blood of Jesus, which ever serves as the atoning sacrifice for our sins, no one has a cause for boasting (Eph. 2:9); yet boasting is precisely what many Christians do when they claim that somehow, gay people cannot be saved as long as they're still gay, even though they themselves are saved and yet still have sin in *their* lives.

> *"If we say that we have no sin, we are deceiving ourselves*
> *and the truth is not in us."*
> *1 John 1:8*

The only way someone can claim that gay people aren't saved and saved people aren't gay is to conclude that 1) they themselves are not saved, seeing as they also have sin in their lives, or 2) while they may have sin in their lives, at least theirs is not as bad as being gay.

On the first point, I seriously doubt people would call their own salvation into question. They're like the Pharisees of old—quick to point out the problems in other people's lives, and slow to focus on their own. Sure, they give the veneer of humility by calling attention to the fact that they still sin, but they quickly turn it around and make the issue about gay people. God, however, doesn't have so favorable a view of those who consider other people's sins worse than their own.

> *"I have spread out My hands all day long to a rebellious*
> *people... [5] Who say, 'Keep to yourself, do not come near*
> *me, For I am holier than you!' These are smoke in My*
> *nostrils, A fire that burns all the day."*
> *Isaiah 65:2a, 5*

*"Why do you look at the speck that is in your brother's eye,
but do not notice the log that is in your own eye? [4] Or how
can you say to your brother, 'Let me take the speck out of
your eye,' and behold, the log is in your own eye? [5] You
hypocrite, first take the log out of your own eye, and then you
will see clearly to take the speck out of your brother's eye."*
Matthew 7:3-5

In no uncertain terms, God declares that people who believe themselves to be holier than others anger Him. Why? Because all of us are filthy before Him unless and until we baptize ourselves in the blood of Jesus, so having our sins washed away.

The simple fact is that everyone, Christian or not, gay or not, has sin in their lives. This is testified to in 1John 1:8 and Romans 3:23. Therefore, the implication of what Jesus said in Matthew 7:5 was not that once you get rid of the sin in your life, you can go ahead and focus on other people's sin. It wasn't even that it's okay to focus on other people's *big* sin (the log), as long as you only have *small* sin (the speck). His point was simple. "You'll never be without sin, so quit bothering about everybody else's and focus on your own!" If you start reading at verse one, you'll see this point more clearly.

*"Do not judge so that you will not be judged. [2] For in the
way you judge, you will be judged; and by your standard of
measure, it will be measured to you."*
Matthew 7:1-2

That people boast about their spiritual condition in their condemnation of others is a sin in and of itself. In truth, the only part of the righteousness process we're involved in is faith—our humility and dependence upon the sacrifice of Jesus. To take our eyes off of the cross and place them upon ourselves—which is precisely what people do when telling others that something they *are* or *do* prevents them from being saved—is to place ourselves in danger; for what we are doing at that point is attributing our own righteousness to self, rather than wholly to God.

All of this being said, are they somehow right? Are we, in fact, made righteous by virtue of our own nature or actions, e.g. being straight?

"He [God] made Him [Jesus] who knew no sin to be sin on our behalf, so that we might become the righteousness of God in Him."
2Corinthians 5:21
"Even as Abraham believed God, and it was accounted to him for righteousness."
Galatians 3:6 (KJV)

We are not righteous as a result of anything we've done. Our righteousness comes from God through Jesus Christ, and only results from our faith in Him. Being straight or gay, being sober or drunk, being chaste or promiscuous... All of these things are incapable of producing righteousness in our lives, or of taking it away.

Christ took upon Himself the coat of our sin when He died on the cross, and gave us the coat of His righteousness. Indeed, it's not *our* righteousness that we possess, but is, rather, the righteousness of God in Christ (2Co. 5:21). We are *His* righteousness! So, how can someone who has faith in Jesus be disqualified from righteousness by virtue of his sexual orientation or even his sexual activity, when the supposedly holy orientation (being straight) plays no part whatsoever in securing that righteousness in the first place?

"But now apart from the Law the righteousness of God has been manifested, being witnessed by the Law and the Prophets, [22] even the righteousness of God through faith in Jesus Christ for all those who believe; for there is no distinction; [23] for all have sinned and fall short of the glory of God, [24] being justified as a gift by His grace through the redemption which is in Christ Jesus; [25] whom God displayed publicly as a propitiation in His blood through faith. This was to demonstrate His righteousness, because in the forbearance of God He passed over the sins previously committed; [26] for the demonstration, I say, of His righteousness at the present time, so that He would be just and the justifier of the one who has faith in Jesus."
Romans 3:21-26

The richness of this passage cannot be overstated. Consider the following points.

16

1) We possess God's righteousness, not our own (v. 22).

2) This righteousness comes by faith in Jesus (v. 22).

3) This righteousness is available to *all* who believe, not all who believe and are straight, or all who believe and have conquered certain areas of sin, or all who believe and _____ (fill in the blank) (v. 22).

4) Because we are all in the same boat—dependent upon the righteousness of God—there is no distinction between us. No one who has this righteousness by faith is better or more righteous than another (vs. 22-23). Consequently, the drawing of lines of distinction or comparison is a form of boasting that no one is qualified to engage in (Eph. 2:9).

5) Being just in the eyes of God is a gift from God, not an act of labor that we earn (vs. 24- 25).

Saying that people aren't saved because of the presence of particular sins in their lives is an act of gross sacrilege. Sacrilege is the act of depriving something of its sacred character. It's taking something holy or consecrated to God and calling or treating it as though it's a common thing, not something peculiar, special, and of utmost value. This is an offense against God.

> *"And there were in it [an object like a large sheet] all kinds of four-footed animals and crawling creatures of the earth and birds of the air. [13] A voice came to him, "Get up, Peter, kill and eat!" [14] But Peter said, 'By no means, Lord, for I have never eaten anything unholy and unclean.' [15] Again a voice came to him a second time, 'What God has cleansed, no longer consider unholy...' [28] And he said to them, 'You yourselves know how unlawful it is for a man who is a Jew to associate with a foreigner or to visit him; and yet God has shown me that I should not call any man unholy or unclean.'"*
>
> *Acts 10:12-15, 28*

When we speak against the work of the Holy Spirit in making people righteous through faith in Christ, we are calling common what God has cleansed. We are demeaning a work of grace, despite the fact that it was and is that very grace that is preserving *us* in righteousness.

God gave this revelation to Peter in a vision, and recorded it in Acts for our edification; yet so many modern Christian leaders find themselves committing the same act of sacrilege, except that the target of their hypocrisy is gay people, rather than Gentiles.

What's so amazing is that some of these people recognize the danger in levying so daring an attack against others. Still, even the "careful" ones, who put on an air of humility, ultimately say the same thing. Consider that Joe Dallas, who said that "gay" and "Christian" are not compatible, went on to talk of gays and lesbians being "won *into* the kingdom of God,"[3] the implication being that if they're gay or lesbian, they aren't a part of God's kingdom yet. But then, to shield his hypocrisy, he says in the same breath that homosexuality is no better or worse a sin than some of his own.[4] Following his logic to its conclusion certainly left me wondering if he believes he's a Christian at all, seeing as 'gay' and 'Christian' are incompatible, yet his own sins are just as bad as homosexuality!

Dallas concludes his salvo against gay Christians by stating, "It's a waste of time to argue intangibles, such as whether or not a 'gay Christian' is truly born-again, or 'saved.'"[5] Well, it certainly didn't seem a waste of time, considering how much time he actually spent attempting to prove that gay people *aren't* truly Christian. Note the quotes he places around "gay Christian" and "saved," which reinforce his belief that the two terms are incompatible. He seems to have thought it *quite* worthy of his time.

Robert Gagnon agrees with Dallas—that one could hardly consider truly saved a gay person who engages in what he calls "homosexual behavior." He goes so far as to claim that "Jesus' teachings make clear that repentance, transformation, and obedience to the will of God are essential for salvation."[6] One is

---

[3] *The Gay Gospel?*, 142.
[4] Ibid., 143.
[5] Ibid., 149.

left to wonder if anyone at any time could, by such a standard, have any degree of assurance of his/her salvation; and if so, would it be hubris speaking, rather than humility.

Humility doesn't look inwardly to determine one's status with God. It looks wholly to God's divine act of grace, bestowed upon all who believe. As demonstrated by an Old Testament foreshadowing of Christ, when deadly snakes bit the children of Israel, they needed only to look upon the bronze image of a snake fashioned by Moses at the instruction of God in order to live (Num. 21:4-9). They did not look inward. They looked upward, toward the snake, which was placed atop a pole. And so it is today. To survive the sin that plagues us, we must not look to ourselves. We must look *up* to live! We must look to Christ, who was lifted up on the cross.

> "The past tense 'such *were* some of you' cannot be ignored. Paul does not address 'homosexual Christians.' He addresses former homosexuals who were *now* Christians. A transition had taken place, a supernatural movement *from* the practice of homosexuality *to* the Christian faith."[7]

White and Niell completely misunderstand Paul's words in 1Co. 6:11. Because of the passage's proximity to a supposed reference to homosexuals in verse 9, they erroneously conclude that a saved person can't be gay, since Paul referred to the acts in past tense.

We'll discover in Chapter 8 that Paul wasn't referring to homosexuals in verse 9; however, even if he were, White and Niell's interpretation of "such were some of you" would still be wrong. They seem to believe that Paul's intention was to teach that once people become Christian, they never engage in the acts listed in this vice list. To them, Christians never fornicate, commit adultery, steal, covet, get drunk, or commit any of the acts listed in this vice list. Now, maybe that's their fantasyland version of Christianity; but biblical Christianity is very different. It's made up of real people who *all* struggle with sin. Even Paul, who wrote

---

[6] *The Bible and Homosexual Practice*, 220.
[7] *The Same Sex Controversy*, 151.

more Bible books than any other individual, struggled with specific areas of sin (Ro. 7:14-8:1) and considered himself a chief sinner (1Ti. 1:15).

In their zeal to prove that gay people can stop being gay, White and Niell completely missed Paul's point. He wasn't addressing acts people commit, but rather, things that define a person—things that characterize their lives. As Christians who have made Jesus Lord (Ro. 10:9), sin should not be our vocation. We should be people who struggle *against* sin, not people who are defined by it. But, the idea that there aren't Christians who commit these sins is simply not true.

Christians live daily in a constant state of civil war, in which the inner spirit (where the Spirit of God resides) battles with the flesh (Matt. 26:41; Gal. 5:17). While the sins we commit no longer define who we are (Ro. 7:20), we should never trick ourselves into believing that we have no sin (1Jn. 1:8). We must also never allow ourselves to self-righteously believe that people who commit sins that made it onto a vice list are less Christian than we are, or aren't Christian at all.

3

On The Wings Of Hate
How Anti-Gay Traditionalism Is Anything But Christian

One of the great ironies in this debate is found in how the anti-gay position rests entirely upon Scripture. As Section 2 will explain in detail, it doesn't rest upon *rightly divided* Scripture; nonetheless, it hinges upon their ostensible acceptance of the absolute authority of God's word, and upon our need to yield to whatever it teaches. I'm all for that, especially the "whatever" part. Yet, the issue isn't whether Scripture should be obeyed or ignored, but rather, whether *their* interpretation and application of it should be submitted to or opposed.

The most crucial sources of authority are Scripture (the word breathed of God—2Ti. 3:16), Jesus' life and ministry (He who is the Word made flesh—Jn. 1:1, 14), and the inner witness of the Holy Spirit (He who makes the word comprehensible—Jn. 1:5; 16:13). Without these, we have no way to grasp God (1Co. 2:11-16), let alone walk out His purpose for us individually and collectively. Yet, this tri-union of the revelation of God's heart, mind, and character is disregarded when it comes to homosexuality. The Scriptures so many anti-gay Christians purport to champion are the very Scriptures that indict their handling of this issue.

What do we learn from the tri-union? Does it teach that holiness is God's standard, and that all Christians must pursue it with all their hearts? Yes. Does it *also* teach that how we deal with the sin in the lives of others is vital? Absolutely. So, whether homosexuality is a sin or not, anti-gay traditionalists have utterly butchered their handling of this issue. What's more, they've called their extreme mishandling of God's word love, thereby creating an image of God in the minds of unbelievers (and even some believers) that is anything but appealing.

Although this entire book is dedicated to their mishandling of this issue, let's explore specifically their violations of the Christian standard of love, as described in 1Corinthians 13.

"If I speak with the tongues of men and of angels, but do not have love, I have become a noisy gong or a clanging cymbal. [2] If I have the gift of prophecy, and know all mysteries and all knowledge; and if I have all faith, so as to remove mountains, but do not have love, I am nothing. [3] And if I give all my possessions to feed the poor, and if I surrender my body to be burned, but do not have love, it profits me nothing. [4] Love is patient, love is kind and is not jealous; love does not brag and is not arrogant, [5] does not act unbecomingly; it does not seek its own, is not provoked, does not take into account a wrong suffered, [6] does not rejoice in unrighteousness, but rejoices with the truth; [7] bears all things, believes all things, hopes all things, endures all things."
1Corinthians 13:1-7

1Corinthians 13 is often referred to as the "love chapter"; yet many traditionalist Christians either ignore or completely warp it in order to force it to fit their socio-religious worldview. They're big on talking *about* love, but someone once said that we are to love not in word, but in *deed* (1Jn. 3:18). Patience, kindness, humility, propriety, selflessness, temperance, forgiveness... these are the traits that are supposed to characterize the love-filled life—the *Christian* life. Yet, traditionalists often fall drastically short of this fundamental mark on this issue above all others.

Consider the evidence. Their cruelty and self-righteousness overshadow the miniscule references to love they obligatorily inject into their rhetoric. Negativity simply cannot hide. It always finds a way to the surface; and the negativity they feel toward gay people is obvious to any unbiased observer.

Let's examine traditionalist characterizations of gay people and hold them to the standard of love—to the standard expressed in Scripture, demonstrated in the life of Christ, and borne witness to by the Holy Spirit.

> "Indeed, the fact we're arguing over homosexuality
> is evidence of, as radio teacher Chuck Smith says,
> 'a sign of weakness within the church. It should
> not even be a question, because the Bible is very
> clear on the subject.'"[8]

So, let me get this right. Joe Dallas believes that the Church shouldn't even be engaging in discourse or debate over this issue. As far as he's concerned, dialog itself is a sign of weakness. It's better to project strength by refusing to engage? Well, that certainly explains why to-date, every invitation I've issued to anti-gay Christians to engage in discourse on this issue has been rejected. They choose instead to send emails cussing at me, and telling me about how I'm going to Hell. What an odd representation of the love of Christ!

Dallas claims that the Bible is "very clear on the subject." In fact, there are, at best, only five passages in the Bible that address homosexuality in any shape, form, or fashion (Lev. 18:22; 20:13; Ro. 1:26-27; 1Co. 6:9-10; 1Ti. 1:9-10). The other few references—like the Sodom and Gomorrah destruction narrative, or the King James Version references to "sodomites" in Deuteronomy and 1 and 2Kings—speak to something totally different. So, we have five total references, at best. This amounts to a level of clearness that makes discourse undesirable? Okay, so what about slavery, which has over a hundred references in Scripture, none of which condemn it? That's a heck of a lot more "clear" than five. Is that subject equally unworthy of debate? What about the subjugation of women? Where does Dallas' logic lead us as far as women's rights are concerned?

Traditionalists believe that the world can only work as they view it. Anything that flies in the face of how things *have* been, or what people *have* believed is wrong and doesn't warrant sincere inquiry. But this is dangerous beyond expression. Their refusal to allow for the evolution of thought holds them captive to how things *are*, regardless of how wrong they may be. That is, in fact, how they earned the name "traditionalists" and "conservatives". God, on the other hand, wants us to always seek to improve

---

[8] *The Gay Gospel?*, 28.

ourselves—to identify the bad and exchange it for the good, and to even exchange the good for that which is better.

Here's an example… Traditionally, people always wore formal attire to church. They wore what came to be known as their "Sunday's best." Casual attire was frowned upon as a sign of disrespect for the house of God. Personally, I think that dressing up for church is good. But, I also think that creating an atmosphere where people can freely make that decision for themselves is *better*. Why? —Because not everyone feels comfortable in suits and dresses. Not everyone can afford suits and dresses. Why make these people hesitant to come to church when God isn't the least bit concerned with their outward appearance, but only what's in their hearts? Dressing up may be good, but reaching out to as many people as possible is *better*. If we lock ourselves into the good, as some churches continue to do when it comes to attire, we can only limit our ability to excel at our greatest commission—making disciples. And how can *that* be good at all?

So, I reject Dallas' contention that this issue is not open to discussion. In fact, I need not reject it. Scripture rejects it for me.

> *"And when I came to you, brethren, I did not come with superiority of speech or of wisdom, proclaiming to you the testimony of God. [2] For I determined to know nothing among you except Jesus Christ, and Him crucified."*
> *1 Corinthians 2:1-2*

Paul's approach was one characterized by humility. Rather than seeking to preserve a *look* or *form* of godliness, his desire was to be relatable and approachable. The only issue that was not debatable as far as he was concerned was that Jesus is Lord, and died on the cross—also known as the gospel. Aside from that, *everything* was open to discourse.

This seems miles away from today's traditionalists, who don't seem to find those who disagree worthy of dialog. Indeed, Dallas apparently has such a low view of gay Christians who support affirming theology that he brings our very integrity into question.

"It [the gay Christian movement] represents a tendency among Christians who are homosexually tempted to yield to that temptation and then try to justify it."[9]

"The interpretations offered are suited to the desires of those who are practicing, who long to practice, or those who are simply not opposed to the practice of same-sex intimacy."[10]

It's interesting how Dallas cannot bring himself to utter the words "gay Christian." He takes the long way around—"Christians who are homosexually tempted." Unfortunately, semantics is a severe, yet unnecessary impediment in bridging the gap with traditionalists.

In their theological arrogance—the opposite of love's humility—Dallas, White, and Niell assume that anyone who disagrees with their interpretation of Scripture must be doing so to justify homosexuality. But where's the evidence? Are they in the tear-filled prayer closets many struggling gay Christians exist in, precisely because they *don't* want to justify sin and only want to know the truth? Were they in my own heart during my studies in preparing to write *Homosexianity*—a book that was intended to be non-affirming, and was only changed after my eyes began to open during my studies?

Now, I'd be dishonest to claim that everyone involved in the gay Christian movement has a firm grasp of affirming theology. Some have no clue as to the "theology" part, and simply accept it on the basis of the "affirming" part. They often say, "I can't fathom a loving God who doesn't accept me as I am." Personally, I don't think that's a good enough reason to subscribe to a belief. There are many things I can't fathom; and in some cases, the reason is, no doubt, that I haven't developed in that area sufficiently. In such cases, *I* am the problem, not theology. I will not—I *cannot*—put God in the box of what I can fathom. So, just because these affirming Christians wind up on the same side of the issue as I do doesn't mean that I endorse a view of Christianity in

---

[9] *The Gay Gospel?*, 22.
[10] *The Same Sex Controversy*, 57.

which the way that *seems* to align with one's worldview is necessarily right. But this criticism cuts both ways.

I also don't appreciate the portrayal of the gay Christian movement as being full of such people. The majority of affirming Christians I know hold Scripture in high regard. They sought answers, not in an attempt to justify a preexisting belief, but in an attempt to seek the truth, whatever it may be. Traditionalists, on the other hand, don't have a "whatever it may be" approach to their quest for truth. They don't want to expose themselves to other views. They only want to conserve traditional thought—what they already believe. While they may consider this a strength, I consider it a serious weakness, and a grave vulnerability in their spiritual health—for whatever we accept as unimpeachable truth will, from that point on, have absolute control over our lives, even beyond the control of the Holy Spirit. I *never* want to exist in that place!

Ultimately, their argument is omnidirectional. I could easily say that all *they're* interested in doing is justifying their poor treatment of gay people. It would certainly ring true to the targets of their vitriol. But, it's really just a meaningless generalization, lacking of any logical potency. So why bother?

One of the most egregious things traditionalists do is blame homosexuality itself for the despair so many gay people feel. Referring to a study done by one Dr. Choon-Leong Seow, an Old Testament scholar and author, White and Niell demonstrate their utter disdain for homosexuals in refuting Dr. Seow's claim that society contributes substantially to (or even causes) the despair many homosexuals experience. They choose, instead, to blame the "homosexual lifestyle."

> "Upon what basis does Dr. Seow conclude that his observation of a higher than normal suicide rate provides sufficient basis for an accusation against society in general and the church in particular? Did the possibility that the lifestyle itself—which requires a tremendous output of energy for the maintenance of the suppression of God's truth and the voice of conscience—ever come to mind as the actual trigger mechanism? Is it possible that Dr. Seow has misinterpreted what he has seen, and that

the 'joy' to which he referred is in reality empty and shallow? The creature made in God's image cannot truly enjoy the twisting of that image on a daily basis... Is it possible that this self-loathing is generated by the lifestyle itself, which forces a person to live contrary to God's creative design, so that when such a person is reminded of their rebellion and their internal pain and misery by outside elements, whether by the church or society, they make an unwarranted connection?"[11]

Traditionalists destroy what little credibility they have when they blame the "gay lifestyle" for what many gay people go through. They ignore their own overwhelming contribution of bitter rhetoric, which has shaped the minds of families, churches, and even society in ostracizing, rejecting, and condemning gay people in what can only be described as an inexhaustible, torturous, emotional abuse.

The higher than normal suicide rate amongst gays does not (and cannot) provide a basis for advocating homosexuality as an orientation equal to heterosexuality. However, it *should* at least stir sympathy and compassion within those who claim to have the beating heart of Christ within them. Unfortunately, I've come to learn that no such kindness actively flows in the hearts of many traditionalists. Their approach to religion, matched only by the merciless legalism of the Pharisees, prevents any such care from extending beyond the scope of semi-kind words born of obligation, rather than sincerity.

Contrary to their claim, living in accord with one's sexual orientation does not require a tremendous output of energy. What requires tremendous energy is keeping such a sensitive part of oneself secret from family, friends, and the church. It's emotionally and spiritually draining to have to live in isolation and fear day after day, especially during periods of emotional and sexual development (i.e. early teenage years). The love, acceptance, and understanding that are freely extended to our heterosexual counterparts are denied to us. All we can do is wallow in the mire of our isolation, hoping for a day when we can be who we are openly.

---

[11] *The Same Sex Controversy*, 189.

It comes as no surprise that many gay Christians, upon being accepted by the unbelieving gay community, assimilate into their culture—a culture in some ways characterized by activities Christians find immoral. But, we must remember that they're unbelievers. It's not as though many heterosexual unbelievers don't also commit all sorts of licentious acts. For every gay pride parade—in which some people bare their bodies in sexually suggestive displays—is a heterosexual festivity like Mardi Gras or Freaknik, in which the same types of displays take place. Contrary to traditionalist claims, then, gay unbelievers don't have a monopoly on sin. They simply do what unbelievers, straight or gay, do.

It's in no way good that some gay Christians engage in the same types of sinful activity; however, the unbelieving community is oftentimes their only source of affirmation and acceptance. The Church, then, is partly to blame for people's bad choices. Rather than providing them with a Christian community that loves and accepts them, gently inviting them on the mutual journey for spiritual growth, gay people are cast out, ridiculed, and left to Satan's devices. Deprived of the godly fellowship that could help them overcome temptation and live a fruitful, godly life, gay people are consigned to forming ties with a community that *will* accept them.

Now, this doesn't excuse gay Christians from the Christian requirement to pursue holiness. Still, we must understand that God would not have prescribed Christian fellowship (Heb. 10:23-25) if He didn't realize that it was an essential component of Christian living. I can only believe that a just and loving God will take such things into account on the day of judgment, not only in being merciful toward those who were denied Christian charity, but also in requiring just recompense from those charged with loving their neighbor as their own selves—people who constantly reject that directive, blaspheming the name of love incarnate in their effort to judge and condemn.

It's incredible how White and Niell claim that the devastation experienced by many gay people isn't about how they're treated by the Church and society, but by their own lifestyle. Considering their logic, it's a wonder that other sinners don't commit suicide at the same rates as young gay people, seeing as sin is supposedly the problem, not rejection by society and the Church.

> "This lifestyle is a prison that leaves many individuals feeling hopeless and abandoned by God, family, and society…"[12]

I cannot bring myself to believe that James Dobson hasn't considered that it's not the "gay lifestyle" (which doesn't actually exist) that leaves gay people feeling hopeless and abandoned, but is, in fact, traditionalist rhetoric and its consequences. Has it really never occurred to him that many gay people feel abandoned by God because people like him feed them that swill? Has it not crossed his mind that they feel abandoned by family and society because, in large part, they *have* been? The traditionalist predilection for blaming the big bad wolf of the gay lifestyle is old and tired. They really need to let it rest.

I don't believe that Dobson is an ignorant man; however, it would be better if he were. Because he's an intelligent man, I have no choice but to conclude that his heart has waxed so cold that he's really not interested in getting to the heart of what drives so many gay people to despair. He's only interested in spreading his propaganda.

It troubles me that traditionalists have been able to convince themselves that they speak this type of foolishness in love. How so fundamental an aspect of Christianity can be so misunderstood defies comprehension, except to say that religiosity has destroyed the Church's ability to examine itself… that even the most important aspect our faith—love—totally escapes us. Amazing… and horrifying!

---

[12] *Marriage Under Fire*, 72.

4

The Lost Art of Exegesis
How Anti-Gay Christians Incessantly Read
Into Scripture What's Not There

There are two very good, albeit unfortunate reasons so many Christians believe homosexuality is a horrible sin. First, surveys have demonstrated that most Christians do not engage in even a modicum of personal Bible study. Tiny minorities attend Bible classes offered by their local churches, and people rarely study privately—not only because of a general lack of interest and commitment, but also because many Christians simply do not know *how* to study the Bible.

Second, even amongst the minority who actively studies the Bible, an enormous percentage don't know how to properly interpret and apply what they read, especially when it conflicts with what they hear from behind the pulpits of the local churches, or with their socio-religious worldview. This is evidenced by the large numbers of denominations that exist within the Christian community, and by the number of divisions within single denominations. The majority of these divisions are rooted in doctrinal and theological disagreements.

We must ask how so many people can read—for all intents and purposes—the very same Bible, and yet come to contradictory conclusions on a myriad of issues. Does Scripture truly say so many different things to so many different people; or does it speak with one perfectly harmonious voice, thereby placing the blame for theological differences on *our* shoulders?

There are certainly a number of Christians who believe that Scripture itself is contradictory and is, therefore, at least partly to blame for the innumerable theological divisions that exist within the Church; but I'm not one of them. I believe very firmly that

Scripture is without error, and that it, when rightly interpreted and applied, does not contradict itself. In my mind, the fault lies with us, for we rarely read, interpret, and apply Scripture objectively.

The branch of Christian study that deals with how to "rightly divide" (2Ti. 2:15) God's word is called hermeneutics. This is what we'll examine in this chapter—the poor hermeneutics exercised by our profiled authors, as well as how to exercise sound hermeneutics.

In order to properly interpret and apply Scripture, we cannot simply read it. We must *study* it—taking into account the social and religious context existing at the time each passage was written, as well as the specific audience the passage was written to. Many modern Christians fail to realize that Scripture was not written directly to them, but to a large number of people spanning a large divide of geographic locations, cultures, and time periods.

For example, the Pentateuch (the first five books of the Bible) was written over 3,000 years ago to an ancient Israelite society that existed within an exceedingly different culture and religious system than we live in today. Fast-forward 1,000+ years and you'll find the gospels and epistles of the New Testament being written to a much different audience, one comprised of both Jews *and* Gentiles. One of the main purposes of the New Testament texts was to free its readers from the notion that they were required to live by the former religious code contained in the Pentateuch (called the Law of Moses). So, not only did the audiences differ, but so did the purposes of each segment of Scripture. These types of differences must be taken into account in order to exercise sound hermeneutics.

Inaccurate interpretations of Scripture are largely the result of **eisegesis**—reading *into* Scripture what one presupposes it says, or *wishes* it said. When reading the Bible, people have a tendency to connect dots where none exist, or to take a passage out of its textual or cultural context in order to force their preexisting views onto what they read. As you'll soon discover, our profiled authors made this error quite frequently.

On the other hand, the process of critically reading and objectively interpreting Scripture is called **exegesis**—reading *out* of Scripture what its writers put there. This skill does not come naturally, and it certainly doesn't come by simply reading the Bible.

We must commit ourselves to prayerful study, and to thoughtful contemplation of all that we read. We must be careful to not project our personal views into what we read. We must also consider the cultural and textual context surrounding any particular passage. Not everything applies within the modern context, even if it's written in the New Testament. The only way to properly determine what applies is to understand how and why a passage was written in the first place, and to understand the culture of the audience it was initially addressed to.

The Reverence of God's Word

Joe Dallas claims that gay-affirming Christians do not hold God's word in high regard—that we "generally negate its authority or its sufficiency."[13] I strongly disagree with this assertion. It has been my experience that there are both affirming and non-affirming Christians who believe Scripture to be of divine origin, while there are also those who believe it a primarily human work. So, his attempt to characterize the affirming community as a movement comprised of people who don't take God's word seriously shows the limited scope of his own experience as an "ex-gay" Christian. That many affirming Christians advocate the careful study of Scripture shows the level of reverence we have for it. Ironically, it's the anti-gay traditionalists who tell people to simply read Scripture and take it at face value. *They're* the ones who seem to have a lackadaisical approach to God's word.

Dallas goes on to say that because affirming Christians don't want to *appear* to reject Scripture, we settle for revising it. "The pro-gay theology's scriptural arguments are, therefore, basic revisions of the biblical texts traditionally understood to forbid homosexuality."[14] Once again, I disagree. Why is it that those who interpret a passage differently than Dallas are "revising" it, whereas those who agree with his interpretation are simply reading it?

It appears to me that there's been plenty of revising in Church history; but what's been revised is not God's word, but rather, the human tendency to use His word to oppress others. Was it a revision that allowed women to teach in the church and

---

[13] *The Gay Gospel?*, 160.
[14] Ibid., 160.

pastor local congregations, contrary to the letter of New Testament law (1Co. 14:34-35; 1Ti. 2:11-12)? Was it a revision that permitted women to wear gold and pearl jewelry and expensive clothing, contrary to the letter of New Testament law (1Ti. 2:9)? Was it a revision that compelled us to celebrate the heroism of abolitionists, and people like Harriet Tubman, who led countless slaves to freedom, contrary to the letter of New Testament law (Col. 3:22)?

I submit that gay-affirming Christians are not revising anything. Like many who came before us who recognized the cultural subjectivity (and, therefore, the obsolete status) of particular biblical passages, affirming Christians certainly *revisit* the texts traditionally understood to forbid homosexuality; but I strongly disagree with the characterization that we revise these texts.

The Interpretive Role of the Holy Spirit

Dallas goes on to espouse one of the most dangerous beliefs I've ever come across—a belief that cuts to the most fundamental aspect of how we approach Scripture. If I hadn't read it from his own book, I would have sworn it was a misquote. He actually advocates that we rely solely on our own natural logic when interpreting Scripture, to the exclusion of the voice of the Holy Spirit.

> "Now, I think the Holy Spirit is wonderful, and I said as much. But I also said that when it came to matters of doctrine, I could not trust my ability to discern the Spirit's voice. That, I argued, was exactly why God gave us a written standard (inspired by the Spirit)—so we need not guess at what He requires of us... I contend we have to objectively rely on the written Word alone. (In that vein, I can't count the number of people who've said to me, 'I've prayed earnestly on this issue, and I really feel I'm doing what God has told me to do!' The implication, of course, is that earnest prayer or an attempt to discern God's voice can somehow override Scripture's plain teaching.)"[15]

---

[15] *The Gay Gospel?*, 103.

Although I'm stunned by the assertion, Dallas does present a practical concern that all students of Scripture can relate to. Does reliance on an inner voice open the door to subjective interpretations? In truth, it does. I can't tell you how many times I've heard people attribute thoughts or feelings to the Holy Spirit, which have proven to be nothing of the sort, e.g. the Spirit supposedly instructing someone to marry a particular person. So, it's true that people have a tendency to mistake strong desires for the voice of the Spirit. That being said, Dallas fails to realize a number of exceedingly important points.

First, the same potential for interpretive subjectivity exists with logic-based approaches to Scripture. Nine justices sit on the U.S. Supreme Court precisely because people interpret legal documents differently, even people who have made the law their profession. There's no reason to believe that natural logic is any more reliable than listening to the Spirit, especially when one is practiced in hearing His voice correctly.

Second, it's exceedingly ironic that the very Scripture Dallas claims to objectively interpret contradicts his contention. Jesus said that God's word is truth (Jn. 17:17). He also told us that it's the Holy Spirit—called "the Spirit of truth"—who will guide us *into* all truth (Jn. 16:13). As the apostle Paul put it, the Holy Spirit is the only one who knows the mind of God (1Co. 2:10), and it is only through Him (the Spirit) that we, too, can know the deep things of God.

Dallas would have us approach Scripture in a simple, practical way—relying solely on natural logic to interpret it. But, 1Co. 2:14 expressly states that the natural man *cannot* receive or take in the things of God because such things are *spiritually* (by the Holy Spirit) understood. God's word is a spiritual book; therefore, it requires spiritual thinking to grasp it.

I was particularly shocked by the contention that we shouldn't rely on the Holy Spirit *at all!* He contends, "We have to objectively rely on the written Word *alone.*" If affirming Christians ever made such a claim, we'd be all but burned in effigy. But, a traditionalist makes it, and nobody flinches. My view is quite different than Dallas'. I believe that we must rely on the Holy Spirit primarily, and rely on our natural logic as an element that, although involved in the process of interpretation, is secondary to our reliance on the Spirit. It appears that God agrees with this hermeneutical approach.

> *"For this is the covenant that I will make with the house of Israel after those days, says the Lord: I will put my laws into their minds, and I will write them on their hearts. And I will be their God, and they shall be my people."*
>
> *Hebrews 8:10*

This passage reminds us of an Old Testament prophecy that God would establish a new covenant with His people, writing it into our minds and hearts (Jer. 31:33). It would be a covenant that couldn't solely be contained on pages of parchment or tree sap, but would be etched on the tablets of our hearts. However, because our hearts are fallible, it's essential that we rely on the Spirit to open our eyes to what God has deposited within. That's why Jesus said that by allowing the Spirit to guide us, we would be guided into all areas of truth.

In Dallas' mind, Christians make an error when they rely on the Holy Spirit, especially when what one feels the Spirit has spoken contradicts the "plain teaching" of Scripture. I, on the other hand, believe that the "plain teaching" of Scripture is not so plain at all. We must be diligent in our examination of God's word if we plan to interpret it correctly (2Ti. 2:15).

> *"I have many more things to say to you, but you cannot bear them now. [13] But when He, the Spirit of truth, comes, He will guide you into all the truth; for He will not speak on His own initiative, but whatever He hears, He will speak; and He will disclose to you what is to come."*
>
> *John 16:12-13*

Jesus made an amazing statement in this passage. Reflecting on it is one of the things that saved me from my legalistic, face value approach to Scripture. I've always regarded Him as the best teacher ever to walk the earth; so for Him to say that there were things He had to say that they could not yet bear is astonishing to me. Jesus knew what Dallas still stands to learn—that sometimes, words alone are insufficient. The fact is that no written code is sufficient for dealing with every nuance of circumstance that we will possibly be faced with. Therefore, reliance on the Spirit is critical to sound hermeneutics—to practicing the art of exegesis.

Ultimately, Dallas is guilty of condemning one extreme—the subjective perception of the Holy Spirit's voice as the sole indicator of God's truth—with another—the supposedly objective interpretation of the "plain teaching" of Scripture without the guidance of the Holy Spirit. He would likely disagree with this characterization, but he did, in fact, state that we must "rely on the written Word alone"—a statement made in the context of the Holy Spirit's role in biblical interpretation.

Now, although I disagree rather adamantly with Dallas' view, he did raise a legitimate concern. Some people do, indeed, dismiss or minimize Scripture based on their internal feelings, be they ascribed to the Holy Spirit or not. This is a grave error. Jesus stated in Jn. 16:13 that the Spirit will not speak on His own initiative, but only what the Father speaks. So, the Spirit will never contradict Scripture, which has God as its ultimate source (2Ti. 3:16). If it appears in a given scenario that the Spirit contradicted the word, it only demonstrates our need to 1) study more intently and more prayerfully, and 2) spend more time developing spiritually so that we can be sure we heard the voice of the Spirit correctly.

We absolutely cannot afford to ignore God's word; but at the same time, we absolutely cannot afford to ignore God's voice! Both are essential to the exercise of sound hermeneutics, and to a healthy Christian life.

> "The Scriptures cited above [Lev. 18:22; 20:13; Ro. 1:26-27; 1Co. 6:9-10; 1Ti. 1:9-10] are so clear and specific that they defy misinterpretation of any sort."[16]

It is this kind of approach to Scripture that has produced so many theological schisms within the Church. Based on the last two quotations, Dallas clearly believes that unstudied, face value readings that do not involve the Holy Spirit are adequate for

---

[16] *The Gay Gospel?*, 106.

discerning biblical truth. Consequently, I'm compelled to state that Dallas is the last person anyone should take seriously on any matter of theology or doctrine. It may be that a particular conclusion he draws is correct, but his methodology is so irresponsible—so admittedly deprived of due diligence—that to give his interpretations any measure of confidence in this debate would indicate a lack of care on our part.

Unlike Dallas, authors White and Niell believe that the Holy Spirit has an important role in helping us rightly interpret Scripture. On this point, we agree. However, the way they understand His role presents a very dangerous potential with regard to interpretation.

> Do we read the Scriptures so as to hear what *they* [emphasis in original] say, or to hear what others are saying? Should not what we hear from the Spirit in His Word inform how we hear what others say, or should what others say cause us to 'reread' the Scriptures? Which is the ultimate authority?[17]

White and Niell challenge believers to reject out of hand any arguments that run counter to what they already believe Scripture teaches, since such claims apparently violate the authority of the Spirit, who is the source of Scripture. But, this approach is extremely dangerous, for it assumes that whatever one *believes* he heard from the Holy Spirit in relation to Scripture is absolutely what the Holy Spirit said, and is absolutely *all* He has to say on the subject.

Why should we not consider what others say, and reexamine Scripture in an effort to see which view is correct? There's nothing worse than believing that something wrong is right. White and Niell would have us believe certain things to the point of refusing the very possibility of being wrong. But, it is theologically arrogant to assume that what we believe the Spirit told us is all there is to know. We should remain open to having our beliefs challenged. Not only do such challenges compel us to

---

[17] *The Same Sex Controversy*, 187.

reexamine our own beliefs, but they also position us to correct errors or fill gaps that may exist in our thinking.

Scripture is very direct in its admonition that we test *all* things (1Th. 5:21). Should not our interpretation of Scripture be included among the things we should test? Shouldn't our belief regarding what the Holy Spirit may or may not have said to us likewise be tested (1Jn. 4:1)?

The Essential Relevance of Context

Before continuing, let's consider Dallas' argument that the passages believed to condemn homosexuality defy misinterpretation of any sort. One of the keys to sound hermeneutics is to not only know *what* is stated, but to understand *why* it's stated. Intent is a central part of interpretation, and a crucial part of application. Without it, we can never be sure we're pulling from Scripture *only* what God placed in it.

The first two passages Dallas referenced (Lev. 18:22; 20:13) are a great case in point. Both verses prohibit sex between two men. For Dallas, this is enough to pronounce all same-sex sexual activity sinful; but for a serious student of Scripture, every reference to a text requires consideration of its contexts in order to discern intent.

The Religious Context

The religious context places these passages within the ancient Israelite religious code—the Mosaic Law. But, Christians are not to submit to this code because we are in covenant with God through our *new* code: the new covenant (Ro. 6:14; 7:1-4). Dallas, White, and Niell disagree with this contention, believing that the Mosaic Law is still in effect.

> "We as believers are not under the Law, and in fact, we cannot keep it no matter how hard we try. Nonetheless, the Law itself is good, and the New Testament in no way nullifies it."[18]

---

[18] *The Gay Gospel?*, 184-185.

> "Since God is the One who gave His Word (in this case, the Law), He is the only One who has the right to annul or repeal it."[19]

Their point is that because God supposedly did not annul or repeal the Mosaic Law, it is still in full force. The only problem is that God *did*, in fact, annul the Law. Scripture expressly states that God has declared the Law null—obsolete. It was good during the time in which it was in effect, but it is no longer in effect.

> *"For, on the one hand, there is a setting aside [KJV: disannulling] of a former commandment because of its weakness and uselessness."*
>
> *Hebrews 7:18*

> *"When He said, 'A new covenant,' He has made the first obsolete. But whatever is becoming obsolete and growing old is ready to disappear."*
>
> *Hebrews 8:13*

As these passages demonstrate, the ancient Israelite code has been nullified (made obsolete) by the new covenant. Therefore, on the basis of religious context, the modern application of these Levitical passages is out of the question.

The Textual and Cultural Context

In this example, the textual context raises a cultural concern that allows us to consider both contexts together. By beginning our reading at the first verse of each respective chapter, we can clearly see the purpose for the proscriptions that follow. Both chapters express the same concern—that the Israelites maintain a separate religious and cultural identity from the idolatrous Egyptians and Canaanites (Lev. 18:3-5; 20:7-8). This was a very serious demand by God, and violation of it required death in many instances.

But, the ancient Egyptian and Canaanite cultures no longer exist; neither does the ancient Israelite culture. Therefore, the textual *and* cultural contexts make a modern application out of the question.

---

[19] *The Same Sex Controversy*, 75.

The Conclusion

All three contexts—textual, religious, and cultural—indicate that the Levitical proscriptions don't apply to Christians. But, this couldn't be ascertained by taking isolated proof texts at face value, which is obviously how traditionalists prefer to approach Scripture.

The moral is that we must never assume that a passage, no matter how "clear and specific," defies misinterpretation. We must *study* Scripture, rather than simply read it. We mustn't be so spiritual that we neglect to engage in logical and critical thought, but we also mustn't be so natural/practical in our thinking that we fail to rely on the Holy Spirit. Ultimately, our guard against misinterpreting—and thereby misapplying—Scripture should always be up, contrary to Dallas' perfunctory hermeneutics.

The Verification of Translation

Another hermeneutical issue that must be surmounted by any serious student of Scripture is the issue of translation. Should we trust the translations we read, or should we critically analyze them, particularly as it relates to our subject matter, homosexuality?

> "On something as important as sexual ethics, however, are we really to believe that the Bible translators we rely on got it wrong five different times, in two different testaments?"[20]

> "...this argument [that one must examine the Greek and/or Hebrew in order to get a good understanding of what the Bible teaches about homosexuality] 'fails to account for the fact that the Bible has not been translated by modern English speakers with little knowledge of classical languages.' Rather, large numbers of experts and highly qualified scholars have put their best efforts into most Bible translations... To cast doubt on one part of a translation without scrutinizing the rest of it in a similar manner is inconsistent; it must be taken as a whole, or not at all."[21]

---

[20] *The Gay Gospel?*, 106.
[21] Ibid., 164.

Dallas would have us place all of our trust in the translators who rendered the Hebrew and Greek texts into various forms of English. In his view, it's safe to simply *assume* that they got their translations correct. But, I wonder if he would advocate the hinging of our belief in the tri-unity of the Godhead on such assumptions, or our belief in the bodily resurrection of Jesus from the dead.

Ultimately, Dallas is attempting to avoid the need for in-depth study. He tries to overwhelm his readers by claiming, in essence, "If we go that route, we'll have to scrutinize every passage too much for Bible study to be practical; therefore, let's not scrutinize it at all and just trust that our translations are accurate." This attitude is as reckless as his belief that we needn't rely on the Holy Spirit, as well as his view that certain passages "defy misinterpretation."

Rather than deal with the evidence that the words related to homosexuality in 1Co. 6:9 and 1Ti. 1:10 were translated incorrectly (a fact that is undeniable when comparing translations side-by-side), Dallas uses this argument to prevent having to deal with the problem at all. But contrary to his position, limited-scope scrutiny is legitimate because 1) it's dealing with a specific subject matter, as any topical or word-study does, and 2) it's only *necessary* when mistranslation is evident. In other words, one should only be obliged to scrutinize a translation when the translation is legitimately brought into question.

Dallas then offers a ridiculous scenario to demonstrate the strategy gay-affirming Christians supposedly use when discussing what Scripture does and doesn't say about homosexuality. His example is obviously an attempt to plant a subconscious seed of doubt in his readers' minds so that any such arguments they come across are automatically discredited, no matter how legitimate they may be.

> "Now supposed someone tells you that they have done an extensive word study on this verse ['I am the light of the world'], and have discovered that Jesus was really saying, 'I am a hair dryer.' That seems ridiculous; the context so clearly points to something else. But if you haven't taken the time to

study the original Greek in this verse, you can't technically refute the 'hair dryer' idea, though common sense tells you it's nonsense. [p] That's the power of the pro-gay theology. It takes scriptures we're all familiar with, gives them an entirely new interpretation, backs its claims with the words of well-credentialed scholars, and gives birth to a new sexual ethic. Common sense may reject it, but until it's examined more closely, it's difficult to refute."[22]

Dallas wants his readers to assume that their existing beliefs are right—provided that they believe what he believes. He never encourages them to do a word study for themselves so that they can confirm or refute the claims of affirming (pro-gay) Christians. It's much easier to make them believe that any such arguments are as ridiculous as the claim that Jesus is a hair dryer.

There's one argument Dallas uses that I want to address more directly. Referencing credentialed scholars is a common way to argue a point. But, it's one that I don't find compelling when it comes to matters of theology. If credentials mattered in the scope of faith, we'd expect that most, if not all well-credentialed individuals would believe the same things, especially on the more important theological matters; however, this is not the case. People's practical experience or level of scholastic achievement doesn't tell us anything at all about the veracity of their conclusions. Christians in Berea were considered noble because they searched the Scriptures for themselves every day to confirm that what the apostle Paul was teaching them was correct (Acts 17:11). If Paul's words needed to be confirmed, surely those of some Th.D. from Timbuktu Seminary need confirmation, also.

My problem with how Dallas raises this argument is that he directs it solely at affirming Christians, as though anti-gay Christians never quote credentialed individuals. It's not an equitable use of a legitimate criticism. That being said, let me state emphatically that I'm not against referencing credentialed individuals. We simply must be careful not to take at face value whatever a credentialed individual claims.

---

[22] *The Gay Gospel?*, 172.

Further, Dallas uses words like "commonsense" in a crafty attempt to invalidate arguments without having to actually prove them wrong. But, as we've already found, Scripture warns us that "a natural man does not accept the things of the Spirit of God, for they are foolishness to him [i.e. in his mind, they defy 'common sense']; and he cannot understand them, because they are spiritually appraised" (1Co. 2:14). Dallas uses natural logic alone to understand spiritual truths. Is it any wonder he winds up on the wrong side of this issue?

The Pieces of the Law

Another problem we need to address is our anti-gay authors' wildly inaccurate belief that the Mosaic Law is separated into multiple components, with a certain component containing laws that are still in effect today, while the other components have been nullified. It amazes me how popular this belief is amongst anti-gay believers.

According to the theory, the Mosaic Law contains laws of a moral, ceremonial, dietary, and customary nature. The ceremonial, dietary, and customary laws are no longer applicable, but the moral laws are still in full force and effect.

> "A commonsense approach to the Bible shows that certain ceremonial and dietary laws in the Old Testament, such as those quoted by [Troy] Perry, aren't necessary to follow today."[23]

Dallas employs more colorful language in his attempt to validate a view that he either cannot prove, or simply doesn't want to take the time to prove. He never offered a basis for his belief, choosing instead to hide behind the word "commonsense." But, what exactly makes his belief that certain ceremonial and dietary laws aren't necessary to follow today commonsense? As faithful stewards of God's word, we have a responsibility to have a basis upon which to draw conclusions. Common sense (which isn't all that common when it comes to homosexuality) just isn't good enough.

---

[23] *The Gay Gospel?*, 165.

So, let's table common sense for a moment and see what God's word has to say. Does it validate the belief that any portion of the Mosaic Law is still applicable today?

"Now we know that whatever the Law says, it speaks to those who are under the Law..."
Romans 3:19a

"For sin shall not be master over you, for you are not under law but under grace."
Romans 6:14

Whatever the Law says, it's only saying to those under its authority. For example, Canadian law doesn't speak to me because I'm an American in America and am, therefore, not in its jurisdiction. However, if I traveled to Canada, portions of it *would* speak to me. So then, we must find out if we're under the Mosaic Law, because if we are, then it's speaking to us.

This is where the second point comes in. We are *not* under the Law, but under grace. Therefore, the Law wasn't written to us. If the Law were a person, it would tell modern Christians to stop obeying it because "I wasn't talking to you!" Nothing it says applies to us. Obeying the Mosaic Law, then, is as improper for Christians as American citizens obeying Chinese law while in America.

Now, this doesn't mean that we are *without* law. As a U.S. citizen, there are, indeed, laws that I must submit to. I simply don't have to bother obeying Chinese law because I'm not Chinese and am not in China. It may be that some Chinese laws are also U.S. laws, e.g. laws against murder. But, I won't obey those laws as provisions of Chinese law, but as provisions of applicable American law. In the same way, Christians are not lawless. After stating that we are not under the Mosaic Law, Paul immediately stated that such an admission does not mean that it's okay to sin (Ro. 6:15). Being under grace doesn't mean that we have no code that we're required to live by. We simply don't turn to the Mosaic Law to discover the provisions of *our* code. Our code is the new covenant—the law of Christ (Gal. 6:2), also called the law of liberty (James 1:25; 2:12).

> "Though God has changed His Law with respect to the dietary regulations, and other matters that distinguished between the Jews and other nations (laws concerning the separation of fabrics and seed), He has not done so with homosexuality."[24]

White and Niell offer no evidence to back up their claim. I imagine they consider the condemnation of same-sex sexual activity in Ro. 1 and the seeming condemnation in 1Co. 6 and 1Ti. 1 as proof; however, there are two problems with such a contention.

First of all, we've already examined multiple New Testament passages that explicitly teach that we are no longer under the Law of Moses. None of them make a distinction between components of the Law; rather, they nullify it in its entirety.

Second, the Levitical proscriptions condemned sex involving two men. Nothing was said, however, about female-female sex. This requires us to consider whether the text condemns homosexuality, in general, or specific sexual acts taking place within a specific context. This vital question is examined in detail in Chapter 6.

So, with no supporting evidence whatsoever, White and Niell apparently believe that God carried over a supposed condemnation of homosexuality into the new covenant simply because they choose to. But, this cannot suffice serious students of God's word, whose only desire is to let Scripture speak for itself, despite their existing views.

> "The defender of homosexuality must produce a viable criterion for distinguishing between the moral and ceremonial laws, or else consistently reject them all (contrary to the emphatic word of Christ)."[25]

Surprisingly, White and Niell are actually right. One must, indeed, make the choice they present. But, there really is no choice

---

[24] *The Same Sex Controversy*, 73.
[25] Ibid., 84.

at all. We must consistently reject *all* laws of the old covenant, moral *and* ceremonial, dietary *and* customary. But, such a rejection is not contrary to the word of Christ. It's in perfect keeping with Christ's words—which declare His purpose in fulfilling the Law (Matt. 5:17; Gal. 3:24-26)—as well as with the teachings contained in the apostolic epistles, which we've already examined.

Now, in all of my studies, I have not come across a single verse that makes the distinction between moral and ceremonial laws that White, Niell, Dallas, and so many other anti-gay Christians claim exists. But, I recognize that I could be missing something, so I take care to pay attention when reading anti-gay arguments that make this claim. To date, I've only found one attempt to actually prove the case biblically.

> "Recognizing this distinction between the ceremonial and moral law is vitally important in properly understanding such passages as 1 Samuel 15:22: 'Has the Lord as much delight in burnt offerings and sacrifices as in obeying the voice of the LORD? Behold, to obey is better than sacrifice, and to heed than the fat of rams.' The Lord has commanded of His covenant people adherence to both His moral and His ceremonial law; however, in this passage, obedience 'is *better* than sacrifice.' How can this be since God has commanded both? The answer is that, even for the children of Israel who were commanded to offer sacrifices in accordance with the ceremonial law that regulated their lives and worship, loyalty to the Lord by obeying His moral law came first."[26]

White and Niell's understanding of 1Sa. 15:22 is faulty. The passage isn't making a distinction between moral and ceremonial laws, but between empty religion and a sincere heart. The point is that religiosity (the empty shell of religion) is infinitely inferior to a sincere heart, which, by its very nature, *produces* obedience (Jn. 14:15). The apostle Paul offers the same critique in 2Ti. 3:5, where we're told to avoid those who have only a *form* of godliness.

---

[26] *The Same Sex Controversy*, 82.

In attempting to prove their point, White and Niell also reference two passages in the book of Psalms. But, both passages demonstrate the same lack of understanding regarding what the writer was getting at, which is the same point being made in 1Sam. 15:22.

> *"Sacrifice and meal offering You have not desired; My ears*
> *You have opened; Burnt offering and sin offering You have*
> *not required. [7] Then I said, 'Behold, I come; In the scroll*
> *of the book it is written of me. [8] I delight to do Your will,*
> *O my God; Your Law is within my heart.'"*
>
> Psalms 40:6-8

> *"For You do not delight in sacrifice, otherwise I would give*
> *it; You are not pleased with burnt offering. [17] The*
> *sacrifices of God are a broken spirit; A broken and a*
> *contrite heart, O God, You will not despise. [18] By Your*
> *favor do good to Zion; Build the walls of Jerusalem. [19]*
> *Then You will delight in righteous sacrifices, In burnt*
> *offering and whole burnt offering; Then young bulls will be*
> *offered on Your altar."*
>
> Psalms 51:16-19

Of the second passage, White and Niell state, "The Lord desires 'righteous sacrifices' offered by one whose heart is broken and contrite—by one who is striving after righteousness. God desires adherence to His moral law before ceremonial offerings are made." They repeat the statement made in the passage, but in the very next sentence, assign their own interpretation to it.

This presents a perfect case study for eisegesis—reading into the text what one presupposes it says. They force their view of moral laws onto the text, when all that the psalmist is saying is that God isn't interested in religious form if a person's heart isn't right. He's only pleased with our religious lives when we're motivated out of love for Him and for our neighbor (Matt. 22:36-40). So, whether the law that's being obeyed is moral, ceremonial, dietary, or customary, it's secondary to the heart with which we obey it. The Pharisees were masters at obeying the letter of the text, but their heart was so far from God that they couldn't see love in personal form when He was standing right in front of them!

"In addition, one more very significant matter in
Scripture firms up the category into which laws
against homosexuality must fall: the death penalty."[27]

To White and Niell, the imposition of the death penalty in
Lev. 18:22 and 20:13 serves as evidence that the proscriptions are
of a moral nature, rather than of a ceremonial, dietary, or
customary one. Surely, if God prescribed the death penalty, we
must be dealing with something inherently sinful, unlike eating
shellfish. By their logic, then, we must conclude that touching
Mount Sinai (Ex. 19:12), hitting or cursing a parent (Ex. 21:15; 17;
Lev. 20:9), and even failing to keep the Sabbath day (Ex. 31:14-15;
35:2) are all moral laws and should require the death penalty today,
as lasting provisions of the Mosaic Law. Interestingly, the
imposition of the death penalty for adultery (Lev. 20:10) would
subject many anti-gay theologians to execution!

That White and Niell so utterly miss the interpretive mark
on these passages is ironic because when rightly interpreted, these
very passages, which are often used to criticize homosexuals, offer
stinging indictments against people on *their* side of the aisle. They
demonstrate over and over again that they are motivated out of an
unsympathetic, blind religiosity, rather than a loving and
compassionate concern for fellow humans. One need only
consider their advocacy of capital punishment for gay people[28] to
prove their warped version of love!

The Changing Tides of Sound Doctrine

I'm going to make a statement that will, no doubt, shock you. In
many of my discussions about homosexuality, people have levied
the argument that God's word doesn't change. But in fact, it
does—or more precisely, the application and relevancy of His
word changes. The very truths that comprise what Scripture calls
"sound doctrine" are subject to the socio-religious context within
which they exist!

---

[27] *The Same Sex Controversy*, 86.
[28] Ibid., 87-89, 95.

"But as for you, speak the things which are fitting for sound doctrine. [2] Older men are to be temperate, dignified, sensible, sound in faith, in love, in perseverance. [3] Older women likewise are to be reverent in their behavior, not malicious gossips nor enslaved to much wine, teaching what is good, [4] so that they may encourage the young women to love their husbands, to love their children, [5] to be sensible, pure, workers at home, kind, being subject to their own husbands, so that the word of God will not be dishonored. [6] Likewise urge the young men to be sensible; [7] in all things show yourself to be an example of good deeds, with purity in doctrine, dignified, [8] sound in speech which is beyond reproach, so that the opponent will be put to shame, having nothing bad to say about us. [9] Urge bondslaves to be subject to their own masters in everything, to be well-pleasing, not argumentative, [10] not pilfering, but showing all good faith so that they will adorn the doctrine of God our Savior in every respect."

Titus 2:1-10

This passage enumerates a number of instructions that many modern Christians would find quite problematic, particularly those pertaining to women and to slaves. The following is a list of the things classified in this passage as "sound doctrine"—a notion that, in my mind, *seems* to indicate their universal applicability, but which, in fact, does not.

Older men are to be:
1. Temperate
2. Dignified
3. Sensible
4. Sound in faith
5. Sound in love
6. Sound in perseverance

Older women are to:
1. Be reverent in behavior (presumably to their husbands)
2. Not be malicious gossips
3. Not be alcoholics
4. Teach what is good

Older women are to encourage *young women* to:
1. Love their husbands
2. Love their children
3. Be sensible
4. Be pure
5. Be workers at home (homemakers)
6. Be kind
7. Be subject to their husbands

Young men are to:
1. Be sensible
2. Be an example of good deeds
3. Have a sound understanding of doctrine
4. Be dignified
5. Be sound in speech

Slaves are to:
1. Be subject to their masters in *all* things
2. Be well-pleasing
3. Not disagree/argue with their master
4. Not steal, but show their good faith (trustworthiness)

Now, if you carefully read this list of obligations that fell under the umbrella of "sound doctrine," a few things likely stuck out to you. Both older and young men were to "be dignified", but women were never told to. Also, both older and young women were to be submissive to their husbands; yet, the men were not told to submit to their wives. While this, along with the instruction for males to be dignified, does not invalidate the appeals, the absence of the same appeals to the opposite sexes is quite revealing of the patriarchal context within this passage was written.

Amongst the widely (although not exclusively) misogynistic traditionalists, there is no expectation that husbands submit to their wives. I, however, believe that in a society in which men and women are social equals, marriage should entail mutual submission, regardless of the sexes of those involved in the marriage. But, many traditionalists still believe that the man is the head of the house; and it's difficult to prove them wrong theologically because a face value reading of the Bible supports that view. So, let's table that discussion and consider the other points of "sound doctrine."

According to sound doctrine, young women are to be homemakers. I guess ultra-conservatives had it right that women are supposed to stay at home and raise the children. God's word never changes, right? So, why do so many traditionalists who *aren't* ultra-conservative allow their wives to work? Some say that it's not the ideal, yet, it's not a practical expectation for most households to be sustained by one paycheck in the modern economy. Others go so far as to say that this particular point of "sound doctrine" is outdated—based on a patriarchal social structure that doesn't exist in our society. Either way, they're left with a problem—something that once made for sound doctrine is no longer considered so to most people, even traditionalists (except those on the fringes).

Of particular relevance to me as a Black man in America is that slaves are told to be subject to their masters in *all* things. That puts me in mind of the command that wives obey their husbands in all things, as though he's the Lord Himself (Eph. 5:22). Slaves aren't told to escape to freedom, seeing as in Christ, there is neither slave nor free, just as wives aren't told to stop submitting to their husbands, seeing as in Christ, there is neither male nor female (Gal. 3:28). So, why would sound doctrine contradict this core principle of the faith—our equality in Christ?

Ultimately, both women and slaves were told to yield to the prevailing culture, even though that culture contradicted fundamental Christian precepts. But why make doctrine subject to culture? Why would it encompass commands that offend modern sensibilities (or rather, *should* do so)? Of course, not so long ago, a number of Christians believed slavery was an honorable institution—fitting for sound doctrine. So, why the change? How is it that rather than telling an escaped Sudanese slave in modern America to return to his master and submit, we'd open our homes and churches as places of refuge, and report the enslaver to the appropriate authorities? Has the evolution of our social worldview rebelled against God, and against sound doctrine?

So many questions. Some would say that this illuminates the contradictions in the word of God—that Scripture is subject to the fallibility of its human writers. I wholly disagree. I believe Scripture is the only thing ever to pass through the agency of man and be truly infallible. So, how can I say such a thing, given some of the elements of sound doctrine that appear anything but sound?

Five years ago, I would have struggled to give you an answer. My legalistic approach to Scripture would have presented me with a conundrum—do I deny modern ethics, or do I maintain fealty with God's word? Do I engage in theological gymnastics in order to make the two mutually exclusive perspectives gel?

Thankfully, God has opened my eyes and heart to a truth that has revolutionized my theological worldview. Doctrine isn't universal or absolute. It is subject to the context within which it's meant to apply at any given time. What are absolute and unchanging are the principles upon which the doctrines of Scripture stand; but the doctrines themselves necessarily change.

But how could this possibly be the case? How is it that God's word, which never changes, actually does change? The answer was in this very passage all along, but we stopped reading too soon.

> "For the grace of God has appeared, bringing salvation to all men, [12] instructing us to deny ungodliness and worldly desires and to live sensibly, righteously and godly in the present age, [13] looking for the blessed hope and the appearing of the glory of our great God and Savior, Christ Jesus, [14] who gave Himself for us to redeem us from every lawless deed, and to purify for Himself a people for His own possession, zealous for good deeds."
>
> Titus 2:11-14

In the very context of these commands, the reason for their issuance is provided. God has offered salvation to the entire world, with the intent of saving as many as possible. The problem is that the entire world doesn't look at things the same way. Some societies (like the ancient Greco-Roman world) were (and are) patriarchal, whereas others, like the modern Western world, view men and woman as equals. Some societies practiced and practice slavery, whereas others view it as a disgusting stain upon the human soul (and rightly so).

Ultimately, the point is quite simple. In a world where the social context (prevailing worldview) changes dramatically over space and time, it's vital that the gospel message, which alone is able to lead to salvation (Ro. 1:16), changes with it. In order for the gospel to be received by people in different parts of the world, and at different points in time, the institution for which it is presented (the Church) must remain relevant. But relevant to whom? To Christians? Absolutely not! We're already saved. It must remain relevant to unbelievers, for God's desire is that *none* would perish (2Pe. 3:9).

If you re-examine the list of sound doctrines Paul delineated, you'll notice something interesting. From time to time, he injected a notice to his readers that the purpose for these commands was to present to the unbelieving world a Christian community that was honorable (by *their* standards).

- verse 5 – "...so that the word of God will not be dishonored."

- verse 8 – "...so that the opponent will be put to shame, having nothing bad to say about us."

- verse 10 – "...so that they will adorn the doctrine of God our Savior in every respect;" in other words, so that they'll make Christian doctrine look good.

As Titus 2:11-14 states, God's purpose is ultimately to ensure that unbelievers are given the best opportunity to hear and receive the gospel, resulting in their salvation. This requires submission to the prevailing ethic, even in contexts within which that ethic contradicts Christian ethics—like the equality of the sexes, or the immorality of slavery. Basically, if it's the way of the world, deal with it. Just be relevant and get the people born again. It is then, after they have received salvation, that we can show them the *better* way.

Now, I'm intimately acquainted with the concern associated with believing that God's holy word, and the doctrines derived from it, can be subject in any way to the changing character of secular societies; but given the biblical testimony, it's absolutely true. That's precisely why Paul continuously adjusted himself in order to stay relevant to the various audiences he ministered to during his missionary journeys.

*"For though I am free from all men, I have made myself a
slave to all, so that I may win more. [20] To the Jews I
became as a Jew, so that I might win Jews; to those who are
under the Law, as under the Law though not being myself
under the Law, so that I might win those who are under the
Law; [21] to those who are without law, as without law,
though not being without the law of God but under the law
of Christ, so that I might win those who are without law.
[22] To the weak I became weak, that I might win the
weak; I have become all things to all men, so that I may by
all means save some. [23] I do all things for the sake of the
gospel, so that I may become a fellow partaker of it."*
1 Corinthians 9:19-23

Why would Paul go through the trouble of becoming all
things to all people? Why wouldn't he simply be himself and
minister according to his personal socio-religious worldview? Why
would he act as one under the Law, even though he was not? Why
would he behave as a weak person around weak people? It was all
for the sake of the gospel, so that he would maximize his
evangelistic results. It's really a shame that the modern Church has
become so legalistic and rigid, requiring that others change to fit
our beliefs rather than us changing to become relevant to them.

We could learn from Paul's example, but we'd have to
accept the principle espoused in Titus 2 and 1Co. 9—that doctrine
and ministry are (or should be), in many ways, subject to the
societies within which they exist. Christianity *must* remain relevant;
but for legalists and literalists, this is a difficult, if not impossible
thing to accept. Because of the Church's inability to adjust, we're
not seeing the types of evangelistic results that Paul witnessed, and
it's primarily the fault of how we interpret and apply God's word.

Christians must understand that because the world
changes, it's absolutely essential that "sound doctrine" change with
it. If our goal is to save as many people as possible, we cannot treat
women as inferior and expect for the gospel to be received by
those who abhor sexism. Likewise, we cannot send our Christian
Western women, free though they may be, to countries where
women are still perceived as inferior to men, and allow them to
behave in ways that would offend local customs. To do so would
damage the local population's ability to receive the gospel.

A principle emerges here. Sound doctrine can literally contradict itself when compared at face value from one culture to another. The overarching principle remains consistent—saving souls—but how that principle applies produces drastically different doctrinal specifics. Therefore, we cannot judge sound doctrine solely on the basis of how we view the world. We must judge it on the basis of the principles that undergird it, and upon those principles alone. Biblical literalists and others who take the word at "face value" have a hard, if not impossible time doing this; but it's absolutely essential for interpreting and applying Scripture in a manner consistent with its original intent.

As we apply this hermeneutical principle to the question of homosexuality, we must take special care to determine what principles we can derive from the biblical statements about same-sex sexual activity. Worldviews on this subject are too strong and emotional to give a passing consideration to what "sound doctrine" should entail. It's certainly not enough to simply read the text and believe that whatever we read is right and good for our time. We've proven that this isn't necessarily true in all cases. As with the texts regarding slaves and women, we have to recognize that the statements were made for a reason. Discovering that reason is the secret to knowing if and how to apply the specific statements within the modern context.

Most traditionalists are incapable of perceiving what they read in Scripture as being isolated to a particular context. For example, Gagnon acknowledged this principle, and then summarily dismissed it—not because he had evidence to the contrary, but because he chose to interpret the data in a way that gelled with his existing beliefs.

> "The passage of time produces changing conceptions of what is detestable to God (as well as changing civil penalties) but, in this case, what is striking is the high degree of continuity between the values of Israelite culture and post-Enlightenment culture."[29]

---

[29] *The Bible and Homosexual Practice*, 120.

Gagnon crosses a line that few traditionalists are willing to cross, and for that I give him credit. He admits that even what is detestable to God—he preferred not to use the actual word, abominable—changes over time. But, where he sees continuity as evidence of a continuing condemnation of homosexuality, I see an example of how bad theology often persists throughout generations. Both slavery and the status of women (subjective "values") also continued from the ancient Israelite culture through the post-Enlightenment culture. In fact, slavery wasn't ended in the United States until the latter half of the 19th century, while the heyday of the Enlightenment was 150 years prior. Does this fact lead Gagnon to question the social evolution that upset support for slavery? Probably not, proving the unsustainability of his argument. In effect, he used a specious argument to dismiss an admittedly legitimate principle. I can think of no greater example of theological desperation.

The moral of the story is that persistence of belief does not validate belief. How many people believe something for years, only to discover that they were wrong? What does it say about the Christian community that we refuse to evolve and grow? What does it say that our traditional beliefs are all that matters, truth be damned?

This underscores the vital importance of understanding *why* Scripture condemns (vis-à-vis homosexuality), advocates (vis-à-vis the subjugation of women to their husbands), or tolerates (vis-à-vis slavery) something during a given period. Only when we address this question can we determine whether any such judgments are consistent with the dramatically changed social context existent today. And only when we determine such consistency can we ensure that our greatest commission—making disciples—is not negatively impacted by our refusal to adapt.

With this in mind, let's turn to the specific passages in the Bible that are thought to refer to homosexuality. Let's do better than our traditionalist authors. Let's apply this (seemingly anathema) principle of subjective doctrine to the issue of homosexuality and see if the condemnations of same-sex intercourse truly indicate a universal rejection of homosexuality, or if we must necessarily accept it as a perfectly benign aspect of human nature.

Section

2

The Vying of the Verses

5

Genesis 19
The Destruction of Sodom and Gomorrah

Having intensely studied the six traditional passages often interpreted as condemning homosexuality, I've come to believe that not a single one actually does so—at least, not when interpreted and applied correctly. But, out of all of the misinterpretations that exist, those involving Genesis 19, which records the destruction of the sister cities, Sodom and Gomorrah, are the most inexcusable, in my view.

An objective reading of Scripture identifies Sodomite sins that don't involve homosexuality at all. The fact that so many anti-gay Christians believe that Genesis 19 even remotely reflects negatively on homosexuality tells me that either 1) these people clearly haven't studied the issue enough to see the glaring truth, or 2) they reject the truth because it doesn't uphold their view.

If the first explanation is the case, it's horrible because people are using their platform to oppress and, in some cases, devastate the lives and families of gay people. How dare they speak out with such hurtful and often hateful rhetoric if they obviously haven't studied the issue enough to interpret the texts correctly?

The second option is no better. If these preachers and scholars have been presented with the truth, the fact that they refuse to accept it smacks of pride and a willingness, even if subconscious, to twist Scripture into any fiction that validates their worldview. That these people have the audacity to accuse the affirming community of twisting Scripture is extremely frustrating.

Before we look at the massive problems with the anti-gay interpretation of the destruction narrative, let's examine what the Bible actually tells us about who the Sodomites were and why God judged and destroyed them.

> **PLEASE NOTE:** When referencing the "Sodomites" throughout this book, I am not referring to homosexuals—a popular modern usage of the term, which is wholly derived from the misinterpretation of the destruction narrative. Instead, I am referring solely to the residents of the ancient city-state, Sodom.

Sodom and Gomorrah were Canaanite cities during the time of the great patriarch, Abraham. Although no one knows for sure where they were located, biblical clues indicate that they were in the southeastern region of Canaan (Gen. 10:19; Ez. 16:46). They were a wealthy people, which likely resulted from their being a Canaanite border city, where much trade would have taken place.

The inhabitants were very wicked. They were known for their oppressiveness (Gen. 13:13; Ez. 16:49-50), so much so that a great outcry against them rose to the throne of God. (Gen. 18:20)

One fairly major problem exists, though, when attempting to specify the nature of their heinous sins against God. While Ezekiel 16:49-50 identifies five specific sins of the Sodomites (pride, greed, laziness, indifference to the poor, and haughtiness), the sixth sin is anything but specific: they committed abominations.

It's from this generic reference that anti-gay Christians ascribe homosexual motives to the Sodomites, based in no small part on their misreading of the destruction narrative. The problem is that Scripture paints an altogether different picture of the Sodomites and their sins.

I strongly suggest that before you read on, you pause and read Genesis 19 in its entirety in order to familiarize yourself with the subject matter. In short, the narrative tells us that two angels, who were in human form, went to Sodom and were met at the city gates by a man named Lot (Abraham's nephew). He invited the angels to stay the night in the safety of his home. While they were enjoying one another's company, all the men of Sodom surrounded Lot's house, demanding he send out the visitors to them so that they could have sex with them—what ultimately would have amounted to rape (Gen. 19:5). Something of an argument between Lot and the mob ensued, as he pleaded with them not to commit so wicked an act. As the mob grew angrier, the angels pulled Lot inside the house and struck the mob with blindness so that the assaulters wouldn't be able to find the door. The angels then informed Lot that their assignment was to destroy the city, advised him to get his family out immediately, and proceeded to carry out their duty. Sodom, Gomorrah, and other neighboring city-states were utterly destroyed.

There are a few reasons traditionalists read this narrative and conclude that the great sin of the Sodomites was homosexuality. First of all, many believe that although the visitors were actually angels, because they were in the form of human men at the time (Heb. 13:2), the Sodomites were intending homosexual rape. Because male-male sex was identified in Lev. 18:22 and 20:13 as an abomination, they view such an intention as being abominable. The fact that Ez. 16:50 explicitly states that the Sodomites committed abominations before the Lord only serves to validate their interpretation—at least, in their view.

The apostle Jude states that the Sodomites' sin involved the pursuit of "strange flesh" (Jude 7). That, coupled with the use of the phrase "sexual immorality" in the same verse, leads people to conclude that the "strange flesh" pursuits of the Sodomites were of a sexual nature. They interpret "strange" as meaning contrary to the natural order of male and female—homosexual.

Now, the first thing I want to say is that this interpretation seems very reasonable on the surface. So, although I don't excuse the lack of study people engage in before drawing their conclusions, I can certainly understand how they can so easily believe the "homosexual" interpretation. Having said that, an objective reading of the biblical texts that reference Sodom and Gomorrah leave no doubt as to what their abominable sin actually was, and it was *not* homosexuality. To see this, though, people mustn't be blinded by a need to see homosexuals around every corner, as our profiled authors show themselves to be.

Let's begin with the apostle Jude's reference to Sodom, and work our way backwards. Jude 7 does not exist in a vacuum. It's part of a greater context involving human-angel interactions.

"And angels who did not keep their own domain, but abandoned their proper abode, He has kept in eternal bonds under darkness for the judgment of the great day, [7] just as Sodom and Gomorrah and the cities around them, since they

63

in the same way as these indulged in gross immorality and went after strange flesh, are exhibited as an example in undergoing the punishment of eternal fire. [8] Yet in the same way these men, also by dreaming, defile the flesh, and reject authority, and revile angelic majesties. [9] But Michael the archangel, when he disputed with the devil and argued about the body of Moses, did not dare pronounce against him a railing judgment, but said, 'The Lord rebuke you!'"

Jude 6-9

In each of these verses, Jude references both humans and angels. In verse 6, he mentions angels who copulated with human women during the days of Noah (Gen. 6:1-4). In verse 8, he deals with humans who speak ill of angels. In verse 9, he mentions two angels, Michael and the devil, who argued over the body of a human—Moses. Are we to conclude that Jude broke with his context of human-angel interactions in order to deal with homosexuality in verse 7? Sound hermeneutics require us to interpret verse 7 based not on our assumptions about the Sodomites, but upon the context in which the verse resides.

If angels were not involved in any biblical account of Sodom, it would be difficult to understand why Jude referenced the city in this context. However, Genesis 19 does, in fact, involve an attempt by the Sodomites to have sex with two visitors who were, indeed, angels; therefore, their being mentioned in the context of Jude 7 makes perfect sense. The Sodomites attempted to have sex with beings of a non-human created kind, an act that's referred to as bestiality.

Jude 7 says that the Sodomites went after "strange flesh." The Greek word translated "strange" is *heteras*, which means different or other. It's the same word from which we derive "heterosexual", which means, "sexually oriented toward the *other* sex."

Now, 1Co. 15:39-40 states that not all flesh is the same; in other words, some flesh is *heteras*/different. Yet, when it describes how flesh differs, it doesn't draw the dividing line on the basis of biological sex, as traditionalists do in their interpretation of Jude 7. It draws it on the basis of species. *All* human flesh is one flesh—the same flesh—whether associated with the same or opposite sex. So, when Jude said that the Sodomites went after strange flesh (*sarkos heteras*), he meant that they pursued flesh that wasn't human. If we examine the destruction narrative, as well as the context of Jude's words, they harmonize perfectly on the fact that the Sodomites did, indeed, pursue sex with an *other/different* kind—the angelic kind.

Bestiality is, undoubtedly, the "strange flesh" pursuit of the Sodomites. What we must ask is if it's an abomination, because if it is, it would certainly qualify as the abomination mentioned in Ez. 16:50.

> "*Also you shall not have intercourse with any animal to be defiled with it, nor shall any woman stand before an animal to mate with it; it is a perversion... [26] But as for you, you are to keep My statutes and My judgments and shall not do any of these abominations, neither the native, nor the alien who sojourns among you...*"
> Lev. 18:23, 26

Bestiality is, indeed, called as an abomination. This, coupled with Jude's confirmation that the biblical view of their sexual sin was a pursuit of human-angel sex, lends substantial credence to the identification of bestiality as the "abominable acts" that Ezekiel accused them of committing. But, do anti-gay theologians, scholars, and leaders acknowledge this biblical reference to Sodomite bestiality? Do they conclude that bestiality was their abominable sin, rather than homosexuality, seeing as Scripture provides explicit support for this interpretation, unlike the homosexual one?

> "There cannot be any doubt that the sinfulness known in Genesis 13, the wickedness of which God speaks in Genesis 18:20, is here seen in its full expression in the lustful, homosexual desire of the men of Sodom for these visitors."[30]

White and Niell expressed absolute certainty in the belief that Sodom's sin was homosexual desire. But, they offered no

---

[30] *The Same Sex Controversy*, 34.

evidence whatsoever, unlike I have offered above. They trusted, instead, that their simple declaration would suffice their readers. Unfortunately, it's human nature to automatically accept claims that you already agree with. Red flags are only raised in our minds when something *challenges* our existing beliefs. We must all take care to turn off this reflexive response and critically consider every claim that's put before us.

One may think that White and Niell were simply unaware of the human-angel context of Jude's reference to Sodom. It's certainly not as though a number of traditionalists haven't "overlooked" it. But actually, they *were* aware. They simply chose to ignore the contextual evidence, further demonstrating their bias.

> "How should this [sarkos heteras; flesh of a different kind] be understood? Given the background, this would surely be in reference to homosexuality... The 'unnatural lust' or 'perversion' here referred to is that which causes a man to lust for *different* flesh than that which God intended."[31]

Once again, no evidence is offered, save the word of White and Niell. The fault hardly lies with these particular authors alone, though. It's a widespread abuse of the biblical record, as evidenced by these additional "oversights" in the evaluation of the Noachian-era human-angel bestiality, as compared to the Abrahamic-era bestiality.

> "Just as one form of illicit copulation (between angels and women) contributed to the earlier cataclysm of the great flood in Genesis 6 (an important element in the general 'wickedness of humankind,' 6:5), so too another form of unnatural sexual relations (between men) served as a key contributing factor in the cataclysmic destruction of Sodom and Gomorrah."[32]

---

[31] *The Same Sex Controversy*, 49.
[32] *The Bible and Homosexual Practice*, 75.

What contributed to the destruction of these cities was not "*another* form of unnatural sexual relations", as Gagnon claims. It was precisely the *same* form as that which contributed to the earlier cataclysm—(intended) sex between humans and angels. Jude 7 explicitly states this, saying "in like manner"/"in the same way". This is an important acknowledgement because since it was the exact same issue, homosexuality cannot be forced onto the text. This isn't to say that other passages don't identify homosexuality as an additional sin, but Jude 7 can't be considered a proof-text for that point because it speaks specifically and only of human-angel bestiality. That's why Sodom was mentioned there, sandwiched between verses that deal specifically with humans and angels.

But, just because the visitors were angels doesn't mean that the Sodomites' *intention* wasn't to engage in homosexual rape, right? After all, if they were in human form, wouldn't the Sodomites have been planning to rape human men, as far as they knew? That's exactly the point White and Niell attempt to make.

> "Some have attempted to avoid the weight of the description of going after 'strange flesh' by saying that the sin here is that the men desired to engage in relations with angels. While this would surely amount to going after 'strange flesh,' there is one rather obvious problem with this idea. *The men of Sodom did not know the visitors were angels.* They believed them to be mere men, like themselves. Therefore, Jude's description is best understood to refer to the homosexual desire of the men to engage in relations with the visitors."[33]

Let me share with you a little secret when it comes to the language anti-gay theologians employ when attempting to convince people of their perspective. Whenever they say that something is obvious, plain, or evident, make sure to read extra-carefully because you're probably going to be hit with an unsubstantiated argument. The use of such language is often (though not always) a psychological tactic employed by people to convince an audience of something that they cannot actually prove. It's like a tell in

---

[33] *The Same Sex Controversy*, 48-49.

poker. It gives them away every time. Now, I'm not saying that the use of such language is an indication of such a tactic in action; I'm just saying to be on guard to not let such assurances subconsciously convince you that what the person is claiming is actually accurate. The late President Reagan may have said, "Trust, but verify," but Pastor Weekly says, "Engage healthy skepticism, *and* verify!" Never allow yourself to consider theological arguments on autopilot, for that's just a recipe for misinterpretation.

At any rate, the authors claim that the "obvious" problem with the notion that "strange flesh" in Jude 7 refers to bestial intentions is that the Sodomites didn't know that the visitors were angels. But, regardless of how obvious this problem is to them, they neglected to provide a single shred of evidence to back up their claim. I, on the other hand, have a couple of points to submit that serve to indicate that the Sodomites were, indeed, aware of the angelic nature of their unknown visitors.

First, the language of Jude 7 indicates intent. It says that they "went after" or "pursued" strange flesh. This demonstrates that the Sodomites knew full well what they were doing, and that it was precisely their knowledge of what they were doing that made their conscious pursuit wicked. They went after strange flesh (of angels) precisely because it was what they wanted to do.

Second, Gen. 19:1 says that when the angels arrived in Sodom, Lot was sitting at the city gate. When he *saw* them, "he rose to meet them and bowed down with his face to the ground." Now, either Lot had some sort of sixth sense, or there was something peculiar about these visitors' appearance that gave away their true nature, even though they were in human form. Lot didn't simply greet them with a kiss or tip his head in respect. He prostrated himself before them, which was the deepest possible respect a person could show; and he did it on sight! We also have to consider *where* he did it. He didn't wait until they were in the privacy of his home to reveal that he knew there was something special about them. The Bible is very specific about the fact that Lot was at the city gates when the angels arrived. So, it was in full view of a very active part of the city that Lot paid homage. If the Sodomites didn't recognize something special about the visitors on sight, as Lot did (and that's a big if), they were certainly tipped off when Lot prostrated himself before them.

But, the evidence runs even deeper. However, before laying it out, I need to back up and give some background on the destruction narrative because the relevant parts begin *before* Gen. 19.

"And the LORD said, 'The outcry of Sodom and Gomorrah is indeed great, and their sin is exceedingly grave. [21] I will go down now, and see if they have done entirely according to its outcry, which has come to Me; and if not, I will know.'"

Genesis 18:20-21

In this passage, God is speaking to Abraham, telling him of His intention to destroy the cities if the outcry of their grievous sins is substantiated. Afterward (in vs. 23-32), Abraham bargains with God, pleading with him not to destroy the cities if from 50 to as few as 10 righteous people are found in the city.

Now, the angels did not arrive in Sodom to reconnoiter the area until chapter 19. This means that God had already determined to destroy the cities prior to the angels' arrival there, and that their only purpose was to get firsthand verification of the type of evil that was taking place in Sodom. Once confirmed, they were to destroy the cities (Gen. 19:13); and we discover in Chapter 19 that that's precisely what took place.

Think back to Jude 7. It says that the Sodomites *went after* sex with angels. This language indicates a pattern of behavior that would have had to precede this final act before the city's destruction. They didn't simply *attempt*, they *pursued*. Coupled with the fact that an outcry arose against the cities, this indicates that whatever the Sodomites were doing, they were doing it long before we arrive to Genesis 19.

Anti-gay theologians agree, except that they unsurprisingly identify the pattern of behavior as homosexuality. We've already seen that Scripture identifies it as bestiality. But, is there any evidence other than the language of Jude 7 that the Sodomites did, indeed, have a pattern of going after angelic flesh?

Luke 17:26-29, 2Peter 2:4-6, and Jude 6-7 demonstrate an interesting pattern of correlating God's judgment against the whole world during the days of Noah with His judgment against Sodom and Gomorrah. A face value reading of these texts would likely lead someone to believe that the connection is simply that both narratives involve total destruction. But, what if the connection runs deeper? In both narratives, human-angel sex is involved—the former by activity, and the latter, at the very least, by intent. If there was, indeed, a pattern of human-angel sex in Sodom prior to Genesis 19—moments when there wasn't simply an intent, but actual activity—it would explain why God's judgment was so drastic.

Think about it. Ezekiel identified five specific sins that the Sodomites were guilty of: pride, greed, laziness, indifference to the poor, and haughtiness. Do you think Sodom and Gomorrah were the only ancient cities with these sins in abundance? Even if we're to expand the scope of sin to include rape or the supposed sin of homosexuality, we're faced with the same problem. Both were known to exist all over the ancient world, with not a single instance of divine, annihilative judgment against the regions.

If we stick to what the Bible actually tells us, and identify the abomination of the Sodomites as human-angel bestiality, a fascinating picture emerges. Wherever instances of human-angel sex took place, God brought total destruction. For example, the world was rampant with it in Noah's day, and God destroyed the whole world with water.

Gen. 6:4 gives us an important clue. It says that the Nephilim (rendered "giants" in the KJV), who were the hybrid offspring of humans and angels, were in the earth in those days (the days just prior to the flood), "and also afterward." But, if Nephilim exist because of the copulation of humans and angels—yet God destroyed the antediluvian Nephilim—where did the other Nephilim, who were in the earth "afterward", come from? Apparently, human-angel sex wasn't a one-time event.

Now, what's so interesting is that wherever Nephilim existed, you were sure to find two things: 1) evil increasing in the land (Gen. 6:5, 11; Gen. 18:20), and 2) total destruction by divine judgment. Note that tribes of giants/Nephilim also existed in Hebron (the Anakim: Num. 13:33), in Moab (the Emim: Deut. 2:9-11), and in Bashan (the Rephaim: Josh. 12:4). People spend a lot of time trying to make sense of how a loving God could order the total annihilation of so many Canaanite tribes; but if we consider all the biblical evidence together, it becomes apparent that God, indeed, judged these cities for engaging in human-angel bestiality, which is indicated by the presence of giants in their territories. The increased wickedness that accompanied the Nephilim (Gen. 6:4-5) certainly qualifies as the cause of the outcry against Sodom attested to in Gen. 18:20.

It's important to note that the judgment against the bestial tribes is not simply a matter of judging them for engaging in sex with non-humans, for other regions engaged in bestiality, as well. It's a matter of the human genome being polluted by this hybridization, which could have eventually led to the corruption of the line through which the Messiah would be born. Total destruction was the only way to ensure the salvation of the world through Jesus—God in the flesh, who saved the world from its sins because He was the second Adam, holy and without blemish (a prophetic fulfillment that required a pure human bloodline).

A pattern of human-angel bestiality in Sodom is evidenced not only by the language of Jude 7, and by the correlations between the Noachian destruction and the destruction of Sodom and Gomorrah, but also by the fact that the apocryphal Book of Jubilees 20:5 indicates that giants may have been in Sodom prior to its destruction. If true, they could only have gotten there through human-angel sex amongst the Sodomite women, or by migration. All evidence considered, I'm sold on the bestiality explanation.

But, let's be very careful here. While the evidence clearly leads to the sin of the Sodomites being bestiality, could it be that the sin simply *involved* bestiality, but also involved homosexuality? Gagnon raises this possibility.

> "Thus three elements (attempted penetration of males, attempted rape, inhospitality), and perhaps a fourth (unwitting, attempted sex with angels), combine to make this a particularly egregious example of human depravity that justifies God's act of total destruction."[34]

> "...no one can say precisely how [the biblical writer] construed the motives of the men of

---

[34] *The Bible and Homosexual Practice*, 75-76.

Sodom (beyond generic evil), though a reasonable conjecture might be a combination of homoerotic or bisexual lust on the part of at least some of the crowd and an aggressive intent to dominate and humiliate strangers to Sodom by forcing on them an abominable and shameful practice. A strict either/or interpretation, *either* homosexual/bisexual lust *or* an aggressive disgrace of visitors, goes beyond the wording of the text and imposes a distinction that did not always hold true in the ancient world."[35]

"The reference to sexual immorality is ambiguous (though it probably refers to homosexual acts), while the clause 'went after other flesh' probably refers to their attempt to copulate with Lot's angelic visitors. In other words, the two actions (committing sexual immorality and pursuing angels) are to be treated as related, but distinct, actions."[36]

Where's the evidence? First of all, Gagnon's claim that three, maybe four elements were involved in God's determination to destroy the cities is decidedly incorrect. It's interesting that the "attempted penetration of males" is nowhere stated as their sin; yet what *is* stated in Scripture—their attempt to have sex with angels—is only considered a *possible* element by Gagnon. He's so set on assigning homosexuality as their sin that he's willing to overlook the biblical testimony in order to arrive at that destination. He's too scholarly to completely ignore the bestiality interpretation, so he feels compelled to at least mention it; but he minimizes it as much as possible so as not to let it interfere with his abomination of choice—homosexuality.

Furthermore, his "reasonable conjecture" that at least some of the townsmen were motivated out of same-sex lust is anything but reasonable. Lust is rarely a compelling factor in rape. It's almost always about domination. People can satiate their lust by having sex with anyone who's willing, including a prostitute. To be

---

[35] *The Bible and Homosexual Practice*, 77.
[36] Ibid., 87.

willing to force someone into sex requires a motive that far exceeds lust.

Gagnon reveals himself as a master tactician, fitting the more reasonable interpretations into the argument, while still holding onto his homosexuality angle. At this point, he's reduced the accusation to at least "some" of the crowd having gay lust, which still doesn't explain why the entire crowd—which included *all* the men of Sodom (Gen. 19:4)—appeared to have the same motive.

Now, unlike the other authors, Gagnon at least admits that "strange flesh" in Jude 7 refers to their pursuit of human-angel sex; although I strongly disagree that they did so unwittingly (the reasons for which I dealt with previously).

Still, I'm baffled by his claim that the reference to sexual immorality "probably refers to homosexual acts." He offers no supporting evidence, leaving me to believe that he simply chooses to believe this. Besides, if the Sodomites were aware that the strangers were angels (and I believe they were), homosexuality would not be involved at all, seeing as they were aware that these were not really men they were attempting to have sex with. Consequently, neither the act nor the intent would have been homosexual in nature.

Gagnon goes on to claim, "a strict either/or approach to the question of motivation (intent to do harm vs. sexual passion) is unwarranted for this story."[37] But, sexual passion cannot be logically derived from the text. The fact that the narrative involves a mob only solidifies the case for harmful intent, rather than sexual passion, else they could have easily had sex with one another.

Joe Dallas offers a rather weak interpretation of why the whole town gathered a mob with the intent of having sex with the visitors. He claims that "for such an event to include 'all the men of the city, both young and old,' homosexuality must have been commonly practiced."[38] But, I'm compelled to ask which is a more reasonable interpretation—that the town was full of gay, or at least bisexual men, or that it was full of men who wanted to assert their dominance by violating foreigners? Given that the Sodomites had

---

[37] *The Bible and Homosexual Practice*, 97.
[38] *The Gay Gospel?*, 176.

recently been humiliated in the loss of a war (Gen. 14), coupled with the fact that they were a very prideful and haughty people (not to mention that nowhere on the face of the earth is homosexuality practiced by a majority of residents), I'm forced to subscribe to the "dominance through rape" view.

This interpretation is solidified by a very similar occurrence of mob-rape, which took place over 500 years later in the Israelite city of Gibeah. This mob demanded a male foreigner, but acquiesced to the offer of his concubine. If it was a mob full of homosexuals, as we're led to believe was the case in Sodom, why did they accept the man's female and rape her instead? Apparently, they were intending to have a foreigner carry the message of their cruelty in order to instill fear in the hearts of outsiders. The sex of the person wasn't important for their purposes. It wasn't about homosexuality. It was about power!

Interestingly, Lot offered women to the Sodomite mob, yet they rejected his offer. Does this mean that the Gibeanites were straight, while the Sodomites were gay? No, it simply demonstrates that both mobs were only interested in raping an outsider—a foreigner. Lot offered his daughters to the mob—women who were residents of the city, unlike the concubine the Gibeanites accepted.

Gagnon also offered one of the most forced interpretations I've ever come across. In relation to how he identified the sin of the Sodomites as, at the very least, *including* homosexuality, he stated:

> "Ultimately, however, since the story is used as a type scene to characterize the depth of human depravity in Sodom and Gomorrah and thus to legitimate God's decision to wipe these two cities off the face of the map, it is likely that the sin of Sodom is not merely inhospitality or even attempted rape of a guest, but rather attempted homosexual rape of male guests."[39]

This is an extremely subjective interpretation. In fact, rather than being an interpretation, it's more accurately considered

---

[39] *The Bible and Homosexual Practice*, 75.

an interpolation. One must simply *choose* to view the story in this way because, as we have seen, Scripture actually tells us a completely different story.

It appears that Gagnon views the narrative as an allegorical fable, rather than a historical account—for he sees it as a "type scene to characterize the depth of human depravity", rather than substantial events that actually took place in the life of Abraham and his kin. Still, even if he's right, why must he force homosexuality into the moral of the story? Was rape or bestiality not egregious enough to serve in this type scene for human depravity? Apparently not. In Gagnon's mind, homosexuality *had* to be the great Sodomite sin because it is the great sin above all sins, including rape—which, to Gagnon, is only bad enough to justify the destruction of the cities *if* homosexuality is also involved. Absolutely astonishing logic!

Take a moment and think about Gagnon's thought pattern. First, because the story is a type scene (which isn't actually indicated by Scripture), it's intended to validate God's judgment on the cities (as though God's judgment needs validation in the first place). To Gagnon, the whole story was apparently conjured in order to get the reader of the Bible on God's side.

But, who gets to decide what sin is wicked enough? Who is Gagnon to say that the rape of a foreigner was not wicked enough in and of itself? Why must the male-male element (which doesn't actually exist because the foreigners were angels, not men—a fact of which the Sodomites were aware) be the determining factor, even though Scripture never makes this claim?

I submit that the best interpretation is that human-angel sex was the great Sodomite abomination, and, in tandem with the other sins mentioned in Ez. 16:49-50, resulted in the destruction of these ancient cities.

Before I close out this chapter on Sodom and Gomorrah, I want to point out one more example of blatant and excessive bias on the part of anti-gay theologians. It just so happens that Gagnon, whose name has been mentioned quite a bit throughout this chapter, offers one of the worst examples of bias I've ever come across, and it relates to Sodom and Gomorrah.

"Canaanite proclivity to homosexual rape is hinted at by [the biblical writer] in Gen 10:19 when he mentions the fact that the territory of the Canaanites extended as far south as Sodom and Gomorrah."[40]

For Gagnon, the mere mention of Sodom and Gomorrah almost 10 chapters before the destruction narrative served as a hint that the Canaanites had a proclivity to homosexual rape. Apparently, as far as Gagnon is concerned, whenever Sodom appears in Scripture, homosexuality is the reason. He's absolutely incapable of divorcing from his reading of Scripture the preconception that "sodomite" refers to homosexuality—a very bad trait for a biblical scholar to exhibit. Therefore, wherever Sodom is mentioned, homosexuality is the reason.

The actual context within which the city is mentioned in Gen. 10 has absolutely nothing to do with sin, morality, sexuality, or anything else. It's simply a genealogical chapter. It deals with who people were and, in some cases, where they settled. There are no moral pronouncements in the chapter at all. So, that Gagnon would see the mere mention of Sodom and Gomorrah—the purpose of which was to provide the reader with a geographical point of reference—as a hint of Canaanite proclivities to homosexual rape is beyond belief, and should adequately demonstrate his consuming bias to any objective reader.

When the Hebrew prophets, Jesus, and the apostles spoke of the Sodomites, they talked about their greed, pride, cruelty, and their pursuit of sex with angels—a form of bestiality. Nowhere is homosexuality referenced in relation to Sodom *or* Gomorrah, not one single time. But for Gagnon, this simply doesn't matter. The prophets, apostles, and Jesus obviously missed the most important element of the Sodom story—their most egregious and abominable sin. Gagnon is determined to make sure to correct their oversight.

Honestly, I expected a more seasoned interpretative approach from someone who is an assistant professor at a theological seminary. My intention here is not to personally attack Gagnon. I only desire to shine a spotlight on the fact that one's

---

40 The Bible and Homosexual Practice, 67.

credentials do not make him/her right. The fact is that when it comes to interpretations of Scripture, you *must* scrutinize what you read, whether the title before the name is pastor or bishop, or the abbreviation after the name is Th.D. or Ph.D.

As Christians, we make a mistake when we give weight to people's interpretation of Scripture based on their credentials. In the secular world, credentials mean a lot; and that's perfectly fine. But, when it comes to God's word, what matters most is that *you* search the Scriptures to confirm what you're being taught. Never forget: The message is infinitely more important than the messenger.

I challenge you in the name of Jesus to take upon yourself the Berean spirit as you continue to consume this information (Acts 17:11). Don't be a lazy Sodomite (Ez. 16:49). Take notes. Highlight noteworthy statements. **Read with a Bible at hand and look up every single passage referenced.** My opponents may want you to take things at face value and summarily accept "obvious" truths; but I implore you to *study* God's word! Engage yourself and demonstrate to God your zeal for the truth. He sees and honors such zeal, and will bless you with a fruitful understanding. Amen!

And now, back to our regularly scheduled program…

6

Leviticus 18:22; 20:13
To Obey Or Not To Obey?

The book of Leviticus contains two passages that are often referenced when condemning homosexuality. Both reflect a provision of the Mosaic Law against men having sex with men. God gave this law code to the children of Israel after delivering them from slavery in Egypt some 3,400+ years ago. Because the language of both verses is so similar, we'll examine them together.

> *"You shall not lie with a male as one lies with a female; it is an abomination."*
>
> *Leviticus 18:22*

> *"If there is a man who lies with a male as those who lie with a woman, both of them have committed a detestable act; they shall surely be put to death. Their bloodguiltiness is upon them."*
>
> *Leviticus 20:13*

Unlike the story of Sodom and Gomorrah, which involves multiple problems of interpretation, the problems surrounding these verses involve both interpretation and application—what it means, as well as who it applies to. In fact, out of all of the biblical passages surrounding homosexuality, these Levitical proscriptions are the most misapplied.

Still, this hasn't prevented people from trying to force the application of these verses beyond all logic and theological integrity. There was certainly no shortage of such attempts during my reading.

> "Both passages unquestionably prohibit any type of same-sex intimacy and even prohibit the *interest* in same-sex intimacy. If God forbids certain deeds—declaring them sinful—we must necessarily conclude that the desire, the longing, or the interest in committing such deeds is sinful as well."[41]

Remember the secret I shared about people's tactical use of reassuring language without actually providing evidence? Well, here we go again. Apparently, we're to believe that both of these passages "unquestionably" prohibit any type of same-sex intimacy, as well as same-sex erotic desires, despite the fact that neither of these points is actually supported by the verses in question.

First of all, there's a big difference between desire and action. White and Niell claim that desire alone is sin, but Scripture explicitly disagrees. James 1:14-15 teaches that desire makes one susceptible to temptation, which, if left unchecked, can *lead* to sin. Therefore, desire produces a *potential* for sin if left unchecked; but in itself, it is not sin. If desire alone were sin, what point would exist in tempting us, when the sin has already been committed—and not only committed, but present as a continual state of being?

Another problem with White and Niell's argument is their assertion that same-sex intimacy is prohibited in both passages. Every book that dealt with Leviticus joined in this popular, yet completely unfounded belief. Neither verse mentions female-female sex, or even condemns same-sex sexual activity in general; yet both verses *are* explicit in their proscription of male-male sex. White and Niell address this rebuttal in their book.

> "If the case is going to be made that lesbianism is an acceptable practice because it is not specifically referenced, then a whole host of other problems will also come to the surface of this immoral well... They seem oblivious to the fact that this realization supports the view that the prohibition against male-male sexual intimacy is also a prohibition against female-female sexual intimacy."[42]

[41] *The Same Sex Controversy*, 53.

"This uncomfortable reasoning is precisely the problem for those claiming that the Bible does not condemn or prohibit homosexuality. They claim that the Bible does not provide a single verse that prohibits the practice, so it must be acceptable. This type of reasoning is a slippery slope into hell. Such is the outcome of the attempt to render Leviticus obsolete."[43]

While their logic seems reasonable, what White and Niell are ultimately contending is that doctrine can be created out of thin air based on the perceived repercussions of *not* creating it. Because "other problems will also come to the surface," they're content to take it upon themselves to add to the word of God. *"God didn't condemn it, and that leaves the door open to other sins; therefore, let's assume He did condemn it so we can close that door."*

I don't like this approach to Scripture. It makes God's word too subjective—allowing readers to add to Scripture anything they want to when they don't like the implications of what it actually says (or doesn't say). That's very dangerous! Besides, Romans 4:15 teaches that where there is no law, there is no transgression. In other words, you can't break a law that doesn't exist. If White and Niell had their way, they'd simply create new laws along the way, based on what they *wish* a verse said; but this verse in Romans says that they do not have authority to do that.

They then make the outrageous claim that if a person believes Leviticus is obsolete, they're going to Hell. This despicable scare tactic consigns the biblical writers, as well as Jesus, to Hell, for they each taught that the Law has been fulfilled and is, therefore, obsolete.

The failure of their argument doesn't end there, though. Consider that in Lev. 18:23, the verse immediately following the proscription of male-male sex in v. 22, both men *and* women are explicitly forbidden from engaging in bestiality. In addition, incest with both the father *and* mother is explicitly forbidden in v. 7. Why would God, through Moses, condemn women implicitly in verse 22, but explicitly in other verses in this same context?

---

[42] *The Same Sex Controversy*, 106.
[43] Ibid., 79.

The same can be said for chapter 20. Cursing father *or* mother is prohibited in verse 9. Also, both male *and* female bestiality is condemned in verses 15-16. Yet, we're to believe that the intention of verse 13 was to condemn same-sex sexual acts, regardless of the sex of those involved? This interpretation simply doesn't fit the evidence.

Now that we understand that only male-male sex was being condemned, we must ask the question: Why was female-female sex not condemned along with male-male sex? Robert Gagnon attempted to answer this question.

> "The primacy of penetration for defining sexual intercourse may *partly* explain why the Holiness Code leaves out lesbian relationships. In such acts there is no penetration by a male organ and no transfer of semen—two acts that effect in a real sense a climactic merger of beings and definitively and unambiguously cross boundaries. A similar rationale helps to explain why the prohibition of bestiality (Lev 18:23; 20:15-16), unlike that of same-sex intercourse, is applied to both men and women: apparently it was thought that women could be penetrated by male animals. There probably were other factors accounting for why lesbian intercourse goes unmentioned. It may have been thought of as a transgression of the covenant but one meriting a punishment less severe than death. Possibly lesbianism was unknown to the Israelites and/or Canaanites."[44]

First, if the problem is one of same-sex penetration, and not same-sex sexual activity, it demonstrates that this verse contained no universal pronouncement that same-sex intercourse is inherently immoral. If there were an inherent immorality about homosexuality, as all of our authors claim, all forms of same-sex sexual intimacy would have been proscribed, whether involving penetration or not. The theoretical need for penetration cements the notion that what is engendering these proscriptions goes

---

[44] *The Bible and Homosexual Practice*, 144-145.

beyond the nature of homosexuality and speaks to the perceptions resident within a particular culture.

Furthermore, Gagnon apparently has trouble backing up his own argument, as evidenced by the use of very uncertain language, e.g. "may", "partly explain", "probably", "possibly". For someone with such a firm position, Gagnon doesn't seem to have any firm substantiating evidence. This doesn't make his contentions wrong, necessarily, but it indicates his acknowledgement of the weaknesses of his own arguments. It would be much easier to simply trust that God was smart enough to condemn female-female sex if that was His intention. At least then, Gagnon wouldn't have to force himself to wade through an ocean of uncertainty, all so that he could hold on to his anti-gay interpretation of these verses.

Before continuing, I must mention the last *possibility* Gagnon raised—that lesbianism was somehow unknown to the Israelites and Canaanites. While I have no historical evidence to the contrary, logic doesn't allow me to accept this explanation. It reminds me of when the president of Iran, Mahmoud Ahmadinejad, spoke at an American university a few years ago. He claimed that Iran didn't have the phenomenon of homosexuality. It was a ridiculous statement, and Gagnon's claim about ancient Israel and Canaan is equally dubious.

The fact is there's a good reason that female-female sex wasn't included in the Levitical proscriptions. If we begin reading chapters 18 and 20 at the first verse, the reason actually becomes quite obvious.

> "Then the LORD spoke to Moses, saying, [2] "Speak to the sons of Israel and say to them, 'I am the LORD your God. [3] 'You shall not do what is done in the land of Egypt where you lived, nor are you to do what is done in the land of Canaan where I am bringing you; you shall not walk in their statutes. [4] 'You are to perform My judgments and keep My statutes, to live in accord with them; I am the LORD your God. [5] 'So you shall keep My statutes and My judgments, by which a man may live if he does them; I am the LORD."
>
> *Leviticus 18:1-5*

"Then the LORD spoke to Moses, saying, [2] 'You shall also say to the sons of Israel: 'Any man from the sons of Israel or from the aliens sojourning in Israel who gives any of his offspring to Molech, shall surely be put to death; the people of the land shall stone him with stones. [3] 'I will also set My face against that man and will cut him off from among his people, because he has given some of his offspring to Molech, so as to defile My sanctuary and to profane My holy name. [4] 'If the people of the land, however, should ever disregard that man when he gives any of his offspring to Molech, so as not to put him to death, [5] then I Myself will set My face against that man and against his family, and I will cut off from among their people both him and all those who play the harlot after him, by playing the harlot after Molech. [6] 'As for the person who turns to mediums and to spiritists, to play the harlot after them, I will also set My face against that person and will cut him off from among his people. [7] 'You shall consecrate yourselves therefore and be holy, for I am the LORD your God. [8] 'You shall keep My statutes and practice them; I am the LORD who sanctifies you.'"

Leviticus 20:1-8

In both chapters, God declares the reasons He proscribes the activity that follows. In chapter 18, He tells the Israelites that He does not want them doing what was done in Egypt, where they previously lived, and that He also doesn't want them doing what's done in Canaan, where He's taking them to. He says that they are to live according to *His* judgments and statutes. He makes the same point in chapter 20. He demands that they not go "whoring" after Molech, an idol god of the Canaanites. Prostitution is often used in Scripture as an analogy for not remaining faithful to God; so what He's saying is that they're not to commit spiritual adultery against Him by engaging in acts of idolatry. They are to remain sanctified—set apart from the world around them and consecrated unto the Lord, keeping His statutes only.

This explains perfectly why female-female sex was not condemned. It was never God's intention to condemn homosexuality in general, but specific activity that had become associated with the custom and/or worship of the idolatrous Egyptians and Canaanites.

To understand the socio-religious context within which this proscription was given, we must have a brief history lesson. Eunuch priests sometimes served in the idol temples, and they would offer their bodies sexually to the male worshipers as a fertility rite. The eunuch would represent Ashtoreth (a fertility goddess), and the male worshiper would represent Molech (a fertility god). The ejaculation of semen would represent the fertilization of the soil, which represented a plentiful crop in the coming season. Because women were not a part of this ritual, it makes sense why God didn't mention them in the proscribing of these acts.

God explicitly states in both chapters that His purpose in the restrictions that follow is to keep the Israelites sanctified—separated culturally (God's judgments and statutes) and religiously (no playing the harlot)—from the cultures of Egypt and Canaan. The problem in applying this rule in the 21st century is that the cultures of ancient Egypt and Canaan no longer exist. The activities that at one time characterized their societies and religious beliefs no longer have anything to do with them (except in history books).

Now, the time and place of a society doesn't matter when it comes to "playing the harlot". Engaging in acts of worship toward false gods is always wrong because God is always the only true God. But, when it comes to the other acts, they can only be considered obsolete at this point, even if the particular acts were, at a time long ago, used in acts of worship.

For example, there was a time when body markings (tattoos) represented idolatrous beliefs—for people would place the symbols of their gods and/or cultures (which were always idolatrous) on their flesh. That's why tattoos were outlawed in Old Testament Scripture. But, most Christians are wise enough today to not hold modern Christians captive to those ancient practices because tattoos are no longer associated with idolatry in any substantial way.

The principle of rescission is not a "liberal" doctrine. Most Christians realize that laws or commands of Scripture get rescinded, either by subsequent passages, or by post-biblical cultural changes (as in the case with tattoos). The apostle Paul, for instance, forbade certain styles of clothing for women (1Ti. 2:9-10);

yet today, these same exact styles of clothing characterize Christian women. It's precisely the image conjured in the minds of people when they think of a Christian woman (pearls, gold, and expensive clothing). Are our women violating biblical commands by wearing such clothing? Sure they are, if one only cares about the letter of the law. But what's more important than the letter of the law is the spirit or *intent* of the law. Seeing as such styles of clothing no longer represent immodesty, as they did in Paul's day, most Christians consider those restrictions obsolete, even though no passage of Scripture explicitly rescinds them.

Joe Dallas raises another objection to the contention that Leviticus 18 and 20 are now obsolete. Some theologians believe that the Hebrew word translated "abomination" in these chapters, *to`ebah*, refers to things abhorred/hated by God specifically because of their association with idolatrous customs or rituals. I, myself, subscribe to this belief, based on the textual and lexicographic evidence. For example, Strong's Bible Dictionary defines *to`ebah* (Strong's Number: H8441) as: "properly something disgusting (morally), that is, (as noun) an abhorrence; especially idolatry or (concretely) an idol: - abominable (custom, thing), abomination."

Noting that the definitions describe God's view of something (disgusting, abhorred, abominable), we must consider *why* He has this view. Is it simply because the particular thing is inherently disgusting, or is there a particular context that makes it disgusting? This is an important question to ask, and is, unfortunately, often overlooked.

The best way to answer this question is to examine the usage of *to`ebah* in Leviticus, as well as throughout the Pentateuch—the first five books of the Bible, which are traditionally viewed as the writings of Moses. The word is used 25 times within the Pentateuch. The two instances in Genesis, as well as the only instance in Exodus refer to things considered loathsome by Egyptian custom (Gen. 43:32; 46:34; Ex. 8:26). They do not reflect a divine perspective at all. The word occurs five times in Leviticus, and all occurrences are in chapters 18 and 20. It explicitly refers to all the acts proscribed in chapter 18 (18:26-30), and implicitly refers to all acts in chapter 20 (20:23—"abhorred" in the KJV is one of the definitions of *to`ebah*, likely making this word—*quts*—a synonym of *to`ebah*). The remaining instances are all found in the book of Deuteronomy, and are quite telling in terms of the Mosaic usage of the word.

I strongly advise you to read each of the Deuteronomic passages. You will see a very clear pattern form, which associates the things called *to`ebah* very concretely with idolatry (7:25-26; 12:31; 13:12-15; 18:9-12; 20:17-18; 23:18; 27:15; 23:16).

The only exceptions to these explicit textual connections are the following passages: Deut. 14:3; 17:1; 22:5; 24:1-4, 25:16; which are too general to define the word's usage with idolatry directly, although the context and other usage certainly suggests such an intent. However, there's a case to be made for each of these exceptions, given the context.

14:3   In conjunction with the previous verse (v. 2), the theme of keeping the Israelites sanctified (set apart) from the cultures around them is reinforced.

17:1   Verses 2-5 deal specifically with idolatry, providing a direct link in the immediate context.

22:5   This verse forbids cross-dressing as *to`ebah*. Given the fertility rites some Canaanite cities engaged in (which involved cross-dressing eunuchs), the passage almost certainly has in view such rituals.

24:1-4   This passage regards divorce and remarriage, saying that it's forbidden for a woman to remarry a previous husband if she divorces or is widowed from a later marriage. Modern Christians tend to think that reconciling a previous marriage is a good thing. But, some things are forbidden not because they are, in themselves, bad, but because they represent something that is. In the Bible, sexuality (e.g. marriage, infidelity, prostitution) is often a metaphor for our covenant with God. So, this proscription is, at its source, a parable for the fact that God doesn't want His people returning to idolatry now that they've turned their backs on it and are in covenant with him.

25:16   In conjunction with verses 17-19, the things called abominations here are so viewed because they were customs of the Amalekites, an idolatrous people.

So, of all the passages in the Pentateuch in which *to`ebah* appears as a reference to God's view of something (15 passages in 22 verses), 10 are explicitly connected to idolatry, and a legitimate case for implication can be made for each of the other 5 instances. The textual evidence is very strong that Moses' uses of *to`ebah* describe things that are hateful in God's eyes because of their association with the custom or ritual of idolatrous people. This is, indeed, explicitly stated in both chapters referencing male-male sex (Lev. 18:30; 20:23).

But Dallas disagrees, arguing that because *to`ebah* was used in Prov. 6:16-19 to describe things that have nothing to do with idolatry (e.g. a proud look, a lying tongue, and hands that shed innocent blood), the word "clearly... is not limited to idolatrous practices."[45]

Dallas is correct in his assertion that *to`ebah* was used to reference acts that did not necessarily involve idolatry. The problem with the conclusion he draws from this fact, however, is that he fails to take into account the evolution of language. One cannot try to understand how Moses used *to`ebah* by examining how Solomon used it some 500+ years later. Language evolves. Words that were specific at one time can become more widely applied one or two generations later, let alone 500+ years later.

So, the best way to understand the use of *to`ebah* in Leviticus is to study its usage *in Leviticus*, or at most, in the books of the Pentateuch, which are, in large part, ascribed to the same writer—Moses. As has been demonstrated, every usage of *to`ebah* throughout the Pentateuch related in some way to the customs or worship of idolatrous people. That's why Dallas had to go all the way to Proverbs in order to find an example that contradicted this fact. Consequently, his counter-argument holds absolutely no water.

White and Niell argue that the notion that in Leviticus, *to`ebah* only refers to actions or objects associated with idolatry "would contend for the acceptability of bestiality because it would not be practiced in a 'religious' manner, and every time bestiality is mentioned in the Bible, it is prohibited in a context of religious, idolatrous practices (as it is in Exodus 22:19-20 and Deuteronomy

---

[45] *The Gay Gospel?*, 184.

27:15-21)." Apparently, for people like White, Niell, Dallas, and others, it's perfectly alright to stretch the application of a passage of Scripture based solely off of the fear of only applying it within its given context. In my mind, there is no legitimate justification for failing to let Scripture dictate the application of its own words. So, unlike these supposedly conservative authors, I do not believe we have the authority to force passages to apply where they do not, simply because we fear the consequences of not doing so.

To the specific point White and Niell raise, it's an unfounded fear. Bestiality *is* condemned in the New Testament—Jude 7. But, since they view this verse as a condemnation of homosexuality rather than bestiality, they believe that bestiality would be left without an applicable condemnation if they don't force the Levitical passages to apply to Christians. Their snowball of bad theology requires them to create new doctrine in order to accommodate their misinterpretations of other passages. If they would just interpret Scripture properly in the first place, all of these problems would disappear.

Still, the sad truth is that pointing out Jude 7 as a New Testament condemnation of bestiality won't be the end of it. The argument can go on in perpetuity, as other sinful actions are given as examples. *The New Testament doesn't condemn this or that deplorable act; so if we don't force Old Testament proscriptions to apply, such actions would become permissible.* But, no matter how bad the act, we still cannot handle Scripture in so subjective a way—forcing it to apply when we hate the act, and considering it obsolete when we like the act (e.g. wearing mixed fabric clothing).

Sound hermeneutics requires us to submit to God's ruling that the old covenant is obsolete. We are then left to test various acts by the standard of our *new* covenant—the law of Christ, which is characterized by love. The standard of love reveals whether or not acts such as pedophilia are permissible. Seeing as children cannot possibly consent to sex, one needn't have an explicit New Testament proscription to conclude that the acts are forbidden, especially because they are exploitative and selfish. Ultimately, Scripture doesn't need our help. It's well able to sustain its standard of right and wrong.

Dallas goes on to state, "...if the practices in these chapters are condemned *only* because of their association with idolatry, then it logically follows that they would be permissible if they were committed apart from idolatry."[46] I disagree. Consider British colonial law. It applied in New England during the early 1700's because those regions were British colonies. After the Revolutionary War, the colonies became independent, and British colonial law no longer applied. By Dallas' logic, we would assume that every act proscribed within colonial law became legal in New England, including theft, rape, and murder. But, just because British law no longer applied does not mean that the former colonies did not come under the rule of another law—an American law. That said, if a person committed murder, he couldn't be tried in post-Revolution New England for violating colonial law, for colonial law no longer applied. He could, however, be tried under whatever applicable laws existed at the time.

So, Dallas' contention that the inapplicability of the Mosaic Law would make anything proscribed therein permissible is wrong. I've found that this argument, which is quite common among anti-gay Christians, is just a scare tactic—intended to convince people that if the Mosaic Law no longer applies, the world will go to hell in a handbasket. But, they either forget or neglect to acknowledge that the abrogation of the Mosaic Law did not leave a moral vacuum. The Law of Moses was replaced with the law of Christ (Gal. 6:2), also referred to in the New Testament as the law of liberty (James 1:25; 2:12). So, while the Law of Moses no longer applies, Christians are still in covenant with God, and required to submit to His *new* law—the law of Christ.

White and Niell, in making the same argument, offer the outrageous example of child sacrifice.

> "If someone were to murder his children for the sake of convenience—doing so in a non-religious way, that is, not in a temple—would the practice be morally acceptable? Can any moral approval be gained when we restrict the practice of child sacrifice to a non-religious type (Deuteronomy 28:54-55; 1 Kings 3:26; 2 Kings 6:25-31; Matthew 2:16)? Certainly not!"[47]

---

[46] *The Gay Gospel?*, 184.
[47] *The Same Sex Controversy*, 102.

Obviously, they've never heard of "thou shalt not kill", which would include killing children. Now, although Exodus 20 no longer applies because it's a provision of the Mosaic Law, murder is most certainly prohibited within our new covenant (Gal. 5:21; 1Jn. 3:15).

But, let's say that murder wasn't condemned anywhere in the New Testament. Would that make it permissible? Absolutely not; however, sound hermeneutics doesn't permit us to make such a determination based upon the condemnation of murder within a covenant that doesn't apply to Christians. Murder does not pass the test of love, which is the chief law and overriding principle of our new covenant (Matt. 22:36-39). Therefore, an explicit condemnation of murder, though present in New Testament Scripture, is unnecessary to rule the act forbidden.

They go on to say that those who believe the proscriptions of male-male sex only refer to idolatrous practices "are assuming the moral acceptability of that which they are trying to prove."[48] The accusation is that we must start from a place of assuming the acts are acceptable in order to find them so. But, is not *every* act to be considered "lawful" unless condemned in Scripture, or fails the test of our new covenant standard of love (1Co. 10:23; Ro. 4:15)? So then, the authors are actually guilty of the opposite of what they accuse us of. They wrongly assume the moral reprehensibility of same-sex sexual acts and, as a result, don't mind forcing related Old Testament proscriptions out of their context and applying them universally.

Gagnon's argument is not only as weak as that of White, Niell, and Dallas, but it's also contradictory and self-defeating. In fact, so defeating is his argument that he literally makes the case for those who believe the Levitical proscriptions no longer apply.

> "Lev 18:22 occurs in a larger context of forbidden sexual relations that primarily outlaws incest (18:6-18) and also prohibits adultery (18:20), child sacrifice (18:21), and bestiality (18:23). These prohibitions continue to have universal validity in contemporary society. Only the prohibition against

---

[48] *The Same Sex Controversy*, 102.

having sexual intercourse with a woman 'in her menstrual uncleanness' (18:19) does not."[49]

"These considerations, both the six salient features of the Levitical prohibitions against homosexual intercourse and the application of the word *toeba* to 'intrinsically evil' acts, should give anyone pause before rejecting the relevance of these commandments for our contemporary setting."[50]

The first question we must ask is where the condemnation of sex with a menstruating woman is repealed. If Gagnon acknowledges that a sin listed in this context is no longer valid, then upon what basis does he determine which proscriptions still apply and which do not?

Furthermore—and this is very important—Gagnon claims that the application of the word *to`ebah* indicates that the acts are "intrinsically evil", which, by his logic, means that they have universal validity. Yet, sex with a menstruating woman was called *to`ebah*, for all of the acts proscribed in Leviticus 18 were called *to`ebah* (vs. 26-29). So, why does Gagnon believe that the prohibition of sex with a menstruating woman is no longer applicable, seeing as it's supposedly intrinsically evil, given the application of the word *to`ebah*?

So, either 1) *to`ebah* doesn't describe intrinsically evil acts, 2) what is considered intrinsically evil changes over time (which means the acts aren't *intrinsically* evil), or 3) sex with a menstruating woman is still forbidden, given the application of the word *to`ebah* to the act. The fact is that the only option that holds true given the biblical witness is that *to`ebah* does not describe intrinsically evil acts. The evidence indicates that the word describes acts considered disgusting and abhorrent because of their association with idolatrous custom, whether cultural or ritual.

Gagnon disagrees with the notion that Leviticus tells us what makes male-male sex an abomination. How he failed to connect these verses to their context at the beginning of each chapter, I don't know; but he, characteristically, offers *possible*

---

[49] *The Bible and Homosexual Practice*, 113.
[50] Ibid., 120.

explanations, which apparently have more weight in Gagnon's mind than the textual context.

> "Some of these commands may have arisen out of traditional taboos regarding the sacral quality of blood and semen, a concern not to mimic fertility practices of the Canaanites, a desire for consistency in maintaining clear social boundaries and the divinely ordained categories of creation, and/or the intent to symbolize Israel's 'set apart' status (that is, its separate and pure devotion to God)."[51]

> "Although Lev 18:22 and 20:13 do not directly specify why homosexual conduct is an 'abomination,' the most likely reasons are that homosexual conduct entails a confusion of genders through violation of the anatomical and procreative complementarity of male and female, that it constitutes a rejection of the pattern laid down in the traditional material in Genesis 1-3, and that it serves to destabilize the integrity of the family and the ordered survival of the species."[52]

Since Gagnon is willing to submit that at least *some* of the Levitical commands *may* have arisen from socio-religious taboos, the obvious question is: Which ones exactly? Not surprisingly, he never answers this question. He's certainly correct in that verses 22 and 13 of the respective chapters do not specify *why* homosexual conduct is an abomination. However, if he would just consider the context, reading each chapter from the first verse, the reasons behind the proscriptions are explicitly laid out. Applying that to the evidence in the Pentateuch surrounding Moses' usage of *to`ebah* leaves absolutely no doubt as to what made male-male sex abominable. So, Gagnon's assumptions simply aren't necessary; yet he continues to offer them, completely ignoring the textual evidence.

He also states, "That Canaanites practised [sic] homosexuality no doubt enhanced Israel's aversion to it… but it is

---

[51] *The Bible and Homosexual Practice*, 121.
[52] Ibid., 348.

not the fundamental motive for it."[53] While he acknowledges that there is "no doubt" that Canaanite practice enhanced Israel's aversion to male-male sex, he refuses to let go of his interpretation. But, whether Gagnon likes it or not, the first few verses of chapters 18 and 20 demonstrate that the fact that the Canaanites and Egyptians practiced the acts being proscribed in the chapters *is* the fundamental motive behind the condemnations. So, while I can appreciate Gagnon's intellectual honesty in acknowledging the legitimacy of the affirming argument, I believe he would do well to let the word direct his view of these passages.

Before concluding this chapter, it's important that I deal with one of the most dangerous, unchristian arguments I've ever heard regarding homosexuality.

> "It is God who has determined that some offenses of homosexuality deserve the death penalty, not the person who is the messenger of God's truth. This divinely appointed penalty is applicable in both the Old and New Testaments. The apostle Paul taught that homosexuality deserved the death penalty as well (Romans 1:24-32). The next point that we need to remember is that the Bible did not require the execution of *every known homosexual.*"[54]

> "Also important to note is that the Bible allows for the execution of homosexuals by a godly and just civil government, *not* the church…"[55]

When I first read these statements, I couldn't believe what I was reading. White and Niell were actually saying that at least *some* homosexuals should be executed! Realizing how horrifying their advocacy for capital punishment for gays is, they made sure to blame God. It wasn't *their* fault that He ordered the execution of gays. They were just "the messenger[s] of God's truth."

The first problem with their dangerous claim is that neither the Old nor New Testaments advocate the execution of

---

[53] *The Bible and Homosexual Practice*, 132.
[54] *The Same Sex Controversy*, 87.
[55] Ibid., 89.

homosexuals. At most, the Levitical proscriptions order the execution of men who have sex with men, specifically because at that time and in that region, such activity was representative of idolatry. As such, it ran the risk of polluting the spiritual purity of the Israelite people—an ethnic field through which the Seed of David, Jesus Christ, would spring forth—which is why such a drastic penalty was prescribed. Nothing was said, however, about women who have sex with women precisely because homosexuality is not inherently immoral. What men having sex with men *represented*—idolatry—was the problem, not same-sex intercourse.

Regarding the claim that the New Testament also prescribed the death penalty for homosexuality, it's simply not true. The authors referenced Ro. 1:24-32 as proof; however, there are multiple problems with their interpretation. First, Paul's "worthy of death" statement referred to the list of vices he enumerated in verses 29-31—acts that he said the idolaters engaged in *after* God turned them over to a reprobate/depraved mind (v. 28). Same-sex sexual acts were mentioned in verses 26-27, *before* God turned them over. The acts were not repeated in Paul's vice list; therefore, they were not among the things he claimed were "worthy of death."

Second, even if same-sex acts *were* in Paul's vice list, he didn't prescribe the death penalty. He simply said that those who commit such acts are *worthy* of death. In the same epistle, he also stated that *all* people sin (Ro. 3:23), and that the wages of sin is death (Ro. 6:23). So, the same writer stated in the same book that *all* people are worthy of death! In their zeal to find an excuse to advocate the execution of gay people, White and Niell completely missed the point Paul was only *beginning* to make by the end of Romans 1. He enumerated the sins of some (Gentile idolaters) in order to lull the Jewish Christians into a self-righteous sense of superiority, only to turn the tables on them in the very next chapter and demonstrate that they were no better!

Paul ultimately said, "You shouted 'Amen' when I said that those who are proud, disobedient to parents, deceitful, full of gossip, etc. are worthy of death. But guess what... So am I... So are you! Jew and Gentile—we're *all* in the same boat, and we all wholly depend on the grace of God!" This was Paul's "let he who is without sin" moment; but White and Niell, blinded by their apparent loathing of gay people, completely missed it. They viewed Paul's "worthy of death" phrase in isolation from his overall point, and in so doing, wound up falling for the same trap of self-righteousness that Paul set for his Jewish Christian readers—being disgusted by the sin of others, while failing to recognize their own sin and need for forgiveness and grace. Paul would turn over in his grave to see his words being used for the exact opposite of their intended purpose—to judge someone else rather than to prove the sinfulness of us all.

They also claim that the Church shouldn't execute gay people, but rather, a "godly and just civil government" should. In making such a claim, they demonstrate precisely what's wrong with theocratic societies, and why religion has no place in civil government. Who is to say that the way a particular police officer, mayor, judge, or other official interprets a particular passage is right? What happens when their view of God isn't dictated by the Bible but, instead, by the Qur'an, or by Joey's Book of Divine Morals?

> "This [capital punishment] is a moral duty that requires that God's standards be known and followed. It is required of civil officials that they search the Scriptures, do careful exegesis, pursue thorough discussion, and even debate the matter before applying God's standards of justice to society."[56]

White and Niell actually believe that people should apply their interpretation of Scripture to their duties as civil officials! Have they ever heard of the establishment clause of the First Amendment? To permit religious views to dictate how a person serves in a society that is supposed to *allow* the free exercise of religion without *imposing* any particular view is not only self-defeating, but is also one of the reasons people fled Europe hundreds of years ago in the first place.

I imagine they would feel differently if they were the victims of someone else's misguided interpretation of Scripture.

---

[56] *The Same Sex Controversy*, 95.

We'd likely see them picketing in front of the local city hall, screaming about the freedom of religion. They prove their hypocrisy by advocating the imposition of *their* brand of Christianity over everyone else. I've got to tell you... Their brand doesn't look so appealing. They can keep it!

7

Romans 1:26-27
Both Male and Female
Same-Sex Intercourse Addressed

Romans 1:26-27 is the only passage in the entire Bible in which female-female sexual activity is either referenced or condemned, thereby making it the only place in all of Scripture that can possibly be said to condemn homosexuality in any general way. To be precise, though, we'd have to first acknowledge that the Bible never actually references homosexuality—same-sex attractions—and that what is being condemned in Ro. 1 is same-sex sexual activity, which both heterosexuals *and* homosexuals can engage in (e.g. heterosexual prostitutes who engage in same-sex sexual activity for pay, or heterosexual men in prison who rape other men to assert their power/dominance).

The problem that has arisen with the traditional interpretation of this passage is that people too quickly take verses 26-27 out of their preceding context, thereby failing to understand *why* the activity was viewed in a negative way. They choose to impose their own personal, modern perceptions onto the text, rather than to see the words through the lens of ancient Greco-Roman culture, within which the writer (the apostle Paul) and his audience (the first century Church) lived. Consequently, they completely miss the fact that according to the biblical evidence, same-sex sex is more analogous to things like long hair on a man or women preachers than it is to moral wrongs like adultery or prostitution. But, I'll prove this a little later.

First, it's important to consider the overall theme of Paul's epistle to the Roman Christians. Only then will we be in a position to understand how the passage referencing same-sex intercourse fits into that theme—a vital step in interpreting and applying the reference.

Romans was not written as a random, disjointed collection of ideas and doctrines, like the book of Proverbs. In fact, Paul gave a strategic presentation on the nature of salvation, particularly how it relates to the two human groups—Jews and Gentiles. Because Christianity was birthed through the Jewish people and faith as the continuing and concluding expression of God's purpose to save mankind, it was only natural that serious theological challenges would arise between the two groups, as each understood salvation through their own cultural and religious eyes. Consequently, Paul, a Jew by birth and upbringing, yet called to take the gospel to the Gentile races, took this opportunity to address, in detail, God's purpose in salvation.

This theme—God's grace extends equally to Jew and Gentile alike—saturates Romans. Paul began in the first chapter by capturing the support of his Jewish readers, which he accomplished by harshly criticizing the Gentile races for their idolatry (vs. 18-27) and for a wealth of other vices they were perceived to succumb to regularly (vs. 28-32). He rightly expected his Jewish readers to be lulled into a sense of self-righteous disgust at Gentile culture, which found uninhibited expression in the epicenter of ancient wealth and power—Rome.

In the next chapter, Paul quickly turned the tables on his readers by declaring that they were no better than the Gentiles—that they had the audacity to judge them, even though they did many of the same things. It's amazing how much Paul's words reflect the state of modern Christianity, where people are quick to point the finger, yet behind closed doors, they're often guilty of the very same things.

While Paul stated in 1:18 that God's wrath was revealed against the ungodliness of the Gentiles, he flipped the script in 2:5 by stating that the Jewish believers were also storing up God's wrath. In vs. 9-11, he sealed the deal by unequivocally stating that both Jews and Greeks (a metaphorical reference to Gentiles) would be judged.

"For all who have sinned without the Law will also perish without the Law, and all who have sinned under the Law will be judged by the Law."

Romans 2:12

Paul's point was that whether someone lived under the Law or not, everyone was going to have to answer for the lives they lived. Jews would receive no special favor with God. He went on to state that a *true* Jew was not someone with a Jewish ethnicity, but one whose heart was turned towards God (vs. 25-29).

Without giving a detailed exposition on the entire epistle, suffice it to say that Paul continued to build his case for biblical salvation—that it was by faith alone, apart from works of the Law. Because the Law was so integral to Jewish life, this wasn't easy for Jewish believers to receive. That's why Paul's strategic use of the Jewish (and in many ways, human) tendency toward self-righteousness in the first chapter was such a brilliant way to present this teaching.

The tragedy is that many modern Christians completely miss Paul's point. There's really only one way to do this—view the first chapter in isolation from the rest of the epistle. Consequently, many in our generation fall prey to Paul's bait and switch tactic, except that they never get to the "switch" part. Their self-righteous ire is raised at the thought of same-sex sexual activity, as Paul originally intended; but they fail to understand that Paul was using those acts, as well as the vices listed in verses 29-31, for the sole purpose of showing believers how their judgmental view would be their undoing!

Of all the authors of our profiled books, Gagnon is the only one who addresses Paul's overall point in Romans in any substantive way. Yet somehow, he still manages to impose his traditionalist view on the text.

> If even Jews cannot be justified 'on the basis of works of the law' but only 'apart from the law' (3:20-21), then gentiles too are justified apart from observing the requirements of the Mosaic law. Paul here has in view primarily those requirements that in the first century were regarded as distinctively

Jewish such as circumcision, special dietary laws, and special holy days (the sabbath, Jewish festivals).[57]

Gagnon acknowledges Paul's overall point, but limits that point to those Mosaic requirements that deal with Jewish customs, e.g. circumcision, dietary laws, and holy days. But, there is absolutely no evidence that Paul's reference to the Law was limited in this way. He had in view precisely what he said: works of the Law.

Ultimately, Gagnon tries to release believers from having to keep Judaic customs, while still requiring them to keep what he sees as the moral components of the Law. Paul, however, does not divide the Law in this way. In fact, Scripture makes it clear that one must either recognize his freedom from the entirety of the Mosaic Law, or keep it entirely—moral, ceremonial, dietary, and all other components (James 2:10-12). Contrary, then, to Gagnon's claim, Christians are subject to the law of Christ (a.k.a. the law of liberty), not to the Law of Moses.[58]

Now that we've considered the overall point Paul was making in Romans, let's examine our authors' arguments concerning the immediate context of his reference to same-sex sexual acts. To do this, we first need to read the passage for ourselves.

> "For the wrath of God is revealed from heaven against all ungodliness and unrighteousness of men who suppress the truth in unrighteousness, [19] because that which is known about God is evident within them; for God made it evident to them. [20] For since the creation of the world His invisible attributes, His eternal power and divine nature, have been clearly seen, being understood through what has been made, so that they are without excuse. [21] For even though they knew God, they did not honor Him as God or give thanks, but they became futile in their speculations, and their foolish heart was darkened. [22] Professing to be wise, they became fools, [23] and exchanged the glory of the incorruptible God for an image in the form of corruptible

---

[57] *The Bible and Homosexual Practice*, 240-241.
[58] See Romans 6:14-15; 7:1-4; 8:2; Galatians 6:2; James 1:25; 2:12

man and of birds and four-footed animals and crawling creatures. [24] Therefore God gave them over in the lusts of their hearts to impurity, so that their bodies would be dishonored among them. [25] For they exchanged the truth of God for a lie, and worshiped and served the creature rather than the Creator, who is blessed forever. Amen. [26] For this reason God gave them over to degrading passions; for their women exchanged the natural function for that which is unnatural, [27] and in the same way also the men abandoned the natural function of the woman and burned in their desire toward one another, men with men committing indecent acts and receiving in their own persons the due penalty of their error. [28] And just as they did not see fit to acknowledge God any longer, God gave them over to a depraved mind, to do those things which are not proper, [29] being filled with all unrighteousness, wickedness, greed, evil; full of envy, murder, strife, deceit, malice; they are gossips, [30] slanderers, haters of God, insolent, arrogant, boastful, inventors of evil, disobedient to parents, [31] without understanding, untrustworthy, unloving, unmerciful; [32] and although they know the ordinance of God, that those who practice such things are worthy of death, they not only do the same, but also give hearty approval to those who practice them."

Romans 1:18-32

The first error our authors make is their failure to understand the connection between idolatry and the same-sex sexual activity Paul condemned. Rather than viewing the latter as an extension of the former, as the apostle did, the authors see them as distinct sins against God.

> "The first subsection (vv. 24-25) refers generally to idolatry, the second (vv. 26-27) describes a specific sexual vice, and the third (vv. 28-32) gives a list of vices destructive to human relationships."[59]

> "God does not judge them for their ignorance but for acting contrary to the knowledge that they do have. This suppression of knowledge shows itself

---

[59] *Straight & Narrow?*, 67.

especially in two ways: idolatry and same-sex intercourse."[60]

"...same-sex intercourse parallels the sin of idolatry since both suppress the truth about God and God's creation."[61]

Both Schmidt and Gagnon err by viewing idolatry as one sin Paul addressed, while seeing same-sex sexual activity as a second. They ostensibly believe that the two are separate and distinct acts. Schmidt contends that they comprise distinct subsections of the text, while Gagnon believes that while they parallel one another, meaning that they ultimately lead to the same destination—suppressing the truth about God and creation—they are not otherwise connected. Both of these views are wholly contradicted by the text, however.

In verses 21-23, Paul made it clear that idolaters were the subject of his criticism. But, he didn't stop there. Every time he mentioned the sexual acts/lusts, he prefaced it with a reference to idolatry, *and* a conjunction to make the connection directly.

In verse 24, he mentioned their (the idolaters') lusts, but he prefaced it in the previous verse with the fact that they changed the glory of God for images of humans and animals. He then connected the reference to idolatry directly to their lust by using the conjunction "therefore" at the beginning of verse 24.

He did the same thing when providing an example of the lusts mentioned in verse 24. Before mentioning same-sex sex in verses 26-27, he referenced idolatry in verse 25—that they worshipped and served the creature rather than the Creator. He then used a conjunctive phrase to connect the sexual acts with idolatry, saying, "For this reason..." at the beginning of verse 26.

It's as though Paul knew people would try to misrepresent his words, so he constantly linked the sexual activity to idolatry at every reference point in an effort to preclude such a contortion. Yet, despite his best efforts, traditionalists like Schmidt and Gagnon demonstrate their determination to separate the two as distinct acts, no matter the cost to sound theology.

[60] *The Bible and Homosexual Practice*, 247.
[61] Ibid., 276.

This begs the question: Why is it so important to anti-gay traditionalists that these acts be seen as separate? Does it matter that Paul's reference connects the acts directly to idolatry? Actually, it matters a great deal, as Schmidt and Gagnon recognize and fear. If Paul's condemnation of same-sex sexual acts was a direct result of his view that the acts were connected with (and the result of) idolatry, as the text indicates, it would make his condemnation inapplicable in social (and, arguably, even individual) contexts in which the activity has absolutely nothing to do with idolatry—as is the case today. Not wanting to cede this point, the authors treat the two sins as distinct sinful acts Paul condemned, contrary to the logical flow of the text.

In a characteristic move, Gagnon references Paul's association of the sexual acts with idolatry; but he distorts the association in order to reinforce his interpretation of the text, completely ignoring Paul's conjunctions, which clearly demonstrate that the acts were viewed as a result or consequence of idolatry.

> "The insertion of 1:25 was Paul's way of reminding the reader of parallels between idolatry and same-sex intercourse that made the punishment so appropriate for the crime."[62]

Initially, I assumed that the authors' zeal caused them to unwittingly miss the connection between idolatry and the sexual acts Paul condemned. However, my benefit of the doubt was washed away upon seeing Gagnon acknowledge the connection. I can't understand how he could view Paul's words as a reference to some supposed parallel between idolatry and same-sex acts, rather than as evidence that Paul viewed the acts as a *result* of idolatry. Paul's insertion of idolatry (v. 25) within the context of lusts (v. 24) and same-sex sexual acts (vs. 26-27) does not remind the reader of a parallel between the two, but of a cause and effect relationship—the only interpretation that explains words like "therefore" and "for this reason."

Even after Paul moved on from the same-sex sexual acts and mentioned how God turned the idolaters over to a

---

[62] *The Bible and Homosexual Practice*, 261.

reprobate/debased mind, he *still* connected God's judgment directly back to idolatry, saying at the beginning of verse 28 that it (God's judgment) was the result of the fact that they "did not see fit to acknowledge God any longer," a clear reference to their having exchanged the truth of God for a lie in worshiping idols rather than the true and living God (vs. 23, 25). Gagnon, however, views this refusal to acknowledge God as a reference both to sex *and* to idolatry.

> "Quite appropriately, an absurd exchange of God for idols leads to an absurd exchange of heterosexual intercourse for homosexual intercourse. A dishonoring of God leads to a mutual dishonoring of selves. A failure to see fit to acknowledge God leads to an unfit mind and debased conduct."[63]

> "Same-sex eroticism functions as a particularly poignant example of human enslavement to passions and of God's just judgment precisely because it parallels in the horizontal-ethical dimension a denial of God's reality like that of idolatry in the vertical-divine dimension. In other words, idolatry is a deliberate suppression of the truth available to pagans in the world around them, but so too is same-sex intercourse."[64]

> "...The fact that Paul singled out homosexual conduct in 1:26-27 does indicate that he found this to be a particularly egregious sin—precisely because it constituted a clear and willful suppression of the knowledge of God's will for humans in the created order."[65]

> "Instead of acknowledging that God had made them 'male and female' and had called on them to copulate and procreate, they denied the transparent complementarity of their sexuality and engaged in

---

[63] *The Bible and Homosexual Practice*, 253.
[64] Ibid., 254.
[65] Ibid., 283.

sex with the same sex, indulging themselves in irresponsible sexual passion on which stable and productive family structures could not be built."[66]

Gagnon's interpretation fails on multiple points. First, his excessively referenced principle of Complementarity isn't taught in Scripture, neither by name nor in principle. Same-sex sexual acts can't, therefore, violate a "biblical" principle that doesn't actually exist anywhere in the Bible. I deal with this in detail in Chapter 10.

Second, this argument fails to account for the large number of gay people who desire to *not* be gay precisely because of their beliefs concerning God's view of homosexuality. They aren't rejecting God. In fact, they're tormented by their belief that God condemns them because of their sexual orientation and/or sexual behavior. They often demonstrate a greater level of commitment to their perception of godliness than many traditionalists, in that they live with this torment every day, yet continue to strive to deny their inherent orientation in an, albeit misguided, effort to please God. But when they have moments of weakness and engage in same-sex lust or behavior (which Paul reasonably anticipated by anyone not gifted with celibacy—1Co. 7:7-9), people like Gagnon excoriate them for supposedly having rejected God. This judgmental view is neither compassionate, nor indicative of even a modicum of understanding of the nature of homosexuality and what many gay Christians live with day after day.

It also doesn't account for those who do not believe God condemns them for being gay and for romantically expressing their same-sex orientation. Traditionalists act as though it's not possible to interpret Scripture any differently than they do, and that any attempts to do so smack of a desire on the part of gay people to live their "deviant lifestyles." But, they fail to consider the large numbers of heterosexuals with no vested interest in "twisting" God's word to support their sexual desires, who also believe that Scripture, when translated, interpreted, and applied correctly, does not condemn homosexuality in any general sense.

Ultimately, there are innumerable doctrines Christians cannot agree on, none of which demonstrate a lack of sincerity on

---

[66] *The Bible and Homosexual Practice*, 291.

the part of any particular group. One need only consider the large number of denominations as evidence. We can't agree on whether to baptize using the Trinitarian formula or in Jesus' name, whether baptism is essential to salvation, whether the prophetic ministry still exists within the Church, whether the bread and wine symbolically represent or are the actual substance of Christ's body and blood, etc. The list could go on and on. These disagreements involve serious issues (like whether a person can lose his/her salvation), as well as insignificant issues (like whether to use grape juice or wine during Holy Communion).

I've always felt that it was pitiful that some Christians think that unless others believe precisely as they do on a myriad of issues, they aren't "true" Christians. I can't help but believe that God views such theological arrogance as a sin in itself, especially when we attack the motives of other believers based solely off of the fact that they disagree with our interpretation of Scripture. People like Gagnon are, in my view, especially guilty of this haughtiness—ironically, one of the sins Scripture explicitly identifies with the infamous Sodomites, unlike homosexuality (Ez. 16:49-50). Although I don't judge traditionalists or feel myself a better Christian than they, I do challenge them to do better—to stop condemning gay Christians as reprobate, and to realize that it is, indeed, possible to have sincere disagreement on this issue without rejecting God or attempting to disregard His word.

At any rate, in the quoted references above, Gagnon also contends that same-sex intercourse denies God because such passions cannot build "productive family structures"—that God calls us to "copulate and procreate," and that gay people reject this commission. But, productive family structures (i.e. procreative productivity, which is obviously what Gagnon is referring to) cannot be naturally built upon through many opposite-sex sexual passions, either. Some heterosexual couples are comprised of men and/or women who are unable to have children. Gagnon's logic condemns such sexual unions in that they also deny God's supposedly procreative intent for sex.

I simply don't believe that Paul's reference to people refusing to acknowledge God is a criticism of homosexuals, but of idolaters. It certainly fits the pattern of idolatry, as well as the description Paul provides in the text. In fact, same-sex sexual acts were only a sidebar to the primary subject of idolatry. That Paul kept mentioning idolatry every few verses indicates that he wanted his audience to clearly understand that idolaters were the subjects of his criticism.

Interestingly, although Gagnon and Schmidt failed to yield to the textual evidence of Paul's linkage of same-sex sexual activity to idolatry, another of our authors took the opposite approach, actually attacking affirming Christians for supposedly failing to recognize this connection.

> "Further, the argument makes idolatry a separate and distinct sin rather than seeing how it is related to everything the passage is addressing. Those who are suppressing the knowledge of God (a universal charge) express that rebellion in many ways, including homosexual behavior and all the other sinful activities listed in 1:28."[67]

White and Niell recognize the link between the sexual activity condemned and their perceived source in idolatry; however, they fail to see the textual distinction between the sexual activity of vs. 26-27, and the vice list of vs. 29-31. The same-sex activity is seen as an extension/consequence of idolatry, while the vice list is seen as a result of being released/turned over by God. In other words, the same-sex intercourse was directly connected to idolatry, whereas the vices were not. They were connected to a rejection by God, which was, in turn, connected to idolatry. To put it another way, idolatry was the source. Same-sex sexual activity and being turned over by God were both consequences of that source. The vices were consequences of the second consequence (reprobation). Ergo, same-sex activity is not analogous to the vices, but to rejection by God. Both are seen as a consequence of idolatry.

History demonstrates that the acts were often engaged in during Bacchanalia—sex orgies dedicated to Bacchus, the Roman god of wine. This is undoubtedly what Paul had in mind, based on the fact that 1) he linked the lust/acts with idolatry every time he

---

[67] *The Same Sex Controversy*, 137.

mentioned them, and 2) he referenced the acts in an epistle to Christians in Rome, which is indicative of the fact that the Bacchanalian festivals had as their source *Roman* religious beliefs! This is no coincidence. It's undeniably what Paul had in view when condemning these acts.

So, contrary to traditionalist claims, Paul perceived the same-sex acts taking place in his society as a consequence of idolatry, as witnessed in Bacchanalia. "For this reason" (v. 26), his words cannot be interpreted as a universal rebuke of homosexuality—a rebuke that includes gay Christians, who are *not* idolaters.

Of course, not everyone believes Paul condemned same-sex acts because he saw them as intertwined with Gentile (specifically, Roman) idolatry. Such an admission would prove their smoking gun no more than a false alarm in relation to modern application. Fear of the implications prevents them from letting the text speak for itself.

> "If we are to say homosexuality is legitimate so long as it's not a result of idol worship, then we also have to say these other sins are legitimate as well...so long as they too are not practiced as a result of idolatry."[68]

I hear this argument over and over again—an argument that I can only describe as ridiculous. Traditionalists seem to believe that the inapplicability of a passage makes everything it condemns permissible; but this doesn't make sense at all. As I argued in Chapter 6, did the rescission of British law in New England after the Revolutionary War make murder permissible, seeing as murder was condemned within that former legal code? Obviously not! It simply meant that we could no longer base murder's impermissibility upon that inapplicable code.

The conjunctions Paul used when referencing same-sex sexual activity undeniably establishes that in his mind, idolatry and same-sex intercourse were inextricably linked. Even if the acts were not committed in Bacchanalia or other forms of idolatrous

---

[68] *The Gay Gospel?*, 207.

worship, he still believed that they developed in a person's life as a result of his/her association with an idolatrous culture. He didn't see the acts as originating from inner desires that a person is born with, or otherwise develops outside of conscious choice, as those who understand the nature of sexual orientation realize today. It doesn't mean that he was wrong. It simply means that his perception was colored by his social context, much as it was when he opposed certain styles of women's dress (1Ti. 2:9-10), women speaking in church or teaching men (1Ti. 2:11-12), or men having long hair (1Co. 11:14).

Now, I disagree with some affirming Christians, in that this evidence indicates to me that Paul's intention was not to condemn same-sex sexual acts only when they explicitly involved idolatry. Paul's view that idolatry was the source of same-sex eroticism demonstrates that he didn't believe the activity existed outside of some degree of idolatrous association. In his mind, *all* same-sex acts were repugnant. I believe Paul viewed same-sex sexual acts as I view the Confederate flag. The context doesn't matter. I absolutely abhor that flag because of what it represents to me as a Black person, and I don't understand why *everyone* doesn't view the flag in the same way. Same-sex sexual acts obviously represented idolatry in Paul's Jewish mind, just as the Confederate flag represents racism and bigotry in my mind. This explains the language he used to describe the acts.

> *"For this reason God gave them over to* **degrading**
> [atimias] *passions; for their women exchanged the natural*
> *function for that which is* **unnatural** [para phusin], *[27]*
> *and in the same way also the men abandoned the natural*
> *function of the woman and burned in their desire toward one*
> *another, men with men committing* **indecent**
> [aschêmosunên] *acts and receiving in their own persons*
> *the due penalty of their error."*
> Romans 1:26-27

The adjectives Paul employed can only lead us to conclude that his contempt was not isolated to acts committed within a particular context, but to the acts in general. Still, the context makes it abundantly clear that Paul didn't believe any other context existed. According to him, the very reason people engaged in the acts was their idolatry. Paul's unfailing use of conjunctions to link the acts to idolatry demonstrates this beyond all doubt. To him, idolatry was, at the very least, a catalyst for all same-sex sexual acts in a person's life.

Roman idolatry and Bacchanalia no longer characterize our culture. Consequently, Paul's view of the acts is now wholly obsolete, much as my view of the Confederate flag may be 2000 years from now. Nevertheless, it probably won't surprise you to know that our traditionalist authors disagree with this contention, finding in Paul's description evidence that his condemnation was universal, rather than culturally subjective. Their reliance on the language Paul employs only emphasizes the weakness of their case.

> "Paul uses the same words here he used of lesbianism: these men have abandoned (another word signifying choice) the *natural sexual use* of the woman ("natural relations," NIV). God's intention in the sexual expression of His creatures is to be between a man and a woman, just as it was with Adam and Eve... There is no possible way of reading this term as referring to anything neutral or simply "unusual" or "out of the norm."[69]

> "Similarly, the reader should expect that the appeal to nature in 1:26-27 has to do, at least primarily, with the visual perception of male-female bodily complementarity (the fittedness of the sex organs)."[70]

The authors make the mistake of failing to divorce their own worldview from how they read and understand Scripture—a difficult but absolutely essential step in sound hermeneutics. They see Paul's appeal to nature and reflexively conclude that he's referring to a universal, God-established order. Gagnon goes so far as to consider Paul's appeal to nature as relating to "visual perception"—in other words, that a penis "obviously" fits into a

---

[69] *The Same Sex Controversy*, 118-119.
[70] *The Bible and Homosexual Practice*, 257.

vagina. They all make the mistake of understanding Paul's word-usage within the framework of their prejudices against homosexuality. They don't fully appreciate the fact that the same writer (Paul) used the same appeal (nature) to condemn men with long hair (1Co. 11:14). In fact, he used a second word in this very same verse in describing "unnatural" hair lengths on men that he used to describe same-sex sexual acts in Ro. 1:26—*atimia*, translated as "degrading" in Ro. 1:26, and as "dishonor" in 1Co. 11:14. Does this mean that long hair on a man is as "morally reprehensible" as same-sex sexual activity? I can't imagine that White, Niell, or Gagnon would support such a contention, yet their reliance on Paul's choice of language can lead to no other end.

Just in case someone would contend that long hair on a man *is* morally reprehensible "because the Bible says so," let's keep in mind that roughly 1,000 years prior to Paul's writing, men of the Nazarite community of the Israelites kept long hair as a point of honor. Not only did God not judge them for their supposedly immoral rebellion against his "natural" order, but also, God made long hair the source of one Nazarite's superhuman strength—the hero Samson! So, either universal moral standards change over time (which contradicts the very notion of their being universal), or the use of *atimia*, *para phusin*, and other descriptive adjectives to describe things or behaviors cannot be considered an indication of the universality of such things.

Indeed, Paul appealed to nature to describe things that were culturally subjective (e.g. men with long hair), as well as things that were of an inherent nature (e.g. having a Jewish ethnicity—Gal. 2:15). We cannot, therefore, rely solely upon his appeal to nature to determine whether or not the acts he described are morally wrong, or simply perceived as wrong based on one's cultural context.

> "There are only two other occurrences of *atimia*, *aschēmosynē* in Pauline ethical contexts, but both are instructive. In 1 Corinthians 15:43 Paul writes of the body being 'sown in dishonor' before it is 'raised in glory.' Surely this implies more than death as social disgrace: death is the penalty for sin. The only other Pauline occurrence of *atimazō* is in

the very next chapter of Romans, where the apostle challenges certain Jews: 'Do you dishonor God by breaking the law?' (2:23). Clearly sin here constitutes an offense against God, not mere social disgrace."[71]

Schmidt attempts to prove that the words were, in fact, used some places in Scripture to refer to things that were not culturally subjective. I don't have a problem with this, but for the fact that he tries to base his opinion of how Paul used the word in Ro. 1 solely on these specific uses. The problem with this approach is that both positions have support for objective or subjective word usage, which means that neither position can actually be proved or disproved on this basis alone. Upon realizing that Paul used the terms in both objective and subjective ways, an unbiased student of Scripture would simply return to Ro. 1 and examine the context to see how Paul used the terms in that particular passage. So, that's what we'll do right now.

We've already seen that every time Paul referenced same-sex sexual acts, he unfailingly conjoined them to idolatry, saying that the latter was the cause or catalyst of the former. The context, then, demonstrates very clearly that the actual object of Paul's disdain was idolatry. This means that his reference to the sexual acts is, without a doubt, subject to the acts' association with that object. *We* are not making this connection. Paul made it for us, and he made it every single time he mentioned the sexual acts. This isn't to say that the acts must be considered morally benign. It's only to say that we can't use the reference in Ro. 1 as evidence to the contrary, seeing as according to Paul, those particular acts were a result of idolatrous beliefs. We can only conclude that the adjectives he used to describe the acts were contingent upon idolatry.

Consider the Confederate flag I referenced before. I have a particular disdain for it, based largely on my perception of it as a Black man. Every time I see one, I want to spit—and some times, I literally do. It's foul, disgusting, and utterly sickening to me, and to this day, I have trouble understanding how some Southerners, who

---

[71] *Straight & Narrow?*, 75-76.

supposedly wave the flag in celebration of their "heritage", can possibly have pride in something so tied to the inhumane treatment of other people. Is it a wonder Black Southerners don't join in that manifestation of "Southern pride?"

Now, I recognize that the Confederate flag represents many things to many people, and I also recognize that there isn't anything inherently immoral about the collection of colors and images that comprise the flag. Still, when reflecting on it above, I used adjectives that described my feelings about what is, ultimately, the source of my disdain—what the flag represents to me: slavery and inequality. That flag flew in places where humans made in the image of God were degraded for generations, and it was waved proudly over armies that fought to retain the right to continue to oppress people. So yes, I hate that flag—not only what it represents, but also the flag itself *because* of what it represents.

I believe that this is an accurate analogy for Paul's disdain for same-sex intercourse. It's certainly true that in the text, the adjectives (*atimias*/degrading, *para phusin*/unnatural, and *aschêmosunên*/indecent) described the acts themselves, not the idolatry they flowed from. But, perception isn't created in a vacuum. It exists *because* of one thing or another. In Ro. 1, the context bears out that the source of Paul's disdain is idolatry. As I said before, this doesn't mean that the acts are benign; but it does mean that Ro. 1 doesn't indicate anything but that Paul hated idolatry, and found same-sex intercourse sordid, at least in part, because of its association with idolatry. The textual evidence leads us to no other conclusion.

Now, if idolatry only explains his disgust for same-sex acts *in part*, it's very important that we figure out the other part, because that will help us determine whether the acts are or are not inherently immoral. If, however, no other part is indicated in Scripture, we are without just cause to consider the acts immoral when they are no longer associated with idolatry, as they were during Paul's day.

We must save this examination of other contributing factors to Paul's disdain for the next chapter, which will deal with the last two passages that appear to reference homosexuality. We discovered that the Sodom and Gomorrah destruction narrative (Gen. 19) is wholly uninformative since it doesn't condemn homosexuality, contrary to popular belief. Also, the Levitical proscriptions of male-male intercourse (Lev. 18:22 and 20:13) are as contingent upon idolatry as the reference in Ro. 1.

I would like to deal, then, with one of the most disturbing anti-gay arguments I've read in relation to Ro. 1. In *The Same Sex Controversy*, authors White and Niell deal with Paul's language in verse 27—that those who engaged in same-sex sexual acts received "in their own persons the due penalty of their error." Some believe that this is a reference to sexually transmitted diseases. While that possibility exists, White and Niell go way too far in their attempt to demonstrate it; and it's weird how they go about it.

They begin by stating that the evidence doesn't indicate that Paul is referring to sexually transmitted diseases because "from Paul's perspective, whatever this punishment is, *all* those who engage in this behavior receive the due penalty for their perversion;" whereas, "not *every* homosexual offender receives this punishment [AIDS]."[72] Seems reasonable enough, especially considering that there is no evidence whatsoever that AIDS dates back to the 1st century A.D., while Paul's perceived penalty was contemporaneous to his own society. The idea that AIDS is God's punishment against gay people, based upon Paul's words in Ro. 1:27, is a perfect example of the traditionalist penchant for reading their modern worldview into Scripture. They *want* to believe AIDS is a gay disease, so they see evidence for it in a passage written 2,000 years ago to a culture in which AIDS didn't even exist. Not only is this a wholly discredited belief based in no small part on people's aversion to homosexuality, but it's also a cruel, bigoted, and unchristian thing to believe (or to wish were so).

For just a moment, I felt that White and Niell were actually going to spare me from such childlike frivolity—that they were, at the very least, reasonable enough not to make such a biased, stereotypical, and bigoted error. Unfortunately, I was wrong. After making their ostensibly reasonable statement disproving AIDS as the evidence of God's judgment against same-sex sexual activity, they spent the next paragraph attempting to actually validate that view.

[72] *The Same Sex Controversy*, 121.

"Since we do not have an utterance from God as to a one-to-one correspondence between homosexual behavior and AIDS, we must be careful about making definitive assertions about their correlation. However, we can assuredly declare that all sin, since it is destructive to individuals and societies, does deserve—and often receives—frightful and deadly penalties; God does judge sinners, He reveals His wrath against all ungodliness and unrighteousness. The fact that some non-homosexuals have AIDS does nothing to overturn the fact of God's holy wrath being exercised against all ungodliness and unrighteousness. Sin, especially that of a public nature, affects others, and often the penalty affects others too…. Jeremiah, for instance, was swept away in Babylonian captivity."[73]

I have a huge problem with White and Niell's analysis of Paul's words in relation to AIDS. First of all, Scripture makes it clear that we are *all* sinners (1Ti. 1:15), and for that reason, we *all* deserve judgment. It is only by the grace of God through the atoning sacrifice of Jesus Christ that we who believe have become beneficiaries of His mercy. So, for White and Niell to claim that God judges sinners, they are ultimately lumping themselves into the same mix. Christians are not subject to God's wrath (Ro. 5:9; 1Th. 5:9), yet there are many out there who have same-sex attractions and are, therefore, gay. Those who were the subjects of God's wrath in Ro. 1 were not simply sinners, but were idolaters who had rejected God (vs. 21, 23, and 28).

Furthermore, their last statement is particularly in error. They claim that because sin "of a public nature" (which they apparently believe homosexuality is) affects others, the penalty often does, also. In this, they demonstrate a failure to understand God's *modus operandi*. Throughout Scripture, He demonstrates a pattern of saving the righteous from His judgment of the wicked. In fact, Scripture explicitly makes this point, holding up Noah and Lot as examples that God, contrary to White and Niell's

---

[73] *The Same Sex Controversy*, 121.

contention, does not punish the righteous (which all Christians are—2Co. 5:21) along with the wicked.

> *"...and did not spare the ancient world, but preserved Noah, a preacher of righteousness, with seven others, when He brought a flood upon the world of the ungodly; [6] and if He condemned the cities of Sodom and Gomorrah to destruction by reducing them to ashes, having made them an example to those who would live ungodly lives thereafter; [7] and if He rescued righteous Lot, oppressed by the sensual conduct of unprincipled men [8] (for by what he saw and heard that righteous man, while living among them, felt his righteous soul tormented day after day by their lawless deeds), [9] then the Lord knows how to rescue the godly from temptation, and to keep the unrighteous under punishment for the day of judgment."*
>
> *2Peter 2:5-9*

White and Niell use Jeremiah's captivity in Babylon as an example of the righteous being punished along with the wicked. On the surface, it seems like a legitimate example, which contradicts the biblical testimony about how God spares the righteous from His wrath. This is why it's vitally important that we prayerfully meditate on God's word, to ensure that what appears on the surface to indicate one thing actually does so. This is especially important when studying something we already have a strong opinion or belief concerning, as is often the case with homosexuality. We don't want our prejudices and existing theological beliefs or assumptions to cloud our interpretive judgment.

Jeremiah's captivity is not a fitting comparison. The kingdom of Judah was conquered by Babylon as a result of God's judgment against the kingdom itself. As a result, all citizens were subject to the repercussions of that judgment because the kingdom, as a collective entity, had fallen into idolatry and wickedness. Jeremiah was a citizen of Judah, and was, therefore, subject to God's judgment of the kingdom. Lot, on the other hand, was not a citizen of Sodom. Even the Sodomites knew that he only sojourned there (Gen. 19:9). He did not share in their collective sin because he was not in covenant with Sodom, as Jeremiah was with

Judah. The same can be said of Noah. The Noachian world had fallen into wickedness; but one doesn't become a citizen of the world, or subject to the world, as though the world is, itself, a sovereign state.

Ultimately, what White and Niell would have us believe is that AIDS is God's judgment against homosexuals, and that heterosexuals who contract AIDS are just collateral damage. Not only does such a contention make God unjust, but it also makes Him fairly unwise, considering that more heterosexuals have AIDS than homosexuals. So, is AIDS just a divine temper tantrum, in which God is so overcome by rage that He haphazardly flings out judgment, not caring how many innocent people are affected, so long as the disgusting fags get what's coming to them? If so, He could have at least made sure to infect all gay people with the disease. Not only did He fail to do that, but He also infected more heterosexuals than homosexuals. For a God whom we claim is characterized by love, mercy, justice, compassion, and loving-kindness, that's a lot of collateral damage.

Take a moment and reflect on the picture traditionalists paint of God. It's radically different than the one presented in the Bible. They appear to be so disgusted by homosexuality that they'll go to any length to oppose it, even if it means making God out to be the villain. Maybe their bigotry, egged on by a zealous religiosity founded upon self-righteousness rather than love, has blinded them to the egregious treason they commit against Christ in how they treat gay people. It's no wonder many unbelievers have such a low opinion of Christianity and of Christians, whom they believe are nothing but hypocrites.

A serious consequence of traditionalist self-righteousness is that so many unbelievers utterly despise the one true faith; and they have reason to, for the most vocal among us also have been the most judgmental and heartless. The only consolation I have is that many Christians are starting to rise up and break their silence, providing a more visible image to the world of what it really means to be Christ's disciples—that we love without condition, and without limitation.

8

1Corinthians 6:9; 1Timothy 1:10
The Pauline Vice Lists

The Pauline vice lists of 1Co. 6:9-10 and 1Ti. 1:9-10 present a unique challenge. Unlike the other passages often believed to condemn homosexuality, the problem here is not one of interpretation (as with Gen. 19; Ro. 1:26-27) or application (as with Lev. 18:22; 20:13; Ro. 1:26-27), but one of translation. Most people take it for granted that what they read in their Bibles is an accurate translation, and that the only concerns involve interpreting and applying the texts; and in a majority of instances, they're correct. However, there are, indeed, times when an incorrect or imprecise translation dramatically effects how a passage is understood.

One of the problems arises when simply trying to discern when a reexamination of a translation is warranted. It's not as though words translated incorrectly have an asterisk attached. When it comes to these two vice lists, a problem of translation isn't evident without a degree of study. But, it *is* made evident when comparing multiple versions side by side, which makes certain inconsistencies plain. But, how many people study with 4-5 Bible translations sitting open on their desks? Thankfully, the research has been done, so we know exactly what we're looking for.

Let's begin by identifying and solving the problem of translation resident in these verses. Then we'll be in a position to rebut the copious errors our authors make when applying these passages to our subject matter.

> "Or do you not know that the unrighteous will not inherit
> the kingdom of God? Do not be deceived; neither fornicators,
> nor idolaters, nor adulterers, nor effeminate [malakoi], nor
> homosexuals [arsenokoitai], [10] nor thieves, nor the

covetous, nor drunkards, nor revilers, nor swindlers, will inherit the kingdom of God."
1Corinthians 6:9-10

"...realizing the fact that law is not made for a righteous person, but for those who are lawless and rebellious, for the ungodly and sinners, for the unholy and profane, for those who kill their fathers or mothers, for murderers [10] and immoral men [pornois] and homosexuals [arsenokoitais] and kidnappers and liars and perjurers, and whatever else is contrary to sound teaching."
1Timothy 1:9-10

The terms in question are indicated by the inclusion of the original Greek word used in the text. We'll examine how each term is rendered in 11 of the most common Bible versions in use today.

Table 1: *malakoi* (1Corinthians 6:9)	
Bible Version[74]	**Translation**
Amplified	combined with *arsenokoites* as "those who participate in homosexuality"
CEV	pervert
ESV	combined with *arsenokoites* as "men who practice homosexuality" (footnoted as "the passive and active partners in consensual homosexual acts")
HCS	male prostitutes
KJV	effeminate
NASB	effeminate (footnoted as "effeminate by perversion")
NCV	male prostitutes
NIV	male prostitutes
NKJV	homosexuals (footnoted as "catamites")
NLT	male prostitutes
YLT	effeminate

---

[74] CEV = Contemporary English Version; ESV = English Standard Version; HCS = Holman Christian Standard; KJV = King James Version; NASB = New American Standard Bible; NCV = New Century Version; NIV = New International Version; NKJV = New King James Version; NLT = New Living Translation; YLT = Young's Literal Translation

These Bible versions present multiple possibilities for the proper translation of *malakoi*. Interestingly, only three render the word as either the homosexual orientation or homosexual activity. Now, some would consider such a distinction arbitrary, but it's vital to know for sure which group is being condemned. As a gay man, I need to know if God condemns me simply for *being* gay, or if the sin only involves engaging in same-sex sexual activity.

But, the variations don't stop with homosexuality. Four versions render *malakoi* as "male prostitutes", a group including heterosexual *and* homosexual men. Three versions render it "effeminate", which doesn't necessarily involve sexual orientation *or* sexual activity. For example, some straight men have high-pitched voices. Finally, one lone ranger (the CEV), renders *malakoi* as "pervert", a generic term without practical specificity.

Seeing how the translations vary, we have no choice but to conclude that the translators were not as certain about the meaning of *malakoi* as we often assume. The implications are too serious to wager a guess, so a deeper examination of the term is definitely warranted. Unfortunately, even after seeing these inconsistencies, some people still won't believe there's cause for further study. They either 1) opt for a majority rule hermeneutic, believing that whichever translation appears most often is the correct one, or 2) consider the translations close enough to give us the gist of what Paul was getting at. Neither of these approaches should suffice a serious Bible student, nor should they sit well with any Christian (whether affirming or not) who cares enough about gay people to want to know specifically what is being condemned in these verses.

Malakos (the singular form of *malakoi*) literally means "soft". In Matt. 11:8 and Luke 7:25, it was used to describe John the Baptist's clothing, as well as clothing worn by royalty and the wealthy. But, the presence of the word in this passage (1Co. 6:9), sandwiched between terms that refer to sexual sins, leads me to believe that Paul used the term to denote some form of sexual activity. We can, at least, begin with the acknowledgment that the translations are right in that the activity appears sexual in nature. Unfortunately, that's all we can state with confidence at this point. The context doesn't provide enough evidence to derive the proper meaning without conjecture, so we'll have to revisit this term after examining the others.

Table 2: *arsenokoitai(s)*		
Bible Version	**1Co. 6:9 Translation**	**1Ti. 1:10 Translation**
Amplified	those who participate in homosexuality	those who abuse themselves with men
CEV	one who... behaves like a homosexual	people... who live as homosexuals
ESV	combined with *malakos* as "men who practice homosexuality" (footnoted as "the passive and active partners in consensual homosexual acts")	men who practice homosexuality
HCS	homosexuals	homosexuals
KJV	abusers of themselves with mankind	them that defile themselves with mankind
NASB	homosexuals	homosexuals
NCV	men who have sexual relations with other men	people... who have sexual relations with people of the same sex
NIV	homosexual offenders	perverts
NKJV	sodomites	sodomites
NLT	those who... practice homosexuality	people... who practice homosexuality
YLT	sodomites	sodomites

Unlike the case of *malakoi*, the translations of *arsenokoitai(s)* from version to version are fairly consistent. They all refer in some way to homosexuality, with the sole exception of the NIV, which translates the word as "homosexual offenders" in 1Co. 6:9, but then as the very generic "perverts" in 1Ti. 1:10.

With the exception of the inconsistent rendering by the NIV, the only version that's a bit ambiguous is the archaic KJV, which refers to people who abuse/defile themselves with mankind. Female prostitutes who have sex with men abuse and defile themselves with mankind, so we can't interpret this particular rendering with certainty. Still, I'm fairly confident that the intended targets of the KJV's language are men who engage in same-sex intercourse.

One problem does carry over from the translations of *malakoi*. The translators cannot seem to agree whether *arsenokoitai(s)* condemns people with a same-sex orientation, *men* with a same-sex orientation, people who actually engage in same-sex sexual activity, or *men* who engage in same-sex activity. Again, some may think these are minor semantic differences, but it poses a serious concern for a number of people. Gay Christians, for example, certainly need to know if they're condemned for simply *being* gay—having same-sex attractions that they didn't ask for—or if only the act of sex with someone of the same sex is what's sinful.

Finally, we come to *pornois*, a word that, like *malakoi*, is only used in one of our two passages. It's not a term that sparks as much debate as *malakoi* and *arsenokoitai(s)*, but because it's used in the same immediate context, I think it warrants examination.

Table 3: *pornois* (1Timothy 1:10)	
Bible Version	**Translation**
Amplified	impure and immoral persons
CEV	sexual perverts
ESV	the sexually immoral
HCS	the sexually immoral
KJV	whoremongers
NASB	immoral men
NCV	those who take part in sexual sins
NIV	the sexually immoral
NKJV	fornicators
NLT	people who are sexually immoral
YLT	whoremongers

Although *pornois* is not as controversial as our other terms, it *should* be. Most of the translations render the term as a type of umbrella for all sexual immorality. Now, that's not so much of a bad thing because that's actually one of the definitions of the word. However, it makes no sense for the word to carry this umbrella meaning in this particular context, given its proximity to another term that is almost certainly of a sexual nature (*arsenokoitais*).

I'm not a linguist, and neither are most Christians, which is why we depend on native translations, trusting that what we read is accurate. But, the inconsistencies surrounding the translation of these three terms justify a more detailed examination, the goal of which is to determine Paul's usage of the terms in these verses.

Since *arsenokoitai(s)* is used in both passages, I think it's best to begin there. Research indicates that this is a very obscure term. In fact, many believe Paul coined the term, because there's no known usage that predates his usage in these two passages. Also, even in later writings, the word is very rarely used, and in such occasions, it's usually used in other vice lists.

One hint does exist regarding Paul's usage. In Koine Greek (common Greek dialect used during Paul's day), *arsenokoitai(s)* appears to be a compound, combining *arsen* ("male") with *koitai* ("beds"). Literally translated, *arsenokoitais* means "male beds"; or, considering the verb form of "bed", it means "those who have sex with men."

It's important to note that every compound word cannot be defined by its constituent words. For example, a butterfly is not a stick of butter that flies, or a fly made of butter. A lady-killer is neither a person who kills ladies, nor a lady who kills people. So, we cannot necessarily assume that *arsenokoitai(s)* can be understood by defining its constituent words. That being said, because of the sexual nature of the words surrounding *arsenokoitai(s)* in these two passages, I think it's relatively safe to literally translate the word as male-bedders. But, even if we do so, we don't know exactly to whom Paul is referring. Wives are male-bedders, for instance. How can we assume a same-sex aspect to the activity?

Dallas doesn't have a problem assuming a same-sex aspect to this word. In fact, he presents his assumption as absolute fact, which isn't very intellectually honest.

> "Though *arsenokoite* is unique to Paul, it refers specifically and unambiguously to sex between men."[75]

---

[75] *The Gay Gospel?*, 213.

Many anti-gay Christians believe that Paul derived the word from the Septuagint—the Greek Old Testament, which he would have, undoubtedly, read. In Lev. 18:22 and 20:13, *arseno* and *koiten* are used in reference to men having sex with men. They assume, therefore, that this is what he had in mind when using the term, *arsenokoitai(s)*. Dallas characteristically presents this assumption as an absolute, undeniable fact when refuting an affirming argument.

> "This makes it impossible to accept [John] Boswell's suggestion that Paul meant anything other than homosexuality when using the term *arsenokoite*, considering that it's derived directly from the Hebrew prohibitions of that very thing!"[76]

This is a very weak argument. Ancient Greco-Romans often spoke of sex using *koitai* (from which we derive coitus); so, it comes as no surprise that Paul used the word to describe the activity condemned in these verses. Consequently, even if the Levitical verses didn't exist, it's likely he would have referred to the activity using identical language, simply because that's how people of the day often referred to sex.

What we *do* know is that Paul had sex in mind, and that it involved men. But, was he was referring to orientation or activity? Because *arsenokoitai(s)* is used in both passages near words that clearly involve sexual activity, it's safe to assume that Paul was referring to activity in his reference, especially considering that sexual orientation is never referenced anywhere else in Scripture. This being the case, at most, Paul was not condemning homosexuals, but men who engage in same-sex sexual activity—a condemnation that would also include some heterosexuals (e.g. heterosexual prostitutes who engaged in same-sex sex for pay, both in ancient times, as well as today).

A final question we must ask is whether Paul was condemning all same-sex sexual activity, or only a specific type. It certainly appears on the surface that he condemned all intercourse involving people of the same sex; however, it would be safer to hold speculation to a minimum.

---

[76] *The Gay Gospel?*, 212.

Actually, there's very strong evidence that he *was* condemning a specific type of same-sex behavior known well to his ancient Greco-Roman audience. Oftentimes, people who don't want to spend a lot of time in the grocery store organize their lists by category. This way, they can get everything they need from each particular aisle or section without having to walk back and forth. Even outside of groceries, humans naturally group things together because it helps us understand the relationships between a number of things.

That Paul grouped the terms in 1Ti. 1:9-10 is obvious once you see it for the first time; and we must be grateful that he did because in so doing, he saved us from the mire of theological uncertainty. By examining the relationships between the terms, we can accurately pinpoint the target of each our terms in question, even in 1Co. 6:9, since *arsenokoitai(s)* was used in both passages.

Table 4: Grouping Analysis of 1Ti. 1:9-10	
Terms	**Type of group**
lawless and rebellious	synonyms for lawbreakers
ungodly and sinners	synonyms for people who transgress God's word
unholy and profane	synonyms for the sacrilegious, those who dishonor the sacred
those who kill their fathers or mothers, murderers	related terms; types of killers
immoral men [*pornois*], male-bedders [*arsenokoitais*], and kidnappers [*andrapodistais*]	*(we will examine below)*
liars and perjurers	synonyms for people who speak untruths

In constructing this list, Paul obviously grouped his terms; so, all we have to do is make sure we've defined the *arsenokoitais* group accurately. There are two words to choose from: 1) *pornois*, which could also belong to the "killers" group, and 2) *andrapodistais*, which could also belong to the "liars" group.

According to the Strong's Bible Dictionary, *pornois* is defined as a male prostitute, being derived from the root word *pememi*, which means "to sell." In a broad sense, it refers to sexually immoral people; however, because it's used in a list of various sins, the more specific "male prostitute" is most likely. Indeed, some variation of prostitute is how the word was translated in the KJV, and YLT versions. Since prostitutes are not a type of killer, *pornois* clearly belongs to the *arsenokoitais* group.

The Strong's Dictionary defines *andrapodistais* as "an enslaver." Its various translations in our examined Bible versions all reflect that basic theme—enslaver, kidnapper, menstealer, slave trader. They all describe people who procure and sell slaves, quite possibly kidnapping free people and selling them into slavery. While such people undoubtedly lie as a matter of course, the "liars" group is comprised of words that more directly refer to lying. Therefore, *andrapodistais* also belongs to the *arsenokoitais* group.

Now that we know the terms in our target group, all we have to do is discover the connection between *pornois* and *andrapodistais*. After accomplishing that, we'll be able to derive a specific translation for Paul's use of *arsenokoitais* in this passage, and quite possibly for his usage in 1Co. 6, the only other place the term appears in Scripture.

So, what do ancient Greco-Roman male prostitutes and slave traders have in common? They are two out of three of the players in a prostitution ring. We have the prostitutes (*pornois*), the ancient equivalent of pimps (*andrapodistais*), and the cryptic *arsenokoitais* (male-bedders). Given some thought, it makes sense that the *arsenokoitais* are the prostitutes' customers. This being the case, Paul appears to have condemned all three players involved in this particular form of prostitution.

Now, a brief ancient Greco-Roman history lesson reveals that a common form of male-male prostitution involved wealthy older men taking younger boys as their sexual slaves—a form of forced pederasty. This is, undoubtedly, what Paul had in mind when referencing *arsenokoitais*. Its pairing with *malakoi* in 1Co. 6:9—a word translated in some versions as "male prostitutes"[77]—o nly confirms the conclusion that the word refers to the customers (bedders) of male prostitutes. It also confirms "male prostitutes" as the best translation of *malakoi*.

---

[77] See Table 1.

Gagnon believes that Paul grouped terms in 1Co. 6:9-10, but completely misses or ignores the more obvious use of grouping in 1Ti. 1:9-10. I don't even believe Paul grouped all of his terms in 1Co. 6. If he did, the associations are much less apparent and, therefore, much more open to subjective interpretation, which is probably why Gagnon opted for its use in his grouping-based arguments.

> "That *arsenokoitai* refers to same-sex intercourse is strengthened by its pairing with *malakoi*."[78]

To Gagnon, the pairing was relevant only in demonstrating the same-sex nature of *arsenokoitai*, but not in indicating its association with prostitution. Of course, there aren't enough clues in the context of the 1Co. 6 vice list to bring us to the realization that the *arsenokoitai* are the customers of prostitutes. Maybe this is why he ignores the obvious grouping in 1Ti. in preference to the interpretatively malleable grouping in 1Co. 6. But, contrary to what he would have us believe, the evidence is strong that what Paul had in mind may have been a *form* of same-sex activity, but wasn't homosexuality in general.

Concerning the vice list of 1Co. 6, Gagnon goes on to say, "If the first vice, *pornoi*, is bracketed off as a Pauline addition to a pre-formed list, a relatively clear sequence develops."[79] He actually asks his readers to believe that *pornois* should be bracketed off so that it doesn't stand in the way of his interpretation of the rest of the list. *If* that twisting of Paul's words is allowed, "a relatively clear sequence develops," by which he really means "a sequence develops that better fits my views than does Paul's clumsy addition of *pornois* to an otherwise perfect vice list." While I'd love to sum up this developing sequence for you, I could never hope to match Gagnon's—albeit tedious—eloquence...

> "If the first vice, *pornoi*, is bracketed off as a Pauline addition to a pre-formed list, a relatively clear sequence develops. As Martin Stowasser has

---

[78] *The Bible and Homosexual Practice*, 316.
[79] Ibid., 316.

shown, the first four vices (in a list minus *pornoi*) are joined together in chiastic sequence. The first (*eidōlolatrai*, idolaters) and the fourth (*arsenokoitai*) are both five-syllable words ending in *–ai* and accented on the penult. The second (*moichoi*, adulterers) and the third (*malakoi*) are words ending in *–oi* and accented on the ultima. The fifth (*kleptai*, thieves) and sixth vices (*pleonektai*, the greedy or covetous) exhibit assonance and share a similar content. The seventh (*methysoi*, drunkards) and eighth vices (*loidoroi*, the verbally abusive) are both three-syllable words ending in *–oi* and accented on the antepenult. They are sometimes paired in Jewish literature, inasmuch as drunkenness leads to abusive speech. Only the ninth vice (*harpages*, robbers or swindlers) is left dangling without a partner. Idolatry and adultery (or *porneia*) are linked in early Jewish tradition. OT prophets frequently compared Israel's idolatry to an adulterous woman. If adultery is paired with idolatry, then *malakoi* and *arsenokoitai* constitute a pair of sexual sins distinct from adultery. Given such a pairing, our identification of *malakoi* with passive homosexual partners confirms the supposition that the term *arsenokoitai* refers to the active partners in homosexual intercourse."[80]

Excuse me, but… *What???* I know I can't be the only person who had to read that passage multiple times, more slowly each time around. Once you get past the tedium, what Gagnon is attempting to establish is a theology based off of the number of syllables used in a list, and off of the letters the words end in? Even if there were merit to this argument, based on some degree of literary style being employed, I fail to see how he goes from this analysis to a conclusion that simply because *malakoi* and *arsenokoitai* are paired (a conclusion that I actually agree with, without having to jump through the hoops of syllables and word endings), they refer to the passive and active partners in homosexual intercourse, respectively.

---

[80] *The Bible and Homosexual Practice*, 316.

Without wanting to appear ostentatious, I have to admit that it seems to me that Gagnon employs convoluted theoretical analyses only to, in a manner of speaking, hypnotize his readers into accepting any conclusion he draws, no matter how baseless. Re-read his syllabic analysis and pay special attention to the uses of "if". His entire theory is based upon a series of assumptions that one must surrender to in order for his argument to even be a possibility. He *may* be right *if* adultery is paired with idolatry—a conclusion that can only be drawn *if* we remove *pornoi* from the list and *if* we then find his syllabic analysis compelling. But, by Gagnon's own logic, *arsenokoitai* is syllabically joined with idolatry, while *malakoi* is joined with adultery. So, even if that wearisome tome is relevant, it disproves his very contention that *arsenokoitai* and *malakoi* constitute a pair. And on the question of the credibility of his analysis, why, if poetic emphasis is the intent, did Paul leave *pornoi* and *harpages* to despairing isolation?

> "In 1 Cor 6:9, the term *malakoi* has most in view males who actively seek to transform their maleness into femaleness in order to make themselves more attractive as receptive or passive sexual partners of men; *arsenokoitai* has most in view men who serve as the active sex partners of the *malakoi*. Neither term can be widened in meaning to include heterosexuals or narrowed in meaning to exclude certain non-exploitative forms of homosexual intercourse."

In continuing his misguided analysis of *arsenokoitais* and *malakoi*, Gagnon proves that he doesn't have a solid grasp on *what* he believes. He spends considerable time attempting to prove that the terms refer to all homosexual sex, only to later state rather plainly that they actually refer only to men "who actively seek to transform their maleness into femaleness in order to make themselves more attractive", and to those "who serve as the active sex partners of the *malakoi*". By this definition, *malakoi* aren't simply gay men who desire to be penetrated (as he initially contends), but are male-to-female transsexuals, who desire to feminize themselves. But even that betrays a faulty understanding of transsexuality because male-to-female transsexuals do not feminize themselves for the sake of potential partners, but for the sake of aligning their biologically male sex with their psychologically female gender. It's an introspective, not interpersonal issue.

This opens a can of worms that is not the point of this book. Suffice it to say that Gagnon obviously doesn't have command of the issues surrounding sexual orientation and gender identity. Thus, his definitions of *malakoi* and *arsenokoitai* are all over the place.

Also, by his logic, the text has in view "soft" men and their sexual partners—a definition that restricts the scope of application. Most gay men are not exclusively active (tops) or passive (bottoms). But, even amongst those who are generally one or the other, many bottoms are not soft/feminized, and not all tops are attracted to soft/feminized men. Likewise, some tops are soft/feminized, while some bottoms are masculine. So, if Gagnon is right and these words only describe feminized men (*malakoi*) and the men who sleep with them (*arsenokoitais*), then a large number of gay men aren't included in this condemnation, e.g. masculine bottoms, feminine tops, and those who are neither tops nor bottoms.

Furthermore, if *malakoi* only describes men who "actively seek to transform their maleness," an even larger swath of gay men are cut away, since most aren't seeking masculinity *or* femininity, but only seek to live genuine representations of who they are on the inside.

> "The reference is clearly here to homosexual (not heterosexual) behavior which in antiquity usually (though not always) took the form of pederasty."[81]

I was amazed to discover that Gagnon acknowledged the historical role of pederasty in Greco-Roman society. That goes a lot farther than many anti-gay traditionalists go. Still, it wasn't enough in his mind to serve as evidence that the scope of Paul's condemnation only encompassed that particular practice. What's very interesting is that Gagnon goes on to admit that in some post-

---

[81] *The Bible and Homosexual Practice*, 318.

Pauline uses, words derived from *arsenokoitais* were used in reference to prostitution.

> "Some of the occurrences of the *arsenokoit-* word group cited in the texts above have to do either with prostitution or rape but other occurrences cannot be so limited."[82]

This admission yields that *arsenokoitais* was, at times, used in relation to prostitution. Bolstered by Paul's use of grouping in 1Ti. 1, it demands a consideration of how he, specifically, used the term. We shouldn't play the numbers game, believing, as Gagnon does, that the most common usage automatically reflects Paul's usage. Instead, we should consider the textual evidence, allowing historical uses to inform but not determine. Historical uses inform us that Paul very well could have used *arsenokoitais* to refer to prostitution; and this is the sole interpretation that harmonizes with all available textual data.

Further, Gagnon wants to impose particular word usages on Paul[83]—usages separated by centuries of time—while ignoring the implications of the usages he doesn't favor. He later contends that we understand what Paul meant by *arsenokoitais* in light of what he said in Ro. 1, not because the word was used in Ro. 1 (it wasn't), but simply because it mentions same-sex intercourse.

> "...The meaning which Paul gave to *arsenokoitai* ultimately has to be unpacked in light of Rom 1:24-27. Scholars who want to adopt a very restricted meaning for *arsenokoitai* usually treat 1Cor 6:9 in isolation from Rom 1:24-27. Is it not logical to assume that what Paul says in Rom 1:24-27 tells us precisely what it is about the *malakoi* and *arsenokoitai* that Paul rejects?[84]

I answer Gagnon's question with an emphatic, "No!" He employs highly circular reasoning, requiring that we determine the

---

[82] *The Bible and Homosexual Practice*, 324.
[83] Ibid., 317-322.
[84] Ibid., 326.

meaning of Paul's words by *assuming* their meaning relative to a comparison with Romans 1. In other words, to find out what the word means, we must first assume that it has something to do with Romans 1. The more logical, responsible hermeneutical approach is to let the context of Paul's statement provide us with the proper meaning of the word. How does it relate to *pornoi* and to *andrapodistais? That's* the question he should be asking.

> "The criminal conduct of *andrapodistai* was hardly confined to feminizing male slaves for masters with same-sex erotic designs. More central still to the derogatory epithet of *andrapodistes* was the illegal kidnapping of freeborn citizens, with or without an accompanying feminization for homoerotic clients. In this connection, Philo treats the sin of *andrapodistai* in *Spec. Laws* 4.13-19 without once mentioning homosexual prostitution."[85]

Gagnon continues to ignore the relevance of context. Despite how Philo, an ancient Jewish historian, may or may not have used *andrapodistai* in a wholly different context, it is precisely its connection to *arsenokoitai* and *pornoi* in the 1Ti. 1:10 context that demonstrates *Paul's* meaning. That meaning is, without a doubt, related to prostitution, most likely of a pederastic nature. This is undeniable *if* the context is allowed to stand. We may, on the other hand, employ Gagnon's hermeneutical skill by bracketing off words here and there in order to force our preexisting beliefs onto the text. Personally, I'd rather consider the immediate Pauline context before Philo's.

> "1Tim 1:10 reinforces rather than provides an additional or alternative understanding to 1 Cor 6:9. It is, however significant because *if* the Pastorals were not written by Paul (as most scholars think), it confirms that Paul's opposition to homosexual behavior continued on in the early post-Pauline churches. Scroggs attempts to blunt the imact of the text by arguing that *pornois*,

---

[85] *The Bible and Homosexual Practice*, 333-334.

arsenokoitais, and *andrapodistais* are to be taken as a topical unit. He gives *pornoi* its more restrictive sense of 'male prostitutes' (normal Greek usage) rather than 'sexually immoral persons' (the broader sense it usually takes in the New Testament), then construes *arsenokoitai* in the limited sense as men who lie with the aforementioned male prostitutes. The word *andrapodistaes* means 'slave dealer, kidnapper' but Scroggs thinks that the preceding context of sexual terms implies that *andrapodistai* has a particular type of slave dealer in mind: people who sell boys or girls to be 'slaves for brothel houses.'"[86]

Gagnon actually acknowledges awareness of the grouping argument—something I assumed he wasn't aware of as I first began reading his arguments. But, he completely rejects the evidence, choosing instead to believe that the syllabic "evidence" for grouping in 1Co. 6 holds more water.

It amazes me that someone so intellectual could be so blinded by his determination to see what he wants to see in Scripture. Even in the face of sound exegesis, he's opted for if's and maybe's. He stands as the perfect case in point that God uses the foolish things of the world to confound the wise (1Co. 1:27). If anti-gay theology requires such blatant compromises of intellectual and spiritual integrity, I want no part of it.

In criticizing a proponent of affirming theology, Gagnon actually acknowledges that normal Greek vernacular supports the "male prostitutes" translation of *pornois*. Yet, he ignores this fact, casting Paul's use of grouping to the wind.

He even appeals to heterosex monogamy as the supposedly solely-sanctioned form of sexuality, contending, "…the context of the passage in 1 Corinthians makes clear why the *malakoi* and *arsenokoitai* belong with other forms of sexual immorality (*pornoi* [those who fornicate, commit incest, or have sex with prostitutes] and adulterers): they participate in a form of sexual behavior other than that sanctioned in the context of a monogamous, lifelong, non-incestuous, opposite-sex marriage bond."[87]

---

[86] *The Bible and Homosexual Practice*, 332.

136

There's one problem with his logic. Barring "lifelong", his conditions for sanctioned bonding have exceptions. People like Jacob, Elkanah, David, and Solomon are exceptions to the monogamy condition. None of them were ever chastised for engaging in polygamous unions, although Solomon was chided for marrying foreign, idolatrous women. The non-incestuous element was made a condition after some time; but prior to that, Adam's children, and even Abraham—the great patriarch of our faith, who married his half-sister, Sarai—were prominent exceptions. Finally, the disagreement over the "opposite-sex" condition is the very subject of Gagnon's book, so it can't be legitimately considered here. His contention is, therefore, without merit.

> "...For Paul the four sexual vices in 6:9 are there because they all constitute forms of sexual intercourse which occur outside of the context of marriage between a man and a woman. In that case, the terms *malakoi* and *arsenokoitai* are meant to signify, at least as representative types, all who participate in same-sex intercourse."[88]

After spending a substantial amount of time arguing that the words describe *all* same-sex activity, Gagnon acknowledges that they, in fact, do not. This is likely a sub-conscious admission on his part. He yields that the words in question cannot be accurately translated as condemning homosexuality in any general sense, else they would *describe*, rather than merely *represent* participants in same-sex intercourse. In other words, he acknowledges the limited scope of the terms as defined, but believes that they *represent* the broader scope.

> "Once again, the derivation of *arsenokoitai* from Lev 18:22; 20:13 (a formulation that is not limited to prostitution), its actual usage in Judeo-Christian literature, and the unqualified Judeo-Christian rejection of all forms of homosexuality make an

---

[87] *The Bible and Homosexual Practice*, 327.
[88] Ibid., 330.

overly narrow interpretation of the word implausible."[89]

Now, this argument is clever; however, he fails to point out that the Judeo-Christian rejection he holds to as evidence is, itself, based on faulty hermeneutics. It's completely circular logic, as if to say, "We know the people are right because the people believe it." The only reason they believe it is because of tradition and assumption!

The Judeo-Christian view will obviously reflect what has been passed down through history, be it right or wrong. For example, the inferiority of women was passed down through at least 3,500 years of Judeo-Christian history. I don't find the appeal to history compelling, especially as one whose ancestors were enslaved by Christians for hundreds of years.

I believe it is our job as students of Scripture to examine the biblical witness free of historical interpretations. At most, they should inform, but never determine. Church history is replete with examples of bad theology and oppression. Just because many have believed "it" (whatever "it" may be) for so long does not make "it" true. If the majority were theologically significant, Jesus wouldn't be the Messiah, Gentiles would have to be circumcised, women could not preach God's word, and gay people could not be Christian. Thank God the Christian majority during each period was/is wrong on all counts!

Speaking quite literally, I'm compelled to shout, "Damn majority rule! Let God be true, but every man a liar" (Ro. 3:4). We must challenge convention, not by the standard of time or numbers, but by the standard of truth—"Thy word is truth." (Jn. 17:17)

Homosexuality Through A First-Century Lens
Toward the end of the previous chapter, I raised the point that Paul perceived homosexuality, at least in part, through the lens of idolatry. I then stated that if there were another perception that informed his view of homosexuality, we must consider it, as well, in order to form a more complete picture of the New Testament

---

[89] *The Bible and Homosexual Practice*, 334.

138

witness. Now that we've considered the other two passages that in any way involve homosexuality, we must draw conclusions regarding how Paul perceived this phenomenon.

The first thing that informed his perception is, undoubtedly, idolatry. I think it's safe to say that this perception influenced his view of homosexuality in general. I cannot subscribe to the view that Paul only considered homosexuality wrong when it involved idolatry. The language he employed in Romans 1:26-27 leads me to believe that as far as he was concerned, homosexuality *always* involved idolatry, whether directly or indirectly. In his mind, there was no same-sex intercourse that did not find its ultimate source in idolatry.

However, the New Testament testimony doesn't end there. We also have Paul's reference to pederasty—a manifestation of same-sex eroticism that history has proven beyond all doubt was a fixture in the ancient Greco-Roman world. While not necessarily condemning all forms of pederasty, Paul definitely condemned those forms that involved prostitution and sexual slavery. An argument can be made that he condemned *all* pederasty, but I don't believe his word usage in the vice lists substantiates this argument. Given the evidence we considered, *malakoi* and *pornois* clearly reference male prostitutes, and *arsenokoitais* clearly references their customers. Still, even in volitional arrangements that didn't involve prostitution (e.g. a wealthy man taking a wealthy young boy as his protégé—a relationship that often involved sexual liaisons), Paul would likely have condemned them as an element of the idolatrous Roman culture.

So, any way you slice it, Paul condemned homosexuality. But, as with women wearing certain clothes, or teaching or having authority over men, we must consider the reason behind the condemnation to determine whether or not it's applicable today.

Because the central theme of idolatry—as it relates to homosexuality—is now wholly obsolete, we're left with the limited condemnation of particular pederastic arrangements that involved prostitution and/or sexual slavery. Any such arrangements would be equally condemnable today, regardless of the sex of the individuals involved. No legitimate case can be made, however, to stretch the application of those condemnations outside of that limited scope.

Consequently, we can produce only one verdict. Looking through Paul's first-century, Jewish lens, all same-sex sexual activity was frowned upon because it was representative of the idolatrous, Roman culture. Among those idolatrous liaisons, he found pederastic prostitution and sexual slavery particularly egregious, not simply because they involved two men, but because of their exploitative nature. From this perspective, Paul's vice list condemnations are still applicable today, in the case of any such arrangements in the modern world, regardless of the sex of those involved. However, his overall condemnation of homosexuality is wholly obsolete because there wasn't a single aspect of his argument that was not culturally subjective, hinged wholly on the acts' association with an idolatrous culture he undoubtedly abhorred—the Roman Empire.

Section

3

Comprehending and Dealing With Sexuality

9

I Think I'll Be Straight Today
The Nature of Sexual Orientation

One of the primary problems in this debate is that so many people don't have a grasp of what sexual orientation really is. Questions abound; and regrettably, guesses proffered as absolute truth abound in equal measure.

It's important that we examine the more pressing questions surrounding the nature of sexual orientation, evaluating the answers presented by our profiled authors. Only upon consideration of these questions will we be in a position to best apply what the Bible does and does not say about sexuality. Among the questions we shall evaluate are:

1. What does biology have to tell us about *how* we are gay?
2. Are people born gay?
3. Would homosexuality have existed in God's ideal Eden, or is it a result/consequence of the Fall?
4. Can sexual orientation change, and, if so, how?

Before probing into these questions, I must first respond to a somewhat disappointing argument posed by Joe Dallas—one that tries to prevent the open-minded examination of these types of questions. I find that many anti-gay Christians approach this issue with the sort of skeptical cynicism represented by Dallas' view; and sadly, they've been successful at preventing open inquiry.

> "But if gay apologists really believe homosexuality is not a biblically forbidden sin, why do they bother arguing, vehemently, that they cannot change? If something is not a sin, after all, then it doesn't matter if it's inborn or chosen, immutable or

changeable… Allow me, if I may, to make a
frivolous comparison. I believe it was all right, in
God's sight, for me to marry an Italian woman. I
have always thought olive-skinned, dark-haired
women are particularly beautiful, and I think that's
perfectly okay. I don't care whether my taste for
dark hair and olive complexions is inborn or
acquired, nor do I see any need to prove that it's
'unchangeable.' Maybe it is, maybe it isn't—but
since I feel good about it, who cares? Now, if
someone came along and told me that the Bible
condemned my attraction to dark hair, I would ask
them to show me where the Bible condemned it. If
I was convinced their biblical interpretation was
wrong—as I'm sure I would be—then I would
leave it at that. I certainly wouldn't bother
explaining any psychological or biological roots
that may have influenced my attractions. If I felt
right about these attractions before God, they
would need no explanation. Which begs the
question: Aren't gay Christian spokesmen betraying
a certain self-doubt when they try so hard to prove
their sexuality is inborn and unchangeable?"[90]

Not only is this a simplistic argument, but it also ignores
the serious emotional and spiritual implications of having a large
number of people ostracize, condemn, and judge you. Whether
homosexuality is a sin or not, people (especially many Christians)
treat homosexuals horribly. So, although Dallas disagrees, it *does*
matter if homosexuality is inborn or chosen, immutable or
changeable. The hope is that such considerations will maneuver at
least some anti-gay Christians to a more compassionate approach
to homosexuality. It's also a serious consideration in terms of
social rights. If sexual orientation is not a chosen characteristic, it
should be granted protected status in all areas of the social sphere.
So, these considerations do, indeed, matter.

I'm particularly disappointed in Dallas' argument because
as someone who is (or at least *was*, as Dallas claims) gay, he should
understand how it feels to have so much of the Christian

---

[90] *The Gay Gospel?*, 120.

community opposed to him. He should remember the hurt caused by rejection, the despairing isolation, and the fearful torment of broken families and friendships. For him to wonder why we care, simply because we believe that homosexuality is moral, is just—for lack of a better term—stupid.

Is it really so inconceivable that gay people could actually want healthy relationships with their families, friends, and church brethren—relationships built on honesty, respect, and transparency, rather than secrets, judgment, and condemnation? I know that anti-gay propaganda claims gay people want to destroy the family; but to the contrary, we want to save it—to save ours, and to save those like ours.

Furthermore, Scripture compels us to educate others—to be ready to give an answer (1Pe. 3:15), and to teach with great patience and instruction (2Ti. 4:2). Dallas tries to turn our noble intentions into a betrayal of non-existent doubt. It's a baseless argument intended to shut down discussion before it even begins.

A Note To Joe Dallas: Sir, we may know that people on your side of this issue are wrong, but that doesn't make their and your treatment of us any less wounding. Of course we attempt to convince you of the error of your ways, not just for your sake, but also for the sakes of all those who could be spared the callousness of your rhetoric and conduct toward us. Self-doubt isn't our motivation. Making the world a better place for others like us is! So, rather than attempting to curtail discussion by impugning our motives, try letting your case succeed or fail on the strength of your arguments alone.

Now that we've dealt with why we should bother engaging in this debate, let's address the common misconception that sexual orientation is defined by behavior. It's a widespread belief amongst most anti-gay Christians, and especially amongst those involved in ex-gay ministry. This is particularly frustrating because many serving in ex-gay ministries are, themselves, gay. They should know better!

> "Is it fair to say that such persons have not
> changed their sexual orientation or to call

145

> conversion therapy in such cases a failure? At the very least, to refer to them as homosexuals or even bisexuals is misleading, particularly if the homosexual urges are neither intense nor acted upon."[91]

Conversion therapy is a spiritual and/or psychological form of treatment aimed at "converting" a person's same-sex orientation into an opposite-sex one. It's often criticized as a misnomer in that it implies that such conversion is possible. Responding to this criticism, Gagnon contends that if a person's urges are no longer as intense as before, and aren't acted upon, it's fair to consider them heterosexual.

This shows an utter failure on Gagnon's part to understand the nature of sexual orientation. By definition, it describes feelings or attractions, totally independent of behavior. For example, there are heterosexual and homosexual virgins precisely because orientation has nothing to do with sexual behavior. Straight people don't need to have sex to realize that they're straight. Likewise, gay people don't need to have sex to realize that they're gay.

The ability to suppress what's inside doesn't stop a thing from being inside. The very admission that same-sex urges remain is an explicit acknowledgement that the individual is still gay! But, you won't find this logic accepted within ex-gay ministries. At best, they admit to struggling with same-sex temptation from time to time; but getting them to admit that they're still gay... you can all but forget it. Yet, the fact that they're *tempted* with same-sex attractions is evidence of a less than wholly straight orientation—at most, bisexuality. But even *that* isn't the case simply because same-sex attractions are suppressed. Bisexuality only exists if same-sex *and* opposite-sex attractions naturally exist concurrently—"naturally" being key.

In our culture of self-identification, many would disagree with my contention that if a person is tempted with same-sex attractions, he/she is, at the very least, bisexual. Our culture all but demands that people take upon themselves whatever label *they* desire, or no label at all. I, on the other hand, believe that what is

---

[91] *The Bible and Homosexual Practice*, 426.

remains so whether a person wants to admit it or not... whether they want to label themselves as such or not. For example, the sky is blue whether people want to call it green or not.

As it relates to sexual orientation, Scripture defines temptation as being drawn away by one's own desires (James 1:14). So, if there is no inner desire for a thing, one cannot be tempted by it. For example, I can be *offered* sex with a dog, but it's not a temptation precisely because I have no desire whatsoever to have sex with animals, neither does the offer awaken me to a desire that may have been present but was unrecognized. Likewise, if a person has no desire for sex with someone of the same sex, he/she cannot be tempted with it. What often is the case is that people's desires are naturally suppressed or dormant because their socio-religious context did not provide those desires with an environment in which to rise to the surface. Consequently, some may have such desires and not even realize it. But, if they're there, which means that the potential for temptation is present, it's indicative of a same-sex sexual orientation, whether they want to claim it or not, or whether they identify with it or not.

So then, based on this *biblical* definition of temptation, people who have, are tempted by, or are struggling with—or however ex-gay people want to characterize it—same-sex attractions are, at the very least, bisexual, and possibly homosexual. Claims to the contrary are either self-deceptions or attempts to deceive others.

In the end, no one knows whether a person's orientation has actually changed, save that individual. The problem is that most who claim such change don't have their definitions and characterizations correct. I've found in my own dealings with ex-gay people that it's all a matter of semantics. In order to get the "honest" answers, you have to ask the right questions. Ask if they're still gay and they'll all say no. Ask if they're still *attracted* to people of the same sex and *most* will say no. Ask if they still *struggle* with same-sex attractions and *some* will say no. Ask if they're still *tempted* from time to time with same-sex attractions and the super-vast majority will say yes.

These questions basically ask precisely the same thing. They simply approach from different angles, using different words. But, ex-gay rhetoric teaches people to not take upon themselves a gay label or identity because their identity is in Christ alone. But, that's like telling people to deny their ethnicity, because their identity is in Christ alone.

My being a 6'1", left-handed, Black, gay Christian man has played a part in shaping the person that I am. None of these things describe the complete Romell, as they can only provide you with a part of my story. Still, they are each components of the total person. Now, I can survive without being tall, left-handed, Black, *or* gay; yet these are still aspects of who I am. The only essential part of my existence that I cannot... that I *will not* do without is my faith in Christ. But, this doesn't mean that everything else about me is not a part of my total identity—what makes me Romell.

Learning who you are, and coming to accept your inherent characteristics are an essential part of the journey into loving yourself. Now, if the second-most important command God has ever given us is to love our neighbor *as* ourselves (second only to loving God), someone tell me how we can fulfill this command *without* first learning to love ourselves!

It has been my experience that those who are angriest at the world around them are those who have least-accepted the world within them. It's always easier to project self-hatred onto others, than to have to admit it to yourself and deal with it. But, ignoring it doesn't stop it from eating away at you, piece-by-piece, quietly... insidiously, until there's nothing left but an empty shell that survives day by day on a diet of criticism—finding fault in everything and everybody... no joy, no purpose, and no ability to love.

Ex-gay ministries enable and reinforce this type of emotional cancer, and that's why it's done so much damage to innumerable people who have actually attempted conversion therapy. Some have gone so far as to commit suicide and can no longer tell their heart-wrenching story; but I encourage you to seek out survivors and hear their stories. Hear the pit that this form of "ministry" put them into, which only Christ Himself could bring them out of.[92]

It's really tragic because the success ex-gay ministries enjoy in getting people to lie to themselves about who and what they are

---

[92] Resource: BeyondExGay.com

can bear no lasting fruit. In fact, it's accompanied by a potential for serious emotional and psychological damage in the long term. You simply *cannot* go on denying a part of who you are and expect that it will produce a healthy individual—spiritually, emotionally, even physically. Jesus told us—in some ways, He *warned* us—that only the *truth* holds the power to make us free. Ex-gay ministry works through the power of lies; and whether homosexuality is an egregious sin or not, no such approach to "ministry" can glorify God in the end.

Cause and Effect

The fact that ex-gay ministries exist is proof that some gay people want very badly to stop being gay. These ministries wouldn't exist if people didn't come to them seeking help. An interesting thing to consider, then, is if these people have *chosen* to be straight, why are they still gay and in need of an ex-gay ministry? If being gay is a choice, why isn't being straight one, as well—a choice that people could make without becoming a part of a support group? Was their initial choice to be gay as much of a struggle as their present choice to be straight? Did they fight with all of their might to suppress their supposedly natural opposite-sex attractions in order to conjure same-sex ones? Did they pray and fast, trying with all their might to stop being straight? These may seem to be ridiculous questions, but the reality is that if sexual orientation is a choice, as so many misinformed Christians believe, ex-gay ministries shouldn't exist, seeing as people have already made the choice before attending one (unless they're forced to attend, which, regrettably, happens also)!

It all boils down to causation. If we don't choose our sexual orientation—and all sound logic concludes that we don't, even though we certainly choose our sexual *behavior*—the question we must ask is how in the world it's determined. Is it a genetic or chromosomal trait determined by the sperm and/or egg? Does it develop in utero from any number of prenatal factors? Is it a result of environment or experiences during critical stages of child development (e.g. during pre- and/or early-teen years)? Is it a combination of any or all of these factors? Theories abound; but the fact is no one knows for sure.

Our authors did much less to assert a belief of their own in regard to causation than to criticize the belief that sexual orientation is in some way biological. The only conclusion I could draw from this is that they don't care what causes homosexuality, so long as it's not biological. That, it seems, is what they fear the most. Gagnon was an exception, however. He did offer a few guesses as to causation.

> "When a proper relationship with the same-sex parent or with same-sex peers is disrupted, the formation of a secure sexual identity in the child is likewise disrupted."[93]

> "Nevertheless, some studies have indicated that poor emotional bonding with the same-sex parent characterizes a significantly higher percentage of homosexuals than heterosexuals."[94]

Gagnon hypothesizes that how children relate to a same-sex parent affects their sexual identities. Many people find this theory compelling; but it doesn't hold up well to scrutiny. If it were true, the Black community, which has more fatherless homes than any other ethnic group, should have a substantially higher rate of gay men than any other group. Yet, there's no evidence to that effect.

Gagnon was quick to question arguments of cause and effect with other theories (particularly the ones he didn't like); but he didn't do so with this one. He didn't consider if a bad relationship could be the result of a parent's view that a child isn't conforming to social norms related to sexuality and/or gender. This is an important thing to consider because parents often go through a phase of blaming themselves if their child is gay, often asking what they did wrong in raising him/her. Inevitably, this can place a substantial strain on the parent-child relationship.

The failure of Gagnon to give due consideration to this very real potential is particularly frustrating because anti-gay rhetoric has led to many unnecessarily strained relationships

---

[93] *The Bible and Homosexual Practice*, 409.
[94] Ibid., 409-410.

between parents and their children, especially when it comes to the accusation of "choice." If anti-gay people care so much about family relationships—like Dobson and his *Focus On The Family* organization claim—they should start promoting love and acceptance, rather than disgust and fear.

Gagnon not only blames how children relate to their same-sex parents, but also how they relate to their peers.

> "When children regard members of their own sex as more 'exotic' than members of the opposite sex, then something is clearly wrong, as the very expressions 'same sex' and 'opposite sex' imply."[95]

Again, he just doesn't focus enough on causation. Obviously, the *reason* children may find members of the same sex more exotic is that something within them produces this attraction. But, Gagnon takes a leap from "exotic"—a term that, in itself, betrays substantial bias—to "clearly wrong," believing that the very words "same sex" and "opposite sex" imply the rightness or wrongness of the attractions themselves. I fail to see how, unless people simply choose to perceive such attractions negatively based on personal worldview.

He finally gets to the question of causation some 60 pages later; but he completely fails to interpret the data he presents properly.

> "Homosexuals experience significantly higher rates of alcohol and drug abuse, major depression, and thoughts of suicide and suicide attempts (often over partnership breakups). There is debate over how much of the fault for these indications of distress rests with homosexual behavior itself (e.g. high relationship turnover) and how much is attributable to social hostility against homosexuality. The fact, though, that significantly higher rates of substance abuse has been documented for homosexuals in San Francisco (as compared to heterosexuals in San Francisco)

---

[95] *The Bible and Homosexual Practice*, 412.

suggests that pinning the lion's share of the blame on societal homophobia is unfair."[96]

Gagnon refuses to see society as the impetus for the negatives he listed, based solely on the enormously flimsy evidence presented for supposedly universal acceptance of homosexuality in San Francisco. It may surprise him to know that bigotry and anti-gay theology exist even in the "gay Mecca", in which a substantial minority of the population is gay, as everywhere else in the world.

Not only does Gagnon acquit society for its contribution to the despair experienced by some homosexuals, but he also believes that people run to the "refuge" of gay relationships to escape the pressures of society surrounding heterosexuality!

> "Homosexual relationships, especially for males may also serve for many as a refuge from the anxiety associated with societal expectations around heterosexual courtship and intimacy. Consistent with this explanation is the fact that promiscuous, casual sex and 'open,' short-term relationships are hallmarks of male homosexual activity. It also fits with the much higher rates of substance abuse reported among homosexuals, inasmuch as the adoption of one self-soothing response to internal distress is usually accompanied by other methods of self-soothing."[97]

You have *got* to be kidding me! The notion that homosexual relationships provide a refuge for people from societal expectations is ludicrous. We're to believe that some heterosexuals are so anxious about being with someone of the opposite sex because of societal expectations that they, completely contrary to their actual attractions, turn to sex and relationships with people of the *same* sex? No one who understands sexual orientation could believe such an absurd thing. If societal expectations were that big of a deal, an individual would hardly pit himself against society by *choosing* to be gay! Anyone who could be moved to such an extreme

---

[96] *The Bible and Homosexual Practice*, 475.
[97] Ibid., 412.

would have a severe anxiety disorder and would require psychological and medicinal therapy. This doesn't describe gay people, who are not defying their orientation for fear of societal pressures, but are embracing it *despite* those pressures.

Societal pressures do not lead to homosexuality. To the contrary, they lead to homosexuals engaging in *heterosexuality*—dating and marrying people of the opposite sex because of the enormous socio-religious pressure brought to bear against them. Society has precisely the opposite effect on some gay people than Gagnon so nonsensically argues.

Further, the inordinate number of short-term relationships and promiscuous individuals within the gay male population is easily understood to be a result of simply being male. "Men are dogs," goes the old adage. I disagree with that characterization; but the fact that two men would be interested in one another romantically does make for a type of perfect storm of testosterone. It's not that gay men are somehow wired to be cheating whores. Men are simply especially sexual creatures; so having two men in a relationship makes for an interesting dynamic.

It's also important to acknowledge the role that society plays in helping to temper people's sexual behavior. When sexuality and relationships have the affirmation of family, friends, and society in general, it helps produce more responsible sexual behavior. What isn't taboo and left to the dark corners of our existence is almost always a healthier and more consistent part of our lives.

The marital state itself contributes to fidelity and long-term commitment because when couples cross the matrimonial threshold, they gain social, psychological, and even spiritual motivation for exercising more discipline in their relationships. This isn't to say that married couples don't cheat on one another; but they certainly do so in smaller numbers than unmarried couples. People also tend to fight more ardently to make their marriages last, as opposed to their dating relationships. So, preventing gay people from getting married doesn't help those who engage in irresponsible sexual behavior to do better. It only deprives them of a fundamental component in maintaining healthy, long-lasting relationships and engaging in responsible sexual behavior.

153

I don't point out these facts to excuse people from bad sexual behavior. I do so to acknowledge reality. Traditionalist Christians love to live in an idealized fantasy—the one that exists in their heads and on paper. But, God and the rest of us live in the real world. In the real world, the affirmation of those around us matters. The human condition compels us into interpersonal relationships, and to feed off of the environment that surrounds us, be it negatively or positively. That gay people could have their relationships recognized by their government and celebrated by their friends, families, and churches would be an important source of positive reinforcement for responsible sexual and relational behavior. Depriving us of such support—which heterosexuals receive without even realizing it—only contributes to the very behavior many believers rightly find morally objectionable.

Admittedly, when it comes to gay Christians, our behavior should be and is tempered by our faith. But, the unfortunate reality is that for gay, as well as straight Christians, faith isn't always enough. In the real world, both straight and gay Christians fornicate. Extending to gay people the same social privileges as their straight counterparts can only lessen the number of those who do.

Gagnon also referenced the higher rates of substance abuse among homosexuals; but I wonder if it has occurred to him that what such people are, in fact, trying to soothe is not internal distress at being gay, but the distress thrust upon them by a society that so relentlessly heaps upon them disapproval, ridicule, and spiritual torment. Could they not simply be trying to cope with being something that so puts them at odds with their families, their perceptions of God (based on what they've been taught), and their friends and neighbors? Under the constant strain of such inexorable pressure, it's no wonder there's a disproportionate number of gay people who are substance abusers. This should invoke compassion from Christians, not reproof. It should challenge them to create a better environment for those with same-sex attractions. Regrettably, it often does nothing of the sort. Some people's self-righteous disgust prevents even a modicum of sympathy.

"The best hope for change in the sexual orientation of homosexuals comes not in attempts to treat homosexuals after years and years of homosexual behavior but rather in limiting the options that young people have in terms of sexual experimentation. Some people will experiment under any cultural conditions. Nevertheless, cross-cultural studies prove beyond a shadow of a doubt that strong cultural disapproval of homosexual behavior can significantly curtail the incidence of such behavior. So perhaps a better question to ask than 'Can homosexuals change?' is 'Can the numbers of self-identifying homosexuals in the population be affected by cultural attitudes toward homosexual behavior?' The answer to that question, I would contend, is 'Yes, significantly so.'"[98]

Rather than pushing for social acceptance of homosexuality, thereby dramatically reducing the instances of drug abuse, depression, suicidal thoughts/attempts, and promiscuity[99] that Gagnon claims to be so concerned about, he actually advocates stronger degrees of cultural disapproval! Now, he's certainly right in that such disapproval would lead to smaller numbers of homosexuals; but not because they would have changed their orientation. It'd be because many more would have died from even greater instances of drug abuse, sexually transmitted diseases, and suicide.

Gagnon's contention that societal disapproval would curtail the incidence of homosexual behavior is, unfortunate though it may be, also accurate. The problem is that while he interprets this fact as hopeful, it's actually tragic. Whether people identify as gay or not doesn't change their orientation. But for those like Gagnon, this doesn't matter. They don't care if people delude themselves and others, so long as they don't allow their gayness to rise to the surface. Whatever the cost to gay people's spiritual and emotional well-being, they must keep their attractions hidden deep inside.

---

[98] *The Bible and Homosexual Practice*, 429.

[99] A poor self-image leads to higher instances of sexually irresponsible behavior.

When it's all said and done, it's not gay people Gagnon is concerned about; rather, it's society. He doesn't want the anti-gay population to have displays of homosexuality imposed upon their "righteous" eyes. That they could have their ideal, gay-free utopia is all that traditionalists really want. The utter despair of gay people who suppress their orientation is but a small price to pay in their minds. While we'll deal with this issue in detail in Chapter 13, suffice it to say that the idea that society would oppress gay people, keeping them hidden from the world, denied the catharsis of self-actualization and transparency just for the sake of public comfort is selfish, malicious, and utterly unchristian. I can't help but think of Jesus' warning concerning "the least of these" (Matt. 25:34-46).

God's Role In Gay

> "The 'inborn theory' takes on special significance when viewed religiously. It implies that if something is inborn, God must have created it. And who are we to argue with the Creator?"[100]

Dallas is correct in his claim that many affirming Christians believe that if/because people are born gay, God made them that way. But, this is one belief I disagree with. I don't believe God determines sexual orientation. I believe that people are straight or gay as a result of natural biological processes, just as with other traits. For example, I believe that I am Black because my mother and father were Black, not because God made it so. My race is a result of biological factors, being explained wholly by natural processes. The same can be said for my handedness, my hair and eye color, and my height. While we may not know the source of every biological trait, it doesn't mean they're any less biological. In this way, I don't believe God determined my sexual orientation.

Some may fear that this detracts from God's providence; but this isn't the case at all. I'm no less His handiwork simply because my height is a result of my genes and not a divine determination. It also doesn't mean that God doesn't determine *anyone's* race, height, or sexual orientation. There may be times

---

[100] *The Gay Gospel?*, 113.

when His purpose is for a particular person to be this way or that, but that doesn't mean that He determines such things for each and every person, outside or contrary to the flow of nature.

One of the reasons I think many people believe God made them gay is that it's a comforting thought. I understand that; believe me. It provides a feeling of validation and encouragement, knowing that because God makes no mistakes, being gay must not be a bad thing. It's certainly not my wish to take away a source of someone's comfort, but I'd rather we be comforted by beliefs that follow the flow of logic, as well.

Consider, for example, the range of various birth conditions, common and uncommon, healthy and deformed. Most people are born straight, while between 5-10% (possibly more) are born gay. Some are born distinctly male or female. Others are born intersex, with ambiguous genitalia or other sex characteristics. Most are born with 10 fingers, while some are born with more or fewer. Most are born with sight, while some are born without it.

The fact is people are born all kinds of ways, some being perfectly natural variations within the human family, while others are abnormalities or deformities. It's not worth debating whether or not homosexuality is a deformity, as there's no way to prove either position. I certainly have a problem believing that upwards of 10% of the human population has a deformity, though. But in the end, it really doesn't matter as far as my point is concerned.

The logic that people who were born a certain way are so because God made them that way fails when it comes to conditions that *are* deformities. For a God who does all things well, I have a problem wrapping my mind around the notion that He created people blind. It doesn't sit with my understanding of how He operates to believe that He created people deaf. But, if we consider that these types of conditions are a result of biological processes gone wrong in some way—nature makes mistakes, whereas God never does[101]—it makes sense. While God certainly providentially *allowed* these things to happen, that doesn't mean He was the agent of their existence.

---

[101] I'm not saying that people born with deformities are mistakes. I'm saying that the deformities themselves are mistakes—mistakes in the natural development of a life, not in the life itself.

When God created the world, He put a natural order in place, providing that all living systems would reproduce after their own kind. To accomplish this, these systems were given biological markers that determine various characteristics a living entity would have (e.g. genes). God is definitely the source of all life, and the master designer of all biological structures; but now that He's put "nature" in motion, there's no reason to believe that He continues to play a determining role as a matter of course (else there is no natural system in place at all, and God simply directs everything down to the minutest detail).

My point is that I don't think we need to inject wishful thinking into the debate in order to find validation and affirmation. Logic itself more than suffices to demonstrate that homosexuality is a perfectly natural component of the human experience.

White, Niell, and Gagnon each believe that the argument that homosexuality is a matter of biology presents a problem for affirming Christians. Of course, they'd probably say the same thing no matter what cause we ascribed to sexual orientation, so it's a no-win situation as far as coming to *any* degree of agreement is concerned.

> "Those who assert that homosexuality is simply a matter of genetics must deal with the fact that there is a vast difference between *disposition* and *necessity*. That is, even if we were to grant the argument that genetics in some way is relevant to homosexual desire or behavior, it is a long stretch to move from being *predisposed* to homosexuality and finding homosexual behavior *necessary*."[102]

> "Few people would argue that violent behavior is so genetically predetermined that humans who engage in it should be absolved of responsibility. Yet this and more is precisely the conclusion that the homosexual lobby wants the general public to draw about homosexual behavior."[103]

---

[102] *The Same Sex Controversy*, 176-177.
[103] *The Bible and Homosexual Practice*, 402-403.

They argue that even if homosexuality results from some biological factor, it doesn't mean that people must express those feelings in their behavior—that we may or may not choose our attractions, but we certainly choose our behavior. On the surface, it's seems true that disposition does not equate to behavioral necessity. However, in all practicality, this argument betrays an unsympathetic, legalistic approach that resembles the Pharisees' approach to issues of their day. To them, it's not unreasonable to conclude that those who are naturally oriented to the same sex must suppress their natural inclination for their entire lives, never experiencing companionship, love, and sexual fulfillment. Because it's not a burden they have to bear, they don't hesitate to require it of others. But this is not the compassionate way Christ would have us deal with such matters. Then again, traditionalists rarely bother themselves with such considerations.

> *"They tie up heavy burdens and lay them on men's*
> *shoulders, but they themselves are unwilling to move them*
> *with so much as a finger."*
> *Matthew 23:4*

Jesus had a problem with religious authorities that so easily placed burdens on others that they did not have to bear. White, Niell, and Gagnon get to go home and live with opposite-sex partners that they're attracted to and in love with, but they expect others to either stay single for life, or to marry opposite-sex partners that they're *not* attracted to or in love with. *"To hell with the happiness of the gay people, or that of their opposite-sex spouses!"* This is a heartless attitude, but is a necessary component of traditionalist thinking.

Interestingly, Scripture disagrees with the contention that sexual desire does not equate to sexual necessity. In Gen. 2:18, God said that it wasn't good that Adam was alone. He realized that He'd fashioned Adam with sexuality, but didn't provide him with an outlet for it. Adam's desire for intimacy, by its very nature, created an unmet need. As far as God was concerned, that *needed* to be remedied. Get it? Need... Necessity...

Furthermore, in 1Co. 7:2, 9, Paul reaffirmed the necessity of an outlet for our sexual desires. While they should only be expressed within marriage, the expression itself is a necessary component of healthy living (spiritually, physically, and emotionally), unless a person is endowed with the gift of celibacy (v. 7). Note that it requires a supernatural *gift* from God to be able to stand against our sexual desires without being subject to the overwhelming temptations that accompany abstinence. He even told those who *are* married not to deprive one another sexually precisely so that they won't be subjected to such temptations even for a moment (v. 5)! There's no way around the fact that Scripture teaches that our sexual needs are a necessity.

If those like our profiled authors had their way, gay people would have to exist in this vulnerable state for their entire lives (considering that opposite-sex marriage would not satiate their desires, since their desires point toward members of the same sex). They only demonstrate their cold-heartedness further in declaring that it doesn't even matter if sexual orientation is a result of biology.

One would undoubtedly counter that these arguments could be used to justify all sorts of sexual desires, including incest, bestiality, and pedophilia. My short-version response is that we cannot deny a biblical truth simply because of the possible repercussions. We must trust that God knows better than we, and that His word alone should be the arbiter of right and wrong.

That being said, this is an illegitimate concern for multiple reasons. Incest involves sexual activity with a family member, not simply being oriented toward family in general. On the other hand, homosexuals are *oriented* toward the same sex in general, not simply involved with an individual who happens to be of the same sex. Finally, incest is defined by action, not by state of being, i.e. a person *commits* incest, but simply *is* homosexual. Just because they both relate to human sexuality in one way or another does not make them analogous. To compare homosexuality with incest, then, is to compare applies with oranges.

The same can be said for bestiality and pedophilia. There is no biological element that attracts people to animals, or to certain human age groups, as though there are zebra-attractive genes, dog-attractive genes, pre-teen attractive genes, or teenage genes. But there *are* biological elements that make us male or female (or, in the case of intersex people, a variation of the two). This consequently impacts the attractions that we experience. Consider that 90-95% of people are attracted to the opposite sex, meaning that biological sex generally determines our attractions, e.g. men are *usually* attracted to women, and vice versa. A 5-10% exception rate is much too high to consider homosexuality unnatural, but much too low to consider it the norm. Yet, for such numbers to exist, biology *must* play a part in orientation, while there's no scientific or logical evidence whatsoever that it plays a part in pedophilia, bestiality, or incest.

Such arguments are fear tactics intended to scare people into opposing homosexuality for fear of some theoretical consequence. The simple fact is that while science has not pinpointed the biological cause of homosexuality, all logical thought points to biology as a primary—if not, *the*—determining factor in sexual orientation. People simply do not choose to be straight, gay, or bisexual. They are because they are.

10

Let Us Make Man
Creation and Complementarity

Without fail, the creation account is referenced by many anti-gay Christians in their attempt to establish that homosexuality is contrary to God's design. It certainly seems like a logical stop in the journey to the truth; but major problems exist with how traditionalists interpret the narrative.

Most common are errors associated with the oft-referenced theory of Complementarity. This theory posits three principles that are supposedly revealed in God's creative work in Genesis 1-2 and are solely applicable to opposite-sex unions: complementary wholeness, complementary fittedness, and complementary procreativeness.

Complementary Wholeness

The notion of complementary wholeness is derived from the account of Eve's creation. In Gen. 2:21-22, it states that God put Adam to sleep, removed one of his ribs, and fashioned Eve from it. The theory puts forth that because Adam's rib was removed, he was no longer whole until he was united with Eve. This holds opposite-sex unions as the only ones that provide wholeness to the two otherwise incomplete sexes.

> "What is crucial is that sexual differentiation is good, and good because the union of the corresponding sexes remedies their incompleteness apart from each other."[104]

---

[104] *Straight & Narrow?*, 44.

Schmidt's use of the word "good" is, undoubtedly, an attempt to convince us that God called opposite-sex union good—a description He used at the end of each creative stage in Gen. 1. However, this isn't true. God certainly called the creation of mankind good, and it's implied that Adam's no longer being without companionship was also good (Gen. 2:18); but that word was never ascribed to any notion of sexual differentiation. No such notion is even implied in the creation account. Schmidt forces this view onto the text. This is an example of how easily Scripture can be stretched beyond its actual intent in order to accommodate a preconceived notion. One can't necessarily blame Schmidt for the human frailty resident in his seeing what he wanted to see; but it underscores our need to objectively approach God's word.

Further, the idea that opposite-sex union "remedies [male and female] incompleteness apart from each other" consequently places the two sexes in a faulty state of being unless and until united in opposite-sex union. The only problem is that no such claim is ever made of the sexes anywhere in Scripture.

> "Only a being made from *adam* can and ought to become someone with whom *adam* longs to reunite in sexual intercourse and marriage, a reunion that not only provides companionship but restores *adam* to his original wholeness."[105]

Gagnon's logic fails in that Eve was made from Adam, not woman from man. She was not fashioned from *adam* (Hebrew for humankind, from which Adam's name was derived). In fact, they—both male *and* female—were called *adam* (Gen. 5:2), which indicates that in relation to creation, *adam* was not representative of maleness, but of both male *and* female—the human species.

If any incompleteness existed, then, it existed in only one man—Adam. If any remedy was exercised, it was exercised in only one union—Adam and Eve. If complementary wholeness rides beneath the surface of the creation narrative, it only applies to one particular man and one particular woman. Any attempt to stretch the application of this theoretical principle results in logical failure.

---

[105] *The Bible and Homosexual Practice*, 61. [emphases in original]

"The missing part of man is found in woman and vice versa. Sexual intercourse or marriage between members of the same sex does not restore the disunion because it does not reconnect complementary beings."[106]

Gagnon's claim that "the missing part of man is found in woman and vice versa" indicts all single people, including many heroes of the Judeo-Christian faith, like Elisha, Elijah, John, Paul, and even Jesus. They were all single and, by Gagnon's logic, existed outside of God's best... outside of what is supposedly "good"—to borrow a referential misuse by Schmidt.

"'Male and female he created them' probably intimates that the fullness of God's 'image' comes together in the union of male and female in marriage (not, one could infer, from same-sex unions)."[107]

This assertion is particularly problematic. It means that many of the heroes of our faith who were single fell short of God's image, even Jesus—a notion that contradicts the biblical testimony that Jesus was, in fact, God's image (2Co. 4:4; Col. 1:15; Heb. 1:3). Are we to offer an exemption to Jesus because of His divine nature, despite the fact that Scripture says that He made Himself of no reputation, having humbled or emptied Himself of that divine station and fashioned Himself as a human being, made like unto us (Ph. 2:5-8; Heb. 2:17)? Surely not! Jesus was not an exception. That He was God's image is a challenge to us to strive to become the same image—something we could not aspire to if He was some sort of supernatural exception (2Co. 3:18). This proves beyond *probability* and *intimation* that the image of God has absolutely nothing to do with our marital state, let alone with the sex of the person we marry.

Understand that what I am offering here are specific biblical statements that directly refute the theory of Complementarity. It only adds to the testimony against this theory

---

[106] *The Bible and Homosexual Practice*, 194.
[107] Ibid., 58.

to consider that it was never once taught in Scripture, but is, at best, simply intimated and/or inferred, based upon how a person understands what they read (the socio-religious lens through which they interpret Scripture)—a fact that Gagnon himself acknowledges. But how faithful are we to the mind of God when we take His words and stretch them beyond their intended scope in order to encompass our personal worldviews, to the extent that we infer *from* the text things that contradict the explicit teachings *of* the text, only to have to then jump through hoops to make room for the exceptions that such a flow of logic necessitates?

Gagnon knew there was no way for his argument to be logically proved; so he settled for mentioning it anyway, even though he was forced to acknowledge how uncertain his interpretation was. He, no doubt, hoped no one would pick up on how his arguments were only "probably intimated." It's bad enough his interpretation is simply intimated (implied) by the text. It's worse that the intimation itself is only probable! This smacks of utter desperation in the face of an interpretive approach that is devoid of all defensibility. Yet, it's an approach that so many anti-gay Christians hold sacrosanct.

My question to Schmidt and Gagnon is whether or not they'd like to indict Jesus as being less-than-whole, or if they'd prefer instead to amend their theory to state: *If* a person gets married, it must be to someone of the opposite sex. The problem with such an amendment is that if complementary wholeness is not required for single people, why would it be required for same-sex couples? Why can't we exist in the same "incomplete" state Jesus existed in? In fact, by their logic, same-sex couples are *more* like Jesus precisely because we're *not* complete in the way mandated by this errant theory. If their brand of incompleteness was good enough for Jesus, it's good enough for me!

The fact is that humankind is not incomplete or in need of a remedy that can only be provided by the opposite sex. At best, Adam was the only such person; but even that interpretation involves conjecture. Was his rib taken? Yes; but that doesn't mean Adam was incomplete. It's not as though Eve ripped the rib from her body and handed it back to him. So, even if he were anatomically incomplete before his union with Eve, he remained so even after it.

I would tolerate such symbolism if Scripture taught it; but it didn't. Though, I was pleased to discover that Schmidt had the intellectual honesty to acknowledge the weakness of this argument. It's just unfortunate that this acknowledgment didn't stop him from avowing the theory anyway.

> "The argument from Complementarity alone, however, has some liabilities. As I explained above, we may reasonably derive it from the Bible, but the Bible itself does not make the point in so many words."[108]

Schmidt is both right and wrong. We may, indeed, derive the theory of complementary wholeness from the Bible; however, he's wrong in his assertion that such a derivation is reasonable. One cannot assert that something is reasonable simply because it can be derived from a text. Derivations are vulnerable to bias and eisegesis, so it's important to judge any such conclusions by the standard of the explicit (underived) teachings of Scripture. Complementary wholeness fails this test miserably.

Complementary Fittedness

This theory espouses a belief often referenced by laypersons, although scholars sometimes make mention of it, as well. It asserts that a penis is made for a vagina, and vice versa—that male-with-female provides anatomical, genital fittedness that isn't possible in cases of male-with-male or female-with-female.

On the surface, the argument seems reasonable, particularly when considering the third component of Complementarity—the ability to procreate. However, if you go beneath the surface even a little, it becomes clear that this theory is unsustainable. Not only is it absent from Scripture—failing to meet something of a requisite when discussing theology—but it doesn't even meet the very test of physical anatomy upon which it stands. But, before dealing with these failures specifically, let's examine the anatomy-based arguments themselves.

---

[108] *Straight & Narrow?*, 46.

> "For Paul, homosexual acts were sinful, first and foremost, because they demonstrated the rejection of God's intention that sexual intercourse be between sexual 'others,' an intention revealed by the anatomical complementarity of male and female sex organs."[109]

Gagnon makes this claim in relation to Paul's condemnation of same-sex acts in Ro. 1:26-27. But, a reading of the text (even of the entire chapter of Ro. 1) fails to bear this out. Nowhere is it so much as hinted to that the "other-ness" or sex-differentiation between male and female had anything whatsoever to do with the condemnation of same-sex activity. What *is* stated multiple times is that the association with idolatry was directly responsible for God's judgment. We don't have to derive this by conjecture or supposition because it is explicitly stated, not implied, inferred, or intimated, as are the supposed principles Gagnon bases his logic on.

Furthermore, he claims that God's intention for intercourse is revealed by the supposed anatomical complementarity of male and female; yet, no such revelation is unfolded in Scripture. Leaving the biblical testimony and looking at the matter biologically, another problem arises. In order for any such fittedness to be indicative of God's intentions, it must be exclusive to the union of male and female, else it could just as easily support whatever other forms of sexual activity such fittedness exists within.

> "Males have a sex organ suited for penetration and no orifice appropriate for sexual receptivity. Females have genital organs suited for receiving male penetration and no penetrating organ of their own."[110]

Gagnon is absolutely convinced that the fittedness of the penis and vagina is an exclusive fittedness, which demonstrates God's intentions for sexual activity. I'm willing to go down this

---

[109] *The Bible and Homosexual Practice*, 270.
[110] Ibid., 365.

road since, like Gagnon, so many anti-gay theologians insist on doing so; but they're undoubtedly not going to like where it leads. You see, the vagina is not the only orifice capable of receiving penile penetration.

In both male-female *and* male-male sex, anal penetration is often practiced. Gagnon, and those like him, believe it axiomatic that the anus is not appropriate for sexual receptivity; however, many Christians do not believe anal intercourse is a violation of created intent when engaged in by married people—heterosexuality being the assumed context. What I've often heard in discussions on the subject is that what married people do in the privacy of their own bedrooms is their own business, and that there's no reason to believe that God would have a problem with it, seeing as Scripture never condemned it. Of course, when you inject a same-sex element to the discussion, beliefs magically change; but leave the discussion in a heterosexual context, and many Christians have no theological problem with anal sex, even if they do not personally engage in it.

In addition to the anus, both opposite-sex and same-sex partners often engage in oral sex. Discussions surrounding oral sex often involve the same logical flow—that if people are married, what's the problem with it, seeing as God never condemned it in the Bible? It's not as though anal or oral sex was unknown to the ancients, which would have given us sufficient explanation for their absence from Scripture.

The fact is that sex involving married couples was not regulated in Scripture. Given the often-tedious specificity with which Scripture condemns various activities, especially in the Law of Moses, it's quite telling that neither anal nor oral sex was condemned.

Traditionalists interpret the fact that a penis fits into a vagina as an exclusive indication of God's intent; but this is simply not the case. Almost every member of the body has multiple functions, many involving eroticism. For example, the hands hold, carry, and clap, but they also tenderly caress. The eyes see; but they also flirt (e.g. winking). The mouth speaks, eats, and facilitates oral breathing; but it also kisses the lips, licks the body, and stimulates the nipple (Song of Solomon 4:5-6; 7:7-8). As for the nipple, in women it provides milk for nursing infants; but it also provides sexual stimulation. In men, it only serves a stimulative end, yet God didn't see fit to create men without them. Ears are for hearing; yet the blowing, kissing, and licking of the ear is often engaged in during sexual foreplay.

My intention is not to survey every part of the body, but to demonstrate that body parts serve multiple functions. Just because the anus is used to excrete waste doesn't mean it's not appropriate for sexual, even penetrative, function. Did it never occur to Gagnon that both the penis *and* vagina also excrete waste? Should we, therefore, believe that God condemns vaginal sex, as well?

> "Sexual intercourse is complementary for males and females, not males with males or females with females. In the contemporary context, one hears repeatedly the objection that not all sexual activity involves penetration by a phallus, even in heterosexual relationships. Why, then, should the absence of such penetration in homoerotic relationships (particularly lesbian) deny their legitimacy? Yet that misses the point. The point is not that sexual intimacy must always and only involve phallic penetration (as if all kissing, caressing, and other forms of sexual contact would have to cease) but rather that the fittedness of the penis and vagina provide clues as to how God desires sexual pairing to be organized by gender. The anatomical clues point to God's intention that human sexuality involves opposite-sex pairing as opposed to same-sex pairing."[111]

If Gagnon is right in his repeated assertions that the male and female anatomies provide clues as to God's intentions for human sexuality, we must consider the two anatomies to see if they in any way facilitate same-sex sexual activity like the fittedness of the penis and vagina facilitate opposite-sex activity. This is a necessary step because we must test the logic of Gagnon's argument to see if it precludes same-sex sex, as Gagnon apparently assumes. To follow the logic properly, however, we must consider

---

[111] *The Bible and Homosexual Practice*, 365.

organs distinct to males and to females, which facilitate sex with the same sex; otherwise, the argument could be seen to facilitate opposite-sex intercourse, instead.

Male-Male Sex Facilitated

Males have a sex organ called the prostate gland, which especially facilitates anal sex among men. Although its primary function is to produce the fluid conveyance for semen, it has a secondary function. When pressed, it provides substantial sexual gratification. But, because of where the prostate is located, the only way to stimulate it is through anal penetration. This is why when a man goes to the doctor for a prostate exam, the doctor must penetrate his anus with a gloved finger in order to feel for the gland and check for abnormalities that may indicate the presence of cancer. Because of the stimulative effect of pressing the prostate, men are often told not to be alarmed if they get an involuntary erection, or even ejaculate during the exam.

Because the prostate provides such an enjoyable sensation, some men, both hetero- and homosexual, purchase a sex toy called a prostate massager. It resembles a dildo/dong, and is used to penetrate the anus and stimulate the prostate. But, the heterosexual users aren't closet homosexuals. They harbor no subconscious desire for penile penetration. They simply wish to feel the sensations God created their prostate with the ability to produce; and anal penetration is the only way for this to occur.

Please Note: I am not advocating the use of sex toys. I am simply presenting evidence in an effort to demonstrate the factual basis for the sexual pleasure provided by the prostate—a sexual organ exclusive to males that especially facilitates male-male sexual activity by way of anal penetration.

Now, one would think that males have no need of a sexual organ that facilitates penetrative receptivity, seeing as the heterosexual paradigm provides no expectation that the male would be penetrated. Still, the prostate exists, and serves its function. It's no coincidence that this gland: 1) is a sex organ, 2) is exclusively male, 3) provides pleasure when stimulated, and 4) is especially positioned so as to require anal penetration in order to achieve stimulation. God did not need to create this gland to meet these criteria; yet He did. By Gagnon's logic, this absolutely demonstrates God's intentions for human sexuality, as it relates to gay men—those whose sexual encounters would, in most cases, involve anal penetration by one partner or the other.

Ultimately, males were designed with anatomies that could experience pleasure via heterosex *and* homosex sexual expressions, making both perfectly natural, and part of the created intent.

Female-Female Sex Facilitated

Like males, females also have a sexual organ unique to them that facilitates same-sex intercourse. This gland is called the clitoris. Unlike the male prostate gland, the clitoris is located on the outside of the female body and provides sexual gratification without the need for penetration—a requirement for natural female-female sex, in which there would be no expectation of natural penetration.

Because of the position of the clitoris, we can't be certain of created intent. A male can stimulate it just as easily as a female can because it's located on the exterior of the body. Still, the fact is that the clitoris facilitates non-penetrative sex; and when considered in conjunction with the prostate in males, it can definitely be seen to facilitate female-female sex.

The conclusion: Both males and females were created with the ability to enjoy sex with members of the same or opposite sex. Therefore, we can only conclude that the human body reveals the anatomical complementarity of humans, and this complementarity affords no regard for the sex of those engaging in intercourse.

> "Since the obvious receptacle given by nature for the male penis was the female vagina, penetration of a male amounted to treating the male as if he were a female and thereby 'emasculating' him—a blatant case of anatomical gender transgression. In effect, the willingly penetrated male takes up a complaint with nature for failing to supply him with a vagina."[112]

---

[112] *The Bible and Homosexual Practice*, 169.

When I read this statement, I laughed out loud. It conjured a mental image of a feminine man complaining to an unseen force that he wasn't given a vagina. The logical consequence of this ridiculous argument is that women who willingly allow a man to penetrate their anal cavity likewise take up a complaint with nature, except that in their case, their grievance is that they weren't given *two* vaginas!

PERSONAL COMMENTARY: Given Gagnon's credentials, and my resulting expectation that he would offer the most legitimate anti-gay case I'd come across to date, I read *The Bible and Homosexual Practice* with the hope of being presented with more reasonable arguments than proved to exist.

If this type of nonsense is the best a well-credentialed traditionalist biblical scholar can come up with, gay people have nothing to worry about, theologically speaking. Our adversaries have stopped grabbing at straws and are now groping aimlessly at the formless wind, hoping that a magical dragon named Falcore will happen by and lift them from the quagmire of their theological desperation.[113]

"...in Paul's view, the fact that sexual intercourse could potentially lead to childbirth only in heterosexual pairing provided clues or insights as to God's design for the sexual complementarity of the male and female organs."[114]

"Procreation is God's clue, given in nature, that the male penis and female vagina/womb are complementary organs."[115]

Where in all of the Pauline scriptures is any such case made? Gagnon likely has in mind Paul's statement that "they are without excuse" because creation itself has revealed certain things

---

[113] In case you missed it, this is a reference to the fantasy book and movie, *The Neverending Story*, which offers both a fitting genre *and* title for traditionalist logic.

[114] *The Bible and Homosexual Practice*, 272.

[115] Ibid., 164.

(Ro. 1:20). But, who are "they" exactly, and what has creation revealed to them? Are they homosexuals? No! Although Gagnon argued multiple points from that assumption, the context clearly bears out that "they" refers to idolaters. Paul's criticism dealt with idolaters, not homosexuals; and there's absolutely no evidence that what creation revealed to them had anything to do with childbirth. Indeed, the context indicates that creation's revelation was the existence of the one true God Himself.

Furthermore, this logic precludes heterosexual anal sex, as well. Gagnon obviously believes it's an ungodly sexual expression, incessantly appealing to a subjective interpretation of anatomy; but he has no chapter and verse to back it up. In fact, it's impossible to condemn anal sex biblically because there simply is no support for such a condemnation. Any attempt to do so isn't worthy of a scholar or Bible teacher. One is certainly allowed a personal aversion to it, but that's precisely what it is—personal.

Complementary Procreativeness

The final element of Complementarity often used to demonstrate that homosexuality is a moral wrong deals with procreation. It asserts, as Gagnon did in the previous quotation, that because the union of male and female is the only one that can produce children, it is clearly the only one God intended humans to engage in. It's amazing how many people hold this to be true, seeing as Scripture never claims, even in its condemnation of various forms of same-sex sexual activity, that procreative potential was a requirement for sex and/or marriage. It also never claims that a lack of procreative potential had anything to do with the few condemnations of same-sex intercourse.

> "The fact that the semen ejaculated by the penis 'takes root' (we would say, 'effects the fertilization of an egg') and nurtures life only when penetration of a woman's vagina occurs is clear and convincing proof of God's exclusive design in nature for heterosexual intercourse."[116]

---

[116] *The Bible and Homosexual Practice*, 169.

As I stated before, the only problem with this interpretation of the procreative potential of opposite-sex unions is that it requires too many suppositions on our part, many of which, if followed to their logical conclusions, would also condemn many opposite-sex unions. For example, consider where the following arguments put forward by Gagnon lead.

> "The pinnacle of God's creative work is thus human beings as creatures capable of receiving and carrying out commands from God in relation to the rest of creation. Filling or populating the earth with humans is a precondition for ruling it, and procreation is a precondition for filling the earth. The Complementarity of male and female is thereby secured in the divinely sanctioned work of governing creation."[117]

> "...the issue of procreation ties in with the command to 'be fruitful and multiply' which, according to the creation story in Genesis 1, is one of two great commands that God gave to the human species."[118]

If homosexuality is invalidated on the basis that it provides no procreative potential and, therefore, violates God's command to "be fruitful and multiply," then so too are all opposite-sex marriages in which either party is incapable of having children. This means that if we want to be obedient Christians, we must question a potential life-partner's ability to provide us with children, else we negligently enter into lifelong unions that put obedience to one of God's "two great commands" out of reach. Post-menopausal widows, otherwise infertile women, sterile men, and people who simply don't want children would be disqualified from any prospect of marriage!

The simple fact is that God's command to be fruitful and multiply was not given to humanity. It was given solely to two individuals—Adam and Eve. We don't find a single instance in all

---

[117] *The Bible and Homosexual Practice*, 57.
[118] Ibid., 132.

of Scripture in which God chastised anyone for not having children. The culture certainly stigmatized barren/infertile women as being cursed by God, but God never punished people for not having children. The sole exception is Onan, whom God killed for marrying his dead brother's wife according to the levirate tradition, having sex with her, yet ejaculating on the ground. His punishment did not result from a refusal to have a child, however. It resulted from his refusal to honor the levirate tradition, dishonoring his brother's widow (and the entire family) in the process[119] (Gen. 38:6-10). Nowhere was a person punished simply for not having children, though.

Now, many traditionalists, like Gagnon, claim that God did, in fact, command the entire human race to be fruitful and multiply, but that heterosexual couples who do not desire children are not living contrary to God's will because this command was ultimately fulfilled by earlier generations. Humanity has, indeed, multiplied greatly since the command was given. The only problem with this attempt to wiggle out of the logical implications of their application of this command is that it would, necessarily, also exempt same-sex couples from any requirement to be fruitful and multiply.

They often counter by claiming that there was no requirement for every individual to have children, but that the procreative potential is only available with opposite-sex partners. But again, their argument has problems. No procreative potential exists for heterosexuals who are already aware that they can't have children. Must they, then, remain single forever?

Furthermore, if traditionalists wish to ascribe intent based on procreative function, consistency requires us to ascribe intent to the prostate gland, based on stimulative function. It can only serve this function through male-male anal sex. By traditionalist logic, then, all men who marry must marry both a male and a female, regardless of orientation—the female to fulfill procreative function,

---

[119] Levirate is from the Latin: *levir*, meaning husband's brother. The tradition required a brother whose married brother died childless to marry his brother's widow and have a son in his brother's name, primarily so that his brother's property would not be lost to the family, seeing as women had no inheritance rights. Though only a cultural tradition at the time of Onan, it was eventually made law as a provision of the Mosaic covenant.

and the male to fulfill anally stimulative function. I didn't realize traditionalists were so freaky!

Ultimately, function reveals options, not requirements. Procreative function shows that opposite-sex intimacy is an option; but it does not necessitate it. It *cannot* be seen to necessitate it, considering that celibacy was commended in Scripture (1Co. 7:1, 7-8)—an elective state that precludes the possibility of procreation. How much more would gay people who did not choose to be gay be given license to leave the procreative potential unfulfilled?

Created Intent

So common is the view that God's intention for human sexuality is revealed in the creation narrative that it really can't be considered a single interpretation among many others. Among traditionalists, it is, without a doubt, *the* interpretation of the text. I doubt you'll find a single non-affirming Christian who doesn't believe that the Adam/Eve model indicates divine intent for a heteronormative sexual paradigm. This wouldn't be quite so surprising but for the fact that there's simply no actual evidence to support this widely held misconception. A third grader realizes that a historical narrative is not a command!

> "Homosexual practice constitutes a denial in practice of the good instituted by God from the beginning."[120]

> "While it's true that this passage does not 'forbid' homosexual relations, it does provide the primary model for sexuality by which other forms of sexual expression must be judged."[121]

> "…a monogamous relation between husband and wife is the standard upheld in Scripture as the ideal. While the often-used phrase 'God created Adam and Eve, not Adam and Steve' seems flippant, it's a fair assessment of created intent."[122]

[120] *Straight & Narrow?*, 48.
[121] *The Gay Gospel?*, 173.
[122] Ibid., 174.

I admit that during my non-affirming days, I, too, fell prey to the misconception that Genesis 1-2 actually told us something of God's intentions for human sexuality. Since those days, I have thankfully come to realize that the passage reveals nothing of the sort. The closest we get to a universal principle in this account is Jesus' statement that the narrative indicates that marriage was originally intended to last for life; however, even *He* provided an exception in the case of adultery—an exception that acknowledged the reality of the world as it exists.

As I once did, our authors assumed that this account tells us many things about God's intentions. Indeed, Dallas even claims that the Adam/Eve model is the standard by which all forms of sexual expression should be judged. That's quite a claim; but let's examine the narrative more closely and see if it's as prescriptive as traditionalists believe.

First of all, as Dallas stated, many believe it tells us of the divine intention that marriage be monogamous. Gagnon repeatedly claimed that monogamy was the only form of marriage sanctioned by God. But Scripture utterly destroys any such notion.

> *"Nathan then said to David, "You are the man! Thus says the LORD God of Israel, 'It is I who anointed you king over Israel and it is I who delivered you from the hand of Saul. [8] 'I also gave you your master's house and your master's wives into your care, and I gave you the house of Israel and Judah; and if that had been too little, I would have added to you many more things like these!"*
> *2Samuel 12:7-8*

Nathan was an Old Testament prophet. In this passage, he rebuked King David for having Uriah (one of his soldiers) killed in order to take Uriah's wife, Bathsheba, as his wife. This unfortunate act of cruelty was, no doubt, precipitated by the fact that David got Bathsheba pregnant while her husband was away fighting in a war.

Contained in this prophetic rebuke is a word from the Lord, in which He states that among the things He gave David when making him king of Israel in Saul's place was Saul's wives (plural). If polygamy is not of God, as traditionalists incessantly claim, how do they explain His giving David multiple wives?

Is our *holy* God, in whom resides no unrighteousness (Ps. 92:15; Jn. 7:18), capable of not simply allowing, but *establishing* things that are contrary to His own will—things that violate His own moral code? Obviously, the traditionalist version of God is capable of such contradiction; however, mine is not. This proves beyond a doubt that although the first model involved monogamy, it could not have been an expression of divine intent. Supporting evidence includes the fact that Jacob, David, Solomon, and many others anointed and blessed by God were polygamists and were never once rebuked for it.

Another supposed principle people derive from the creation narrative is that all humans must be married—for we're required to "be fruitful and multiply." Traditionalists don't explicitly say that it's wrong not to seek marriage, but such an environment definitely exists within the Church. Enormous pressure is brought to bear on single people. They're constantly asked when they're going to start a family; and they're looked at as though there's something wrong with them if they remain single for too long. So, whereas it may not be considered law for everyone to marry, it certainly raises eyebrows if they don't.

I addressed the problems with the idea that procreation is a requirement in the section on procreative complementarity, so I won't repeat myself here. However, consider that Paul commended singlehood on the basis that single people can offer undistracted service to God (1Co. 7:17-8; 32-34). Yet, how are they to be fruitful and multiply if they remain single? Was Paul unaware of this supposed requirement—this "great command", as Gagnon put it—or did he just choose to disregard it?

That's two strikes against the idea of created intent. We can't conclude that the Adam/Eve model tells us that we *must* get married and have children, and we can't even conclude that when we do marry, it can only be to one individual. Now, if the Adam/Eve model is not prescriptive on these particular points, how can we consider it prescriptive with regard to the biological sex of those who choose to get married? How can we point to procreative complementarity in condemning homosexuality and same-sex marriage when God never commanded every human to procreate in the first place? In effect, the creation narrative is *descriptive*, but not *prescriptive* in its witness.

Gagnon acknowledges the descriptive nature of the creation narrative, but still finds a way to apply it in a prescriptive way. What's so amazing is that this isn't done under the radar. He explicitly announces his hermeneutical approach.

> "Unlike stories [like the creation narrative], commands have a definite prescriptive or proscriptive (not just descriptive) function."[123]

> "So great is the complementarity of male and female, so seriously is the notion of 'attachment' and 'joining' taken, that the marital bond between man and woman takes precedence even over the bond with the parents that physically produced them. A descriptive statement about the creation of woman thus provides etiological justification for prescriptive norms regarding marriage."[124]

What Gagnon fails to realize is that Scripture is very good at interpreting itself. When there's a principle to be found, it points that principle out. We're not left to our own devices, theorizing about the point Scripture is *intending* to make. The narrator of Gen. 2 explicitly pulled the principle of one-flesh to the surface for our assimilation. Jesus explicitly pulled the lifelong intent of marriage to the surface. All other attempts to derive principles from the narrative fail because of other contradictory passages. Consequently, there is no created intent as it relates to marriage. The phrase itself is a misnomer.

In the end, it is impossible to find in the creation narrative any principle regarding human sexuality outside of that which Jesus identified—the lifelong intention of marriage, and the principle of one-flesh through marital and sexual union. Using the narrative as a way of condemning same-sex relationships is inconsistent with everything Scripture teaches about human sexuality.

---

[123] *The Bible and Homosexual Practice*, 111.
[124] Ibid., 61.

11

Tackling The Taboo
A Candid Look At Human Sexuality

Sex is among the most off-limit subjects in the Church. The very word makes people uncomfortable, as though it's a revolting, inherently sinful thing. In fact, our aversion to discussions of a sexual nature can almost be described as fearful.

This treatment of sex is not without consequences, the most relevant being the Church's inability to engage in reasonable discourse about homosexuality. People are hesitant to open up about attractions and experiences for fear that such transparency may earn them the scorn of their brethren. This is tragic because our failure to deal with the issue openly has given way to a variety of assumptions about what it is to be gay, and has produced an environment devoid of relevant, relatable moral guidance that would help curb the natural proclivity to engage in irresponsible sexual behavior.

Interestingly, the Bible does not fall prey to our modern socio-religious anxiety about sexual discussion. It's more candid than most churches dare to be.

Our authors certainly had opinions about sex, particularly as it pertains to the biological sex of sexual partners. But, as will become evident, Scripture paints no such picture and is, in fact, our best advocate for same-sex marriage and intercourse.

> "For Paul, the only legitimate sexual union for Christians is that between one man and one woman in permanent, exogamous, and monogamous marriage. All other forms of sexual intercourse, including same-sex intercourse ([1Co.] 6:9), are immoral perversions of this bond (6:18-19)."[125]

Gagnon is a master of ascribing perceptions and intentions to biblical writers that can't actually be supported biblically. He asserts with great confidence that Paul believed the only legitimate unions were those that were permanent, exogamous, and monogamous. This is a great example of Gagnon's tendency to project his personal worldview onto the biblical texts and writers because, in fact, either Paul himself, or other biblical writers, made exceptions for all three of these supposed conditions for legitimate unions. As a result, not a single one of Gagnon's conditions are conditions at all, a fact that weighs heavily against his contention that "*all* other forms of sexual intercourse" are immoral perversions—a bold claim that would, necessarily, include the exceptions resident in Scripture.

Paul makes an exception for permanence in 1Co. 7:15, and Jesus does so in Matt. 19:9. I don't contend that it isn't the ideal, but the fact is that ideals don't always survive realities. Besides, I have a hard time believing that Jesus would offer an immoral basis for divorce. Such a thing would fly in the face of His nature as a holy God, whether manifest in the flesh at the time or not.

Exogamy (marriage/sex outside of one's family, as opposed to incest) has a number of exceptions in early Old Testament people, including Adam and Eve's children, Abraham, and Jacob. It's wrong for *modern* Christians to engage in incestuous relationships (based on 1Co. 5); but it cannot be considered inherently immoral, else we would expect it to have been universally condemned (in all places and all times). This means that God would have necessarily created non-related humans for Adam and Eve's children to procreate with. We also would have found Abraham rebuked at least in *some* degree for marrying his half-sister, who was even more closely related than his grandson, Jacob, was to *his* wives, Leah and Rachel (his first cousins).

Finally, we've already discussed the fact that monogamy is not a biblical requirement on multiple occasions. But, to reiterate, polygamy is never rebuked in Scripture, which means no exception is necessary; yet multiple examples exist, including Elkanah (the prophet Samuel's father), Jacob, David, and Solomon. In addition, Paul placed a requirement of monogamy on bishops and

---

[125] *The Bible and Homosexual Practice*, 293.

elders—they must be the husbands of one wife (1Ti. 3:2; Tit. 1:5-6)—yet, he never made any such rule of the general body of believers. Seeing that the notion of polygamy was certainly in his mind, the absence of such a requirement is quite telling. Apparently, early Christians practiced it (hence the restriction on bishops and elders), yet were never told not to do so.

While Gagnon tries to deem same-sex intercourse immoral on the tri-fold basis of permanence, exogamy, and monogamy—none of which same-sex intercourse violates, by the way—the fact is that no such requirements exist in Scripture, with the exception of exogamy (something that was once not required, which indicates that it's not a moral wrong). Gagnon's persistent appeal to these "requirements" betrays the lack of a better body of evidence on his part, and ultimately proves that Scripture does not share his narrow view of sex and marriage.

> "Scripture presents only two choices for obtaining sexual intercourse: become involved in a lifelong monogamous heterosexual relationship or remain celibate."[126]

This brings us to the heart of the matter. When it comes to sex, what are gay people to do? Is Gagnon correct in his assertion that we must either marry someone of the opposite sex or remain celibate? Does this fit within the biblical framework of human sexuality? What exactly does the Bible tell us about sexuality, and the role that marriage is to play in relation to it?

Interestingly, it says quite a bit; and that witness is of the utmost relevance in the debate over homosexuality. But, in order to interpret the data objectively, without allowing our personal beliefs about homosexuality to cloud our judgment, we must first examine the biblical witness with no mind to sexual orientation. This is the only way we can pull the principles from the text without having our view obscured by the forest of our existing perceptions. We'll then be in a position to apply those principles back to our examination of homosexuality.

---

[126] *The Bible and Homosexual Practice*, 432.

Human Sexuality and Scripture

In Gen. 2:18, God declared that it was not good that Adam was alone. Even in a creation within which everything God made was good, it was *not* good that "the man" had an unfulfilled need for intimacy. This reveals an important truth about God's perspective of sexuality. The human tendency toward emotional and physical companionship preceded sin, and that tendency was "good." God *created* Adam with this need, and He was aware of its potency, which was why it was *not* good that it go unfulfilled.

> "He [Paul] regarded sexual intercourse in marriage as a legitimate (indeed, necessary) activity because it provided an appropriate escape valve for sexual desire that might otherwise result in adultery and promiscuity. Sex did not have to lead to procreation; it had real value as a release for sexual desire."[127]

> "One function of sex within a marriage is to prevent passions from boiling over into 'dishonorable' passions, not to preclude passion altogether."[128]

> "Given this unbroken continuity, one might begin to suspect that something mystical within human nature must be drawing the sexes together—not just for purposes of reproduction as with animals, but to satisfy an irrepressible longing for companionship, intimacy, and spiritual bonding. Indeed, how can it be doubted? Passion finds its fulfillment in the institution of marriage."[129]

With the exception of their assertion that human nature draws "the sexes" together (as opposed to simply two individuals), I agree with all three of these statements. There is, indeed, something within that drives those of us not gifted with celibacy into companionship. This natural, human need for intimacy existed

---

[127] *The Bible and Homosexual Practice*, 272.
[128] Ibid., 387.
[129] *Marriage Under Fire*, 8.

184

before the Fall. The only thing *not* good during that time was that this need was not being fulfilled.

> *"Then the LORD God said, "It is not good for the man to be alone; I will make him a helper suitable* **for him.**" *[19] Out of the ground the LORD God formed every beast of the field and every bird of the sky, and brought them to the man to see what he would call them; and whatever the man called a living creature, that was its name. [20] The man gave names to all the cattle, and to the birds of the sky, and to every beast of the field, but for Adam there was not found a helper suitable* **for him.**"
> *Genesis 2:18-20* **[emphases mine]**

God, being the benevolent, kind Spirit that He is, decided to remedy this ailment. Apropos, He's not only benevolent; He's also wise. He understood that if this need was to be fully satisfied, the companion He provided for Adam would have to be suitable—not to nature, law, principle, expectation, or majority consent, but according to God, "suitable for *him*" ("him" being Adam). If the companion were *not* suitable for him, the union would not be able to serve its purpose, thereby failing to remedy Adam's "not good" condition.

Because God's purpose hinged on the suitability of the companion Adam would be provided with, it was only appropriate for *Adam* to select the companion. Certainly, in His omniscience, God knew what was suitable beforehand; yet, it was so important to demonstrate that Adam had the power of choice that He went through the time-consuming process of bringing every animal to Adam so he could find himself a companion. Naming the animals was only an incidental "killing two-birds with one stone."

Now, if God were the one who determined suitability, this process would have been completely unwarranted. Certainly, the animals needed names, but the process could have (and certainly *would* have) waited until Adam's pressing need for companionship was met first. It makes no sense for God to take weeks (possibly months) to have Adam name the animals, when all He had to do was put Adam to sleep and create Eve. Apparently, it was a necessary, albeit tedious task because it was the only way Adam would be able to exercise the power of choice.

Now, traditionalists would have us believe that Adam's choice was representative of the suitability of all marital unions that would follow—that because his suitable companion was a woman, so too are all men's; and likewise, that all suitable companions for women are men. However, this fails to take into account a couple of points. First, God said that Adam's companion had to be suitable for *him*, not for *us*. Adam was not searching for a companion suitable for the male-kind, but for himself.

Second, what would make the companion suitable would be its ability to solve Adam's need. This meant that the determining factor was Adam's personal longing, else the union would not serve the purpose for which it was created. That's why everything in nature was bypassed, sending God back to the drawing board to create Eve.

We saw Gagnon's claim that there were only two options for gay people—opposite-sex marital intercourse or celibacy. But, he failed to consider if an opposite-sex marriage would fulfill a gay person's need for intimacy, as Adam's opposite-sex marriage fulfilled *his* need. He didn't consider if God would look upon such a union and call it good.

For God, our need for intimacy is a serious concern; but this isn't so for Gagnon. In his mind, a meaningless marriage or celibacy is the only choice gay people have. "Needs be damned" is the attitude his argument betrays. This is in stark contrast to the great care with which God approached Adam's loneliness. It also contradicts Paul's advice that it's *better* for a person who cannot contain himself sexually to marry, than to burn with passion (1Co. 7:9).

Thomas Schmidt takes Gagnon's argument to the next level, putting into words what Gagnon apparently feels about marriage.

> "[For gay advocates] the main thing about sex is pleasure, and homosexual practice is the ultimate expression of this, because it allows a full range of pleasures without the possibility of confusion by connection to children."[130]

---

[130] *Straight & Narrow*, 51.

186

In Schmidt's mind, gay advocates believe that sex is mainly about pleasure. This misguided belief is apparently why traditionalists can't understand that opposite-sex intercourse is incapable of fulfilling gay people's needs. To them, we're only interested in sex for pleasure.

I find this claim ignorant and offensive. It's difficult to not be offended when you're reduced to the status of an animal—devoid of love, and only interested in mindlessly pleasuring yourself.

Since sex is *not* solely about pleasure (although that's certainly a part of it), the question of suitability is made especially relevant. While we can receive pleasure from *any* partner, regardless of sex, the other aspects of intercourse remain unfulfilled if the partner is not suitable.

Does counter-orientational sex fill the need for intimacy that most humans possess? This is the question Schmidt, Gagnon, and the other traditionalists should be asking; and only heterosexuals (and delusional homosexuals) would dare answer in the affirmative. Unfortunately, delusions concerning matters of sex aren't unheard of when it comes to traditionalist thinking.

Schmidt went on to characterize the non-procreative nature of same-sex intercourse as a preclusion of "the possibility of confusion by connection to children." I found this particularly offensive. Many gay people, including myself, desire children, some to the point of seeking adoption or surrogacy at the price of great emotional and financial stress, given the difficulties imposed by society. The idea that gay people view same-sex intercourse as having anything to do with experiencing pleasure without the complication of children is plain stupid, not to mention mean. Besides, condoms afford the same preclusion, so why resort to sleeping with a member of the same sex if that's not where a person's natural attractions lie?

It all boils down to this: marriage is intended to facilitate our need for intimacy. For gay people not gifted with celibacy, singlehood is out of the question according to God and the apostle Paul. It's "*not* good for [a person] to be alone", and it's "better to marry than to burn in passion." But, opposite-sex marriage is also out of the question, for opposite-sex partners are not suitable for gay people, as Eve was suitable for Adam.

Contrary to anti-gay logic, same-sex marriage is the only viable solution for gay people. It's the only way that our God-acknowledged need for intimacy can be fulfilled, thus preventing the natural growth of burning passions that result from unreleased sexual energy—an inevitable circumstance that God intended to prevent by providing the outlet of sex within marriage. To deny same-sex marriage to gay people, then, is to deny God's remedy to a substantial segment of the human community.

> *"Now concerning the things about which you wrote, it is good for a man not to touch a woman. [2] But because of immoralities, each man is to have his own wife, and each woman is to have her own husband... [7] Yet I wish that all men were even as I myself am. However, each man has his own gift from God, one in this manner, and another in that. [8] But I say to the unmarried and to widows that it is good for them if they remain even as I. [9] But if they do not have self-control, let them marry; for it is better to marry than to burn with passion."*
> 1 Corinthians 7:1-2, 7-9

In this passage, the apostle Paul presents one of the best teachings regarding human sexuality that I believe exists in Scripture. In my belief, it single-handedly makes the case for same-sex marriage.

He begins by offering what appears to be very peculiar advice. He says it's good for a man not to touch a woman. This advocacy of singlehood seems to contradict God's pronouncement that singlehood was *not* good. So, who's right and who's wrong? By traditionalist logic, both views *can't* be right, seeing as God's pronouncements concerning Adam apply to the whole of mankind.

If traditionalists are right and Genesis 2 is prescriptive, then it's not good for *any* man to be alone, just as, supposedly, it's not right for any man to love and marry another man, rather than a woman. But, if this is the case, it's not without consequences. It destroys the traditionalist notion of biblical inerrancy (a notion that I personally subscribe to), for Paul clearly contradicted this principle.

There's only one way around this dichotomy, and that's to recognize Genesis 2 for what it is—a narrative description of creation. Only then can we harmonize Paul's statement that it's good for a man to remain celibate (and, by extension, single), with God's pronouncement that it was "*not* good that the man should be alone."

But, even with the two perspectives reconciled, we *must* ask why it's good for people to remain single, with marriage only recommended *if* the individual can't maintain sexual purity (vs. 2, 9). The answer is found in verses 32-35.

> *[32] But I want you to be free from concern. One who is unmarried is concerned about the things of the Lord, how he may please the Lord; [33] but one who is married is concerned about the things of the world, how he may please his wife, [34] and his interests are divided. The woman who is unmarried, and the virgin, is concerned about the things of the Lord, that she may be holy both in body and spirit; but one who is married is concerned about the things of the world, how she may please her husband. [35] This I say for your own benefit; not to put a restraint upon you, but to promote what is appropriate and to secure undistracted devotion to the Lord.*
> *1 Corinthians 7:32-35*

Those who are single do not have their interests/concerns necessarily divided between serving God and seeing to the happiness of their spouses. As a result, Paul concludes that it's preferable for a person to remain single—a reasonable assertion. The only problem is that most humans are not "designed" with the ability to go through life without a strong, compelling desire for companionship.

As with Adam, most people long for intimacy. So inherent to the human condition is this longing that Paul considers the ability to live a celibate life a *gift* from God (v. 7). For those without that special endowment, it's better to marry than to burn with passion.

But what's so special about marriage that it curbs lust? Is there something in the marriage license, or wedding ceremony that stills our sexual desires? Obviously not. It's not marriage that is the remedy for lust; but it does provide *the* God-ordained framework within which sexual intercourse is morally permissible.

This brings up an intriguing notion. In Exodus 20:5, God stated that He's a jealous God, who will have no other before Him. This is repeated elsewhere in Deuteronomy, Joshua, 1Kings, Ezekiel, and Nahum. As the sovereign, self-existent creator of all things, God is absolutely in the position to demand a place of absolute, unchallenged preeminence in our lives… and He avails Himself of that right. So, that He is willing to share us with a spouse, even if it means that we can only render distracted devotion to Him (v. 35), is extremely profound. It tells us that as good (and preferable) as singlehood and undivided service to the Lord may be, the prospect of struggling with lust is a more weighty concern in His eyes.

So, when traditionalists like Gagnon, Schmidt, and others advocate a sexual catch-22 for upwards of 10% of the population, they're not just opposing homosexuality and homosexuals. They're also opposing God's established remedy for our sexual needs—a remedy that is so important that He's willing to share His children with spouses in order to provide it. That's *really* something!

One may say that homosexuality needn't be accommodated to remedy the sexual needs of gay people—that we simply need to marry someone of the opposite sex. This argument betrays a failure to grasp the notion of sexual orientation, as well as the human need for companionship. Both of these go far beyond the physical act of sex. If they were simply a matter of sensation, one could choose the *better* state of celibacy by releasing sexual energy through masturbation; but, self-stimulation, like counter-orientational stimulation, isn't capable of filling our need for intimacy. Suitability is paramount, and only people of the same sex are suitable for homosexuals.

Notice that God, when seeking to remedy Adam's need for intimacy, did not simply assign someone to him. His concern was that Adam was provided with a *suitable* companion. Suitable for mankind, as traditionalists claim? No. Suitable for *him*—one individual. What is suitable for others isn't necessarily what was suitable for Adam.

Same-sex marriage is, therefore, consistent with God's desire to facilitate the homosexual's need for intimacy. We would be faced with a dilemma if Scripture condemned same-sex marriage and/or same-sex intercourse; however, since neither is the case, there is no theological justification for denying this *good* state of matrimony to those who are gay and are not gifted with celibacy. Any such attempt, then, places one in the position of opposing an element of human nature that was pressing enough to merit God's direct involvement.

12

Death To The Family!
Why The Supposed Gay
Battle Cry Doesn't Even Exist

An important aspect of this debate is how these theological issues relate to the world around us. Theology doesn't exist in a vacuum. It impacts the surrounding society. It is, therefore, appropriate that we consider the implications surrounding the socio-religious acceptance of homosexuality.

A substantial degree of traditionalist "ministry" is devoted to painting the gay community as the enemy of all that's noble in the world. They spend more time scaring people about the "gay agenda" than actually teaching anti-gay theology. Let's examine the sociological arguments they use to prove gay people's detriment to society.

Our Deceptive Exploitation of The Family

In the 1993 movie, *Philadelphia*, a gay man with AIDS is fired from his job at a successful law firm in the city of brotherly love. He sues the firm and wins, but the movie ends in tragedy as he succumbs to an AIDS-related illness. In *Straight & Narrow?*, Schmidt draws from this movie a criticism about gay people and their families.

> "But it strikes me as odd that this kind of support must come from the hero's biological family (and such as *Ozzie and Harriet* collection at that!) rather than from the homosexual community. If the message of homosexual liberation is that heterosexual fidelity, childbearing and family

nurture are not necessary to human fulfillment, why does the hero need to go *there* of all places to find strength for the coming crisis? One comes away with the suspicion that this family is being used by a person whose lifestyle symbolizes its negation."[131]

Schmidt's contempt for homosexuals becomes obvious in this unbelievable criticism. He sees in this movie an example of how gay people selfishly use the family for support, yet oppose it by the very nature of their being gay. We rely on families in our minds and hearts, yet oppose it in our sexuality. Ultimately, Schmidt ascribes conscious ill will to gay people on the basis of the unconscious nature of our sexual orientation.

What specifically is it in our "lifestyle" that negates the family? Is it our desire to marry? That sounds like an affirmation of family, not a negation of it. Is it our desire to adopt—yet another affirmation of family? Is it our desire to carry our spouses on medical insurance—a privilege enjoyed by heterosexual couples as a function of family? These things demonstrate our reverence for family, not our desire to destroy it.

I imagine Schmidt is referring to traditionalist misconceptions of what comprises the "gay lifestyle," e.g. drug abuse, promiscuity, and incessant revelry. The only problem is that this is *not* what gay people are about. Do some gay people party and abuse drugs? Yes, but these are things that also characterize a substantial swath of heterosexual life, particularly among the younger (late teenaged and twenties) population. Many gay people don't engage in such living. I, for one, have never stepped foot in a bar or nightclub, and have never used drugs (with the exception of sharing one marijuana joint on two occasions during my early twenties).

Perhaps Schmidt isn't referring to lifestyle-proper, but rather to sexual function. Is the simple fact that we don't procreate naturally a negation of the family? If so, the same criticism can be made of straight couples that either cannot or choose not to procreate.

---

[131] *Straight & Narrow?*, 50.

If Schmidt would put his hostility toward gay people on hold for just a moment, he would see that we're actually fighting *for* family, not against it. We want to have our families recognized and respected by our society. We want to marry and adopt. We want to carry our families on our medical insurance. We want hospital visitation rights so that we can be with our loved ones at their time of greatest need.

If anyone is negating family, it's traditionalists—telling gay people that their marriages aren't real (thereby *negating* family)... Telling a gay couple that they cannot adopt (thereby *negating* family)... By opposing any form of family that does not sit with their narrow, traditional vision, *they* have become the enemies of the family, not gay people. But, they're too blinded by their antagonism of us to see it.

> "...the homosexual population continues to rely on the procreative population for familial support, patterns of relationship and of course the production of more homosexuals. It is as if someone's spleen had declared its independence, departed through an incision in the abdomen, and then periodically returned, leechlike, to draw nourishment from the same body. Are the critics spleenophobic, or is this misplaced organ living in a dream world?"[132]

In making this argument, Schmidt leaked evidence that he believes people are born gay. He stated that homosexuals rely on the procreative population for the "production of more homosexuals." Traditionalists usually claim that homosexuality is a choice, and that we're out trying to convert heterosexuals over to the "gay lifestyle." But, if Schmidt is right that homosexuals are "produced" through procreative function, it seems to me that he, at the very least, acknowledges the likelihood that homosexuality is inborn.

Aside from this point, Schmidt's argument is nonsensical. We rely on familial support because, contrary to popular belief, we're human and our Creator programmed us for such a

[132] *Straight & Narrow?*, 52.

connection. It's the cruelty of traditionalist logic that would deny us the love and support that all others have from their families, even sinners of the worst variety. It's traditionalist logic that views us as leechlike, rather than as people who love their families and have only ever wanted to be *truly* loved in return (truly loved, not given the traditionalist version, which bears very little resemblance to the biblical version).

Schmidt's spleen analogy is hopelessly flawed. Gay people do not "declare" our independence from the family or community. We *want* to be accepted by those around us, especially our families. He obviously holds to the stereotypical view that we hate the very ones we're afraid of losing. This is far from the truth. If any hatred is involved on the part of some gay people, it's an unfortunate reaction to the rejection we've faced at the hands of family members who bought into Schmidt and his ilk's anti-gay rhetoric.

I doubt Schmidt considers heterosexual married couples that choose not to have children equally leechlike. Yet, they, too, rely on the procreative population. So, are they shirking their responsibility to the family and community, as well? In truth, Schmidt should consider their *actual* rejection of procreative intent more offensive than the *perceived* rejection by homosexuals, seeing as we are compelled into relationships that don't involve procreation, whereas the heterosexual couples simply *choose* not to fulfill procreative function, despite their ability to do so. Why hasn't he written a book condemning *them*?

Traditionalists apparently have a deep-seated fear that the gay community desires to destroy the family. They've actually convinced themselves that we hate the notion of family so much that we'll stop at nothing until no one's family is whole. I can't imagine where they got this idea from, seeing as our authors made many claims but provided no substantiating evidence.

> "For nearly sixty years, the homosexual activist movement and related entities have been working to implement a master plan that has had as its centerpiece the utter destruction of the family."[133]

---

[133] *Marriage Under Fire*, 19.

It's an ongoing joke in the gay community that everyone is in the loop about the infamous gay agenda except for gay people. Traditionalists seem intimately familiar with it, whereas none of us who actually are gay have the slightest clue as to what it entails.

The only agenda I'm aware of isn't really an agenda at all. It's simply a desire shared by most gay people to be treated as human beings. We want to live in peace. We want families that don't ostracize or disown us. We want to have jobs without the fear of losing them simply because we're gay. We want to have homes without the fear of people vandalizing them. We want to attend church to worship and serve without seeing contempt on the faces of those we call brothers and sisters in Christ. We want to be able to marry the people we love, carry medical insurance for our spouses, adopt children, and enjoy all the other rights that our straight brethren take for granted. If that's an agenda, then I guess we have one; but Dobson's assertion that our agenda is the "utter destruction of the family" is an absolute lie. It's a scare tactic aimed at rousing his followers, and has no basis in truth.

In fact, gay people have a strong desire for family. Those in the closet live in fear of being disowned should their secret be discovered. Those who *have* come out of the closet did so not to spit in the face of family, but in the hopes that familial relationships could be based on truth and authenticity, rather than fear and deception. So, contrary to Dobson's claim, we love our families and desperately want to be loved and accepted in return.

The accusation that we're out to destroy the family is the epitome of hypocrisy. It's traditionalist teachings that have destroyed families—advising parents to not accept their gay children if they ever want them to change; or convincing people that we have some hidden agenda, thereby creating an "us-versus-them" environment. To be sure, if anyone is a threat to the family, traditionalists are!

Gay people can't win with traditionalists. Schmidt criticizes us for having close relationships with our families, as portrayed in the movie, *Philadelphia*, whereas Dobson and others criticize us for supposedly hating the institution of the family and wanting to destroy it. So, which is it? Do we love our families and seek to draw strength from their love and support, or are we involved in some conspiracy/agenda to wipe the family from the humanity?

Marriage and Relationships

> "The homosexual agenda is *not* marriage for gays. It's marriage for no one. And despite what you read or see in the media, it is definitely *not* monogamous."[134]

> "First, very few homosexual relationships are, in fact, monogamous."[135]

Do all Jews work in finance? Are all Whites supremacists? Are all Blacks unable to speak proper English? Making generalizations about racial groups earns you the title racist, and rightly so. Making generalizations about the sexes earns you the title sexist; and again, rightly so. Yet, for some reason, it's perfectly acceptable to make generalizations about gay people. Apparently, none of us really want to get married, and none of us have monogamous relationships. Dobson may or may not be racist or sexist, but he's definitely orientationist!

Yes, not all gay people want to get married; but the same can be said for straight people. Yet, like straight people, many of us long to find our "suitable companion." It's precisely because we honor marriage that we want to enjoy its blessing in our lives.

On the point of monogamy, Dobson isn't alone in having his view of gay relationships drenched in stereotype. It's very frustrating to see these stereotypes propagated, especially in the name of Christ; but I'm especially disgusted when people who should know better spread such generalizations.

> "If we fail—if we find it too difficult or too intimidating—then I believe there are at least three general and drastic consequences we'll face: 1. The denigration of biblical authority. 2. The sexual exploitation of children. 3. The loss of a coherent definition of *family*."[136]

---

[134] *Marriage Under Fire*, 53. [emphasis in original]
[135] *The Same Sex Controversy*, 51.
[136] *The Gay Gospel?*, 41.

> "Standards such as monogamy and fidelity will
> have to change when the qualifications for 'family'
> change, to make room for a whole new concept."[137]

Shame on Joe Dallas. I abhor, yet understand the ignorance that leads to stereotypes, particularly by those outside of a group, like Dobson in relation to homosexuality. But, Dallas really should know better than to propagate gay stereotypes. That a gay person (whether formerly or presently) could make such hideous and inflammatory statements knowing full well that they're stereotypical can only be interpreted as malicious. It either betrays a substantial degree of self-hatred on his part, or a selfish desire to ingratiate himself to the conservative Christian community.

If Dallas' perception of gay people is accurately reflected in his words, they betray the kind of man he apparently was—living out the very stereotypes he propagates. As a gay man, was he incapable of monogamy and fidelity? Did he sexually exploit children? If he really believes that these things characterize homosexuality, he must have been a truly horrible gay man. His warped perception of gay people, narrowed by his own poor choices, needs serious revision.

> "An ethic that embraces only monogamous,
> lifelong unions between members of the same sex
> will, it seems, encompass such a tiny fraction of the
> homosexual population that heterosexual
> acceptance of homosexual unions in theory will
> have to appear to homosexuals as rejection of such
> unions in reality."[138]

Apparently, it didn't occur to Gagnon, or the other authors, that the lack of societal validation contributes to the failure of many same-sex relationships. It's a fact that marital relationships last longer than non-marital ones. Furthermore, external affirmation is important to the health of any relationship, which is why many churches have fellowship activities for married couples. Gagnon wants to compare non-marital, same-sex

---

[137] *The Gay Gospel?*, 56.
[138] *The Bible and Homosexual Practice*, 481.

relationships to opposite-sex marriages, and then feign surprise at the disparity in the lifespan of the relationships. It's disingenuous, to say the least.

> "...to call a relationship 'loving' in a biblical sense means it is in accordance with God's will and is fulfilling His purpose, resulting in His glory."[139]

> "Forms of sexual expression that deviated form the kind of heterosexual union validated by God at creation can never, by definition, be legitimately construed as 'loving.'"[140]

> "What is a gay 'couple', given God's design of man and woman? How can one describe such a relationship as a 'loving partnership' when the correspondence God himself created in the man/woman relationship is not only absent but also denied?"[141]

These arguments go to the core of same-sex relationships. Are they real? Are they truly loving? Actually, this raises a question of theological significance. Can something outside of God's will exist within the framework of something that He ordained? Now, I believe that homosexuality is *not* outside of God's will; but for the sake of argument, let's consider this. If homosexuality is immoral, does that mean that homosexuals cannot have legitimate, loving relationships?

I answer this question by posing the following questions. Does an incestuous couple not truly love one another, since incest is no longer acceptable to God?[142] Is a marriage between a believer and an unbeliever not truly a marriage[143]; and if not, is the prospect

---

[139] *The Same Sex Controversy*, 51.

[140] *The Bible and Homosexual Practice*, 297.

[141] *The Same Sex Controversy*, 188.

[142] It was acceptable when Adam and Eve's children married one another to "be fruitful and multiply," when Abraham married his half-sister, and when Jacob married his 1st cousin.

[143] 2Co. 6:14-16 forbids Christians from being bound together with unbelievers (which would especially apply to the covenant of marriage).

of divorce, therefore, immaterial? Was David's marriage to Bathsheba not real, seeing as it was established on a foundation of adultery and murder? Questions such as these are so ludicrous that I can scarcely believe there's a need to ask them; but traditionalist logic requires their consideration.

The simple fact is that a couple is not a couple because God approves of the relationship. A couple exists because of the status of the relationship. Likewise, a relationship isn't loving because of divine sanction. It's loving if love exists between those engaged in it. Yes, love exists only because of God (for He *is* love), but that does not mean that where He isn't acknowledged or obeyed, love cannot exist. Even atheists love their children, spouses, and friends. Imagine that!

That something is derived outside of God's will does not mean that what emanates from Him cannot exist within it. We were all made in God's image, even though that image has been distorted by sin. The residue of His essence of love is still resident within the entire human family. That's why people as evil as Adolf Hitler could love an Eva Braun. That's why unbelievers could demonstrate the greatest love possible—laying down their lives for their friends, e.g. falling on a grenade during battle (Jn. 15:13). So, even if our authors are correct in their belief that God's intention for human sexuality is exclusively heterosexual, their logic is completely faulty. Seeing as their belief *isn't* correct, their logic is utterly asinine.

Ultimately, these beliefs betray the irrational logic employed by many traditionalists when it comes to homosexuality. How can we have reasonable discourse when they refuse to even believe we are capable of loving relationships? Their orientation-based xenophobia prevents them from engaging in any degree of rational discourse. This is truly tragic because discourse is so desperately needed. But, if they can't grant us the most basic aspect of the human experience, what hope exists for respectful intellectual and theological discussion?

I can't help but think about American slavery. One way slave owners justified their treatment of Blacks was through a belief that they were, by their very nature, the masters. Blacks were simply beasts of burden that could talk. This way of perceiving other humans allowed them to call themselves Christians while treating Blacks in the most brutal ways. It allowed them to draft a Constitution stating that *all* men were created equal, without believing that Blacks qualified. They fought to remove the yoke of British tyranny while enforcing a much stronger yoke on people within their very own borders!

But to them, this wasn't a legitimate analogy because Blacks weren't worthy human rights or considerations. Their churches taught that we were cursed by God as descendents of Ham[144]—declared inferior by divine decree. This made any manner of wickedness possible, so any manner of wickedness is exactly what Blacks got... not by heathen Aztecs, not by fanatical Mohammedans, not even by uncircumcised Philistines, but by supposedly God-fearing Christians, whose entire religion is characterized by love.

But how could these Christians possibly not recognize evil in their treatment of Black people? —Because they were blinded by a religion-based worldview that viewed an entire group of people as "less than." When people are seen as incapable of intrinsic human qualities, or being cursed or hated by God, it's easy to treat them without all human regard. It's no wonder Christians historically treated Jews with contempt. As far as they were concerned, God cursed the Jews because they killed the Messiah. Consequently, cruelty was not only acceptable, it was noble. They were standing up for Jesus against those He opposed (or so people told themselves).

Traditionalist logic makes gay people inferior in the same way. We're cursed because of our "abominable lifestyle." We're incapable of so basic a human quality as love, so how can anyone consider our relationships valid? Why not deny marriage to a gay couple when they're not *really* a couple?

Slave-owning and anti-Semitic Christians were, in many ways, the traditionalists of their day—people holding to the way things had always been because "if so many Christians believed this historically, it can't be wrong." I've heard this tradition-dependent line of reasoning on multiple occasions, and it really vexes me.

---

[144] Gen. 9:20-25; Historically, some White Christians concluded that the Black race was descended from Canaan and, therefore, cursed as slaves because of Ham's mistreatment of his father, Noah.

Tradition has oppressed too many people for us to put stock in it. We should take our marching orders from God's word—from the standard of love, compassion, and justice—not from what yesterday's fool believed. With tradition as our guide, we'll be forever locked in the errors of the past. This is the destructive potential of traditionalist logic.

Of course, our authors think slavery is a poor analogy for the debate on homosexuality. I'm not too surprised. It's a scathing rebuke of their tendency to create "others" with no burden of conscience. So, I'd hardly expect them not to try to shoot down the analogy.

> "*Slavery* is not a good parallel for the homosexuality debate because the New Testament nowhere affirms slavery as an institution; the best that can be said is that it tolerates slavery and regulates it even in Christian households."[145]

Gagnon's logic actually bolsters the affirming position. He ultimately asserts that New Testament doctrine was impacted by social context—an admission that perfectly explains New Testament condemnations of homosexuality (which are fewer in number than its tolerations of slavery). In his mind, slavery isn't so bad that it's not tolerated biblically; yet homosexuality is evil *beyond* toleration. The treatment of humans as property isn't as bad as consensual, same-sex relationships. But I forgot... Gay people can't have *real* relationships, anyway! Gagnon rationalizes the biblical tolerance of slavery on the basis of social considerations relating to the ancient worldview, yet offers no such consideration to homosexuality. This inconsistency demonstrates why traditionalist theology is anything but trustworthy.

White and Niell present another example of traditionalism's penchant for self-delusion. They claim that "...we should exhibit our disagreement in a loving way,"[146] yet advocate capital punishment for gay people. If this is what they call "a loving way", they can keep it!

---

[145] *The Bible and Homosexual Practice*, 443. [emphasis in original]
[146] *The Same Sex Controversy*, 176.

> "The Bible provides clear guidelines for sexual
> behavior: Intercourse before marriage is forbidden,
> marriage must be monogamous, and divorce is
> permissible only in the event of fornication or
> abandonment by an unbelieving spouse. Any
> serious   believer   has   to   recognize   these
> standards…"[147]

Dallas offers yet another glimpse of traditionalist love. He
legalistically applies the conditions for divorce given in Scripture;
but he fails to consider that at the time the conditions were given,
women were not the social equals of men. Dallas' application of
the letter of the text holds women captive to a 2000-year-old,
obsolete social status. In his world, they wouldn't even be able to
divorce in the event of physical abuse!

The traditionalist hermeneutic is incapable of accounting
for the social environment within which passages were written.
Well, I take that back… Gagnon certainly considered it when
justifying the biblical tolerance of slavery. Apparently, such
considerations are only valid when the subject is *not* homosexuality.

> "With 'love' as the standard for the 'new family,'
> any   one   of   these   groups   [sadomasochists,
> transsexuals, bisexuals, pedophiles], and other
> groups as well, can claim to love their partners.
> Logically, then, bisexual trios, a man and a
> transsexual, an adult and a child, and a 'master'
> with his 'sex slave' should be able to claim family
> status. Is this what gays want when they clamor for
> same-sex marriages? I doubt it. But this is the
> inevitable result of tampering with a God-given
> model."[148]

To Dallas, a standard of love can be used to justify all sorts
of things. Like other traditionalists, he uses the slippery slope
argument, claiming that if love is the standard for family, it will
lead to, among other things, sadomasochists and pedophiles
finding   legitimacy.   This   argument   fails   in   that   neither

---

[147] *The Gay Gospel?*, 103-104.
[148] Ibid., 56.

sadomasochism nor pedophilia passes the test of love. Sadomasochism involves pain and humiliation, which, by definition, falls short of love's character of kindness (1Co. 13:4). Pedophilia involves the exploitation of children, which violates the selflessness of love (1Co. 13:5) in favor of fulfilling the desires of troubled adults. Neither of these things bears any resemblance whatsoever to consensual, same-sex relationships that are based on love, care, and mutual respect, rather than humiliation, domination, or exploitation. That traditionalists can't seem to make this distinction shows the devastating strength of their paralysis of logic.

As for transsexuals, they're a different issue. If people feel a strong misalignment between their psychological and biological sexes (e.g. a male in a female's body, or vice versa), I don't have the right to tell them that seeking medical remedies at their disposal is wrong. If there are visible anomalies that result from some form of biological abnormality (as in the case of intersexuals, who have identifiable dual-sex characteristics, e.g. both male and female genitalia), why is it such a stretch to believe that there are unidentified, nonetheless biological anomalies that lead to transsexuality? If people can be born with a penis *and* a vagina, isn't it possible that people can be born with genitals belonging to one sex, but a psychological identity belonging to the other?

We must ask ourselves how God wants us to respond to this potential. Should we err on the side of compassion, accepting people based on what they tell us is going on in their bodies, or should we condemn them instead, telling them that they're spitting in the face of God by choosing to be something they're not? Do we have the right to make such judgments given that we really have no idea what's going on inside of them? People correct many types of physical abnormalities through surgery all the time and no one accuses them of playing God. Why shouldn't transsexuals be allowed to do the same?

Dallas also refers to "bisexual trios", as though that's the only type of relationship bisexuals can have. But—if I may educate him for a moment—bisexuals don't need to be with both sexes. They're simply *attracted* to both sexes. They can find fulfillment in a monogamous relationship with either sex. It's no different than heterosexuals getting married and choosing to suppress their attraction to others of the opposite sex in preference to their spouses, to whom they are also attracted (which is totally different than gay people having to suppress attractions to the same sex in preference to opposite-sex spouses to whom they are *not* attracted).

> "It [the adoption of same-sex marriage] would change assumptions and expectations by which society has long operated—that men and women are not interchangeable, for example, and that the central reason for marriage is to provide children with mothers and fathers in a safe and loving environment."[149]

Dobson's contention about the central reason for marriage may be supported by his traditionalist ilk, but Scripture heartily disagrees. Both the Creation narrative, as well as 1Co. 7, teach that the central reason for marriage is the provision of a God-ordained framework for the facilitation of the human need for intimacy.

Dobson would make marriage primarily about procreation and child-rearing, which is why so many people (women, in particular) are treated as pariahs when they're incapable of having children. Churches spend so much time celebrating motherhood that they make infertile women feel as though they're substandard. Why can't we learn to celebrate people whether they are married or single, and whether they have children or not?

In Scripture, every state is celebrated because every state provides an opportunity to serve the Kingdom. That's why the apostle Paul taught that people shouldn't overly concern themselves about their present state (1Co. 7:18-24). Married, single, circumcised, uncircumcised, parent, childless… He encouraged people to spend less time trying to change their condition and more time trying to serve God in whatever state they're in. Of course, one of the ways he justified this teaching was his belief that Jesus was returning soon, so there was no need to seek change since the world, as it existed, would soon pass away (1Co. 7:29-31); but the heart of his message still rings true—God can be glorified through our lives in whatever state we find ourselves.

---

[149] *Marriage Under Fire*, 21.

Whether single or married, we are precious and useful to the Lord, and He expects and requires nothing of us in this regard. It is our choice to marry or remain single. It is also our choice to have children or remain childless, even in marriage. Why would a God who has given us such a range of volition as it relates to sexuality and family require us to marry someone of a particular sex, especially if such a union would be incapable of fulfilling the "central reason" for marriage (the central reason according to the Bible, not Dobson)?

Apparently, Men *Are* Dogs

As I read our authors' view of men, I literally laughed out loud at how barbaric they think we are. They paint men as wild beasts, incapable of living civilized, respectable lives without a woman's touch. If their words came from women instead of men, we'd surely call them sexist, blaming the liberal feminist movement dominated by man-hating lesbians!

> "Without positive feminine influence, his [the male's] tendency is to release the power of testosterone in a way that is destructive to himself and to society at large... Stated positively, a man is dependent for stability and direction on what he derives from a woman, which is why the bonding that occurs between the sexes is so important to society at large. Successful marriages serve to 'civilize' and domesticate masculinity, which is not only in the best interests of women, but is vital for the protection and welfare of the next generation."[150]

> "Men need to be 'civilized' and 'domesticated' into such unions by women."[151]

> "Nor is it fair to harshly criticize homosexuals for failing to achieve seemingly unrealistic standards. Males will be sexually stimulated as males, regardless of whether they are heterosexual or homosexual. By this I mean that, relative to

[150] *Marriage Under Fire*, 10-11.
[151] *The Bible and Homosexual Practice*, 459.

females, males have a stronger visual (figural) component to sexual attraction, intimacy needs that require less interpersonal communication, and thus a greater willingness to sacrifice long-term, monogamous relationships for short-term sexual gratification. To put two men together in a sexual bond and then to expect a lifelong union of monogamous fidelity to develop is, to my mind, a recipe for failure."[152]

Apparently, traditionalists view the males of our species as savage animals, tempered by the magic touch that only our females can provide. It's amazing we haven't destroyed the world 10 times over in our testosterone-fueled rages. In Dobson's words, we must be civilized and domesticated or else we will destroy society. *Really?*

Gagnon obviously agrees. In his view, males are inherently dependent upon females. He feigns compassion in a veneered attempt to "stand up for gay men" who are unfairly criticized. In truth, he has such an abject opinion of men that he doesn't see us as capable of fidelity without females. Basically, men are dogs. We cheat, not because we choose to, but because we're programmed to. We're not the masters of our own choices. We're wild animals in need of domesticating. *Surely you jest?*

It appears that the criticism I offered of Dallas must also be levied against Dobson and Gagnon. They betray their own wild abandon in accusing *all* men of being untamed, sex-crazed beasts. Apparently, they're only describing themselves before getting married.

The simple fact is that people are people. Some straight Christian men cheat, and some gay unbelieving men are faithful. While it's true that males are, in general, more sexual in nature compared to females, it doesn't mean that we're incapable of fidelity. It simply means that it takes longer for us to make the emotional connection that leads to fidelity. On that point, it's not the female that tempers the male. It is the emotional bond. It's precisely the same thing that tempers females (who are also known to cheat, even with substantially less testosterone). Now isn't *that* something?!?!

---

[152] *The Bible and Homosexual Practice*, 482.

At its core, fidelity is a choice. One isn't compelled to be faithful or unfaithful. One simply chooses, based on a number of factors. As stated, the emotional connection is a factor. So, too, are personal scruples, which are based, in part, on religious beliefs, upbringing, and experience. There is nothing in the choice to be faithful that precludes fidelity from gay men. Love, faith, and ethics can and does temper all humans—male and female, straight and gay.

It's interesting that none of the authors commented on the needs of females that only males can fill. Do they not consider lesbianism worth refuting on this basis, or was their "oversight" intentional? I'm betting they realized that any statements made regarding females' need for males would rightly earn them a sexist label. So, they chose not to go there. But, they felt it was okay to demean men, painting us as uncivilized cavemen who would destroy society if left to our own devices.

Blacks can call other Blacks "nigga", gays can call other gays "fag", and men can call other men knuckle-draggers. Is that how it works? Personally, I don't care for that version of self-deprecation.

Do Children Need A Mother and A Father?

Traditionalists don't believe that same-sex households are capable of providing children with a healthy home environment. But, as will become evident, their assertions are rooted in antiquated, misogynistic conceptions of what makes for a happy home.

> "The most loving mother in the world cannot teach a little boy how to be a man. Likewise, the most loving man cannot teach a little girl how to be a woman."[153]

This is a common argument used against same-sex parenting. Women just can't teach boys how to be a man, and men just can't teach girls how to be a woman. Here's my question... What exactly is a man, as opposed to simply being an adult male? What is a woman, as opposed to simply being an adult female? Is

---

[153] *Marriage Under Fire*, 99.

not manhood and womanhood a product of social expectations surrounding gender, rather than a true differentiation between male and female? If this is the case—and there's no doubt that it is—why are parents obligated to raise their children in accordance with these social norms? Why should a father force his tomboy daughter to wear dresses, pigtails, and barrettes? Why should a mother force her son to play with fire trucks and toy soldiers instead of the Barbie doll he prefers?

True to their label, traditionalists hold to antiquated standards of what makes for a man and what makes for a woman. They're stuck in yesterday's perceptions of machismo and femininity. To them, real men *still* don't cry, and virtuous women obey their husbands. Maybe someone should drag them kicking and screaming into the 21st century. Nevertheless, they're free to perceive the world the way they choose to, and to live their lives accordingly. My problem is that they try to impose their worldview on others. Ultimately, there are enough single-parent homes in the world to prove Dobson's theoretical social philosophies wrong.

In *The Gay Gospel?*, Dallas quotes various statistics related to single-parent homes, and then asks, "...can we seriously deny the need children have for both a mother and a father?"[154] The statistics do, in fact, bear out that a problem exists; however, Dallas' proposed solution, as well as that given by the other authors, completely misses the mark.

> "More than ten thousand studies have concluded that kids do best when they are raised by loving and committed mothers and fathers."[155]

The problems families have don't result from fatherless or motherless homes, as though both sexes must be present to raise children properly. The statistics he referenced dealt with single-parent homes, in which the weight of managing a family rests on the shoulders of one individual. That's certainly not ideal. Parents must provide financially for the family (usually through traditional, fulltime employment), spend quality time with children, prepare

---

[154] *The Gay Gospel?*, 57.
[155] *Marriage Under Fire*, 54.

meals, help children with their homework, provide transportation to and from extracurricular activities, and be a supportive presence at various events (e.g. sports games, performances, etc.). It's a massive burden for single parents to have to bear alone; and in most cases, they fall short—not because they aren't doing the best they can, but because there's only so much one person can do, and only 24 hours a day within which to do it.

There is no reason to require that someone of the opposite sex share this burden. What would help is having a second parent around—someone to share the financial burden, spend time with the children, support them in their activities, reinforce the other parent's authority, etc. A penis or vagina, testosterone or estrogen—none of these things are pivotal to the successful rearing of children. Time, support, and most importantly, love is what's important—love between parents, and love between parents and their children. Forcing families to fit a certain mold would only damage the peace of the home environment. While traditionalists like Dallas and Dobson focus on the external makeup of families, God is, undoubtedly, focusing on the spirit of the household, whether it's a loving, supportive environment (1Sa. 16:7).

Dobson does address the question of same-sex households, apart from single-parent homes; but the logic he employs indicts more than just same-sex households.

> "Same-sex parenting situations make it impossible for a child to live with both biological parents, thus increasing his or her risk of abuse."[156]

> "How can two men or two women act as 'parents' when the very term from the dawn of creation has referred, in its plural form, to a father and a mother? How can true loving and sacrifice and giving be modeled before children in such a relationship?"[157]

Along with same-sex households, Dobson's line of reasoning delegitimizes single parent households. In fact, it raises

---

[156] *Marriage Under Fire*, 100.
[157] *The Same Sex Controversy*, 188.

objections to households involving stepparents, as well. Should Christians promote singlehood as the only viable option for single-parent widows and widowers, since bringing a non-biological parent figure into the family would increase children's risk of abuse? Is it preferable to require a single parent to shoulder the burden of running the household alone until the children graduate from adolescence? Must they be consigned to the "not good" state of singlehood and celibacy, even if they're burning with passion, contrary to what Scripture explicitly teaches (1Co. 7:9)?

White and Niell's logic is no better. How can single parents model "true loving and sacrifice before children," given that they don't have a partner with which to model such virtues? Should they, then, be encouraged to marry as quickly as possible? But, wouldn't such a marriage violate Dobson's contention that only biological parents should comprise a family's makeup? Traditionalist logic is self-destructive, plain and simple.

I don't envy single parents the catch-22 traditionalists force on them. In desperation, people may respond as the disciples did to Jesus' teaching on divorce: "If this is the case, it's better not to have children at all!"[158] But wait, if we went that route, we would violate the command to "be fruitful and multiply." We just can't win!

There isn't a single sociological objection traditionalists can raise against same-sex parenting situations that can't be raised against opposite-sex ones. So, either they'll throw out every marital form not consisting of biological opposite-sex parents and their children, or they must stop depending on flimsy arguments. Unfortunately, they'll probably opt for Option 3: Continue using paper-thin arguments and hope the audience is too riled up with "righteous indignation" to see the flaws in their logic. So much for theological integrity.

The Family's Saving Grace

> "Among them [those adversely affected by the disintegration of families] are millions of hurting people—husbands, wives, and children—for

---

[158] See Matt. 19:10.

212

whom everything stable and predictable has been shattered."[159]

"Meanwhile, the institution of marriage hobbles along, struggling to survive the assaults being made on it. We must give it a helping hand."[160]

I am a strong advocate of family values. I believe that there are, in fact, standards that, if upheld, will produce healthy and happy home environments. I simply disagree on what those values actually are. I advise strengthening the *spirit* of the family, while traditionalists focus on the outward, visible elements.

Dobson contends that the family is in serious jeopardy. I'm inclined to agree. People have children out of wedlock as a matter of course. They're much too inclined to seek divorce as a quick fix to marital problems. Parents try to live their lives vicariously through their children. Instead of celebrating singlehood along with marriage, Church culture puts pressure on people to get married and have children (start a family), oftentimes before they're ready. Infidelity is widespread, and sexually transmitted diseases are no longer the concern only of single people.

So yes, there are serious threats to the family. The Church is in a position to save the family; but at present, it's spending all of its time and effort accusing the gay community of destroying the family just by virtue of the fact that we want the right to marry. If they would stop whining about the so-called "gay agenda" and would divert their attention to the *real* threats to the family, maybe it would no longer be in danger!

If Dobson really desires to give the family a helping hand, here's some advice for him... Help people *stay* married! Promote marriage over shacking up. Stop advising people to "focus on the family" by not accepting their gay children. Instead, tell them to do what Jesus commanded—love one another unconditionally. Stop turning the gay community into a social boogeyman in order to raise money. Pour your resources into what will save the family, instead of into opposing family types that don't meet with your approval.

---

[159] *Marriage Under Fire*, 36-37.
[160] Ibid., 43.

Nothing on a societal level will be damaged by same-sex marriage. If traditionalists are so concerned about people having stable, loving families, they should be fighting with all of their might to *advocate* same-sex marriage—allowing same-sex attracted people (and their children) to have the blessing of a stable home environment that is recognized and protected by their community and government.

We can either work together to save the *spirit* of the family, or continue the "us-versus-them" struggle to preserve the *look* of the *traditional* family. I, for one, don't care what a family looks like. It can involve a Black husband and a White wife. It can involve two husbands and no wife. It can even involve a sterile husband and an infertile wife. I just want it to be rooted and grounded in love. Traditionalists can keep the "form" of godliness for themselves. I'll fight for the *power* thereof, manifested in: "love thy neighbor as thyself." (2Ti. 3:5; Matt. 22:39)

13

The Community, v. 2.0
The Relevance of Contemporary Society

Traditionalists believe that the gay community poses a dire threat to the wider human community. Consequently, they have turned the gay community into a social and religious boogeyman that the Church must oppose at all costs.

Our Supposed Responsibility To Society

In *Straight & Narrow?*, Thomas Schmidt offers a number of arguments putting forward a belief that people have a responsibility to society as it relates to sexuality.

> "It [homosexual practice] is unaccountable to the implications of creation for the body and for the partner; and perhaps most important, it is unaccountable to the human community. As a variant expression of sexuality, homosexual acts do not advance the good of heterosexual union, nor do they remain neutral. Instead, they undermine heterosexual union and the family."[161]

> "***Responsibility*** is redefined in terms of the self, and perhaps the primary partnership insofar as it serves the self. Personal fulfillment involves no necessary obligation to the wider human community and its procreative family model. Homosexual practice proclaims the independence rather than the interdependence of each relationship or individual. Self-actualized persons

---

[161] *Straight & Narrow?*, 48.

or couples are free to love and serve biological family members or the wider human family, but they do so by choice and not by connection."[162]

Schmidt believes that people are responsible to the human community in the expression of their sexuality. I disagree. We don't owe society anything when it comes to with whom we will spend the rest of their lives. This kind of thinking gave rise to forms of marriage that most modern societies consider primitive, including arranged and levirate marriages. Free societies believe that people's choice in life-partners is their own personal business, primarily because no one else will have to potentially spend the rest of their lives with the people chosen. The only exception to the notion of personal choice I can see is that prospective parents owe it to their future children to not only find a good partner, but also a good parent for their children.

So, the idea that we are responsible to the community is just not true. I find it hard to believe that Adam was responsible to the coming human family in his choice of Eve. For instance, God didn't instruct him to bear in mind procreative potential when presenting Eve. So, where is the responsibility in this narrative? It was only *after* she was chosen that God told them to be fruitful and multiply!

Schmidt contends that homosexual unions undermine their heterosexual counterparts. I can't be alone in my confoundedness as to how exactly this occurs. Do single heterosexuals see gay people getting married and think to themselves, "Heck, if *they* can get married, I want nothing to do with marriage! I think I'll just stay single for the rest of my life." Do married heterosexuals see the gay couple living across the street and decide to get a divorce? Does it change the love heterosexual parents have for their children? Where's the danger?

I assume that one day, a traditionalist will actually specify how homosexuality will destroy the family. Dobson addressed the question directly, yet offered no specifics. In *Marriage Under Fire*, he dedicates an entire section to the question: "How does someone's homosexual 'marriage' threaten everyone else's families?"[163] The

---

[162] *Straight & Narrow?*, 51. [**emphasis in original**]

problem is that not one time in that section (or in the rest of the book, for that matter), did he actually answer the question. This proves that even amongst the most vocal critics of same-sex marriage, no substantive case can be made for how it will undermine or threaten other families/marriages.

> "...for the sake of society, there is some sense to tying the desire for sexual intercourse with the development of responsible and stable family structures. This is not a critique sufficient in itself since it would involve a similar critique of single-parent homes or a woman who marries after menopause, but it is a contributing factor to the overall assessment of the undesirability of same-sex unions."[164]

Gagnon is well aware that his criticism also indicts many heterosexuals. Unfortunately, it didn't prevent him from offering the criticisms anyway. Notice that he cunningly presented it with what appears to be an objective caveat. If he were truly objective, however, he would have allowed the criticism to apply even to the unintended targets, considering that the condition still holds true.

If Gagnon is willing to ignore his own theological conclusions when he has a friendly perception of the victims of his beliefs, why should we take anything he has to offer to this discussion seriously; and even if we do so, why should we take *him* seriously?

This begs the question: Why did Gagnon levy this argument, seeing that it couldn't be consistently applied? All the authors made arguments that also applied to a number of heterosexuals; yet no such criticisms were ever made of them. So, why exercise such intellectual and theological dishonesty? The answer is simple. Their hostility toward homosexuality has so blinded them that they're willing to sacrifice their integrity in order to fire off every argument they can think of. Apparently, they hope their audience isn't smart enough to see through their hermeneutical trickery. I pray that it is!

---

[163] *Marriage Under Fire*, 102.
[164] *The Bible and Homosexual Practice*, 169.

"Most instances of pedophilia and incest pose a threat to the health and stability of families and society. Consequently, the interests of the many must be given priority over the interests of the few. A rigid and visceral societal stance against *all* manifestations of pedophilia and incest is required to banish even the thought of it from the vast majority of people."[165]

Oh the stretches Gagnon is willing to make in service to his worldview—and what a faithful servant he is. First of all, if thoughts toward a thing can be banished, they obviously aren't born of an orientation. Even in societies where homosexuality was punishable by death, it wasn't banished from the thoughts of gay people. At best, it was only suppressed—relegated to the quiet corners of people's lives, away from the public eye. But the desires (or more precisely, the attractions) were still present.

Furthermore, I find his appeal to the interests of the many distressing. Our constitutional republic guarantees the rights of the few, and so does our Christian ethic. I guess they've never heard the phrase "the tyranny of the majority." The interests of the many should *not* be given priority!

Barring these problems, his argument is still fallacious. We don't outlaw pedophilia or incest because of the interests of the many, but because of the danger to the individual—the serious physical or psychological risk posed to innocent people (e.g. children preyed on in the case of pedophilia, or potential children who could be born with serious medical problems in the case of incest). Those are the prevailing interests, not the theoretical interests of the next-door neighbor, the unknown voter, or the religious zealot who feels as though his world has fallen apart because some gay person down the street got married.

Ultimately, every point Gagnon put forward is simply unsustainable. It's yet another example of why it's so important to critically think through what we hear and read, because words are often stylized to appear so reasonable and so absolute, yet are, in fact, so erroneous.

---

[165] *The Bible and Homosexual Practice*, 127.

What About Society's Responsibility To *Us?*

Let's leave this unreasonable discussion of our responsibility to society in relation to our sexual orientation and consider one of the most wildly outrageous arguments I've read (outdone only by White and Niell's advocacy of capital punishment for gay people).

> "If it [religious disapproval of homosexuality] did [lead to violence against homosexuals], these young 'gay bashers' from Christian homes would not have been convicted of hate crimes against homosexuals alone; they'd have also been found guilty of hate crimes against adulterers, gossips, drunks, idolaters, rebellious teenagers, and believers who didn't carefully examine their hearts before taking Holy Communion. Why? Because all of these things are also preached against in church and in Christian homes."[166]

No one's bigoted statements offend me more than those made by Joe Dallas. It's the fact that he is/was gay and should, at the very least, understand what it feels like to be on the receiving end of such vitriol that I find so disgusting. I wonder if his rhetoric is but a cathartic treatment of some degree of self-hatred on his part. His placing "gay bashers" in quotation marks is only one example of the hostility he exudes, as if he doesn't really believe gay bashing happens.

His argument assumes that the sins listed are preached against with the same disgust as homosexuality is. It also presupposes that the people who attack gay people do so solely out of religious zealotry, rather than out of personal bigotry stoked by religious teachings.

Furthermore, the term "hate crimes" applies because they are crimes committed against people based upon an innate characteristic. However, people aren't inherently adulterers, gossips, drunks, idolaters, rebellious, or sacrilegious. These acts must be committed; however, one doesn't *do* gay. It's a state of being, not an act. It exists as a constant, even if idle or dormant aspect of a person's makeup.

---

[166] *The Gay Gospel?*, 141.

Dallas' casual dismissal of the harm that continues to be done to gay people is exceedingly unchristian. Even if he believes that same-sex intercourse is sinful, a tender, Christ-like heart would *require* him to take seriously the acts of violence that have been and continue to be committed against gay people. He should be ashamed that the hatred with which some people preach against homosexuality has egged on such acts. Instead, he dismisses this fact—unwavering, unmoved, and unsympathetic.

NOTE TO DALLAS: No one should be harassed, threatened, or attacked because of who/what they are, whether Black, disabled, gay, or part of any other minority. Your disregard for the suffering of those like you (or at least like you were) is shameful. Yet, I fear you're so clouded by Pharisaical religiosity that you can't appreciate that.

Those who know me know that I'm slow to challenge people on the basis of their Christianity. I find it of poor taste when someone appeals to a person's faith as a basis to invoke a particular response; yet, I'm compel to say this... Whether they believe homosexuality is sinful or not, Christians who are ambivalent to the real harm that is done to gay people seriously need to reevaluate the sincerity and depth of their faith, for it is not as they perceive it to be. The beating heart of Christ does not permit such callousness.

> "Cultures that become increasingly accepting of one or more forms of homosexuality can expect to see over a period of time marked increases in the incidence of homosexual behavior in the population."[167]

> "Given the fact that there still are major cultural reservations about homosexual behavior in the United States, there is every reason to believe that the further erosion of such reservations could lead to significantly higher increases of homosexuality in the population.[168]

---

[167] *The Bible and Homosexual Practice*, 416.

Don't be too taken aback, but I actually agree with Gagnon's contention. It's absolutely true that the continued social acceptance of homosexuality will produce increases in homosexual behavior. The only point I take issue with is that the erosion of such reservations will lead to increases in homosexuality. Whatever causes sexual orientation, it certainly isn't a product of social mores. That said, the problem isn't that declining resistance increases behavior, but rather, how we interpret this fact. Gagnon sees such a society as encouraging homosexuality, rather than simply no longer compelling people to suppress the feelings that exist regardless. It's not that more people will *turn* gay. It's that more people who *are* gay will no longer feel compelled to hide their orientation. I can only applaud such liberty.

Every human has the right to live without fear. Traditionalists may act as though gay people aren't human; but the fact is that we have certain rights, and every Christian should fight to ensure that those rights are protected. No one is required to agree with what they perceive as the gay lifestyle, but they *should* be required to respect the rights that fundamentally should be afforded to gay people.

Land of the Free?

It's ironic that so many conservative Christians claim to be American patriots. They wave their flags and celebrate the ideal of freedom (particularly freedom of religion); yet, they see no inconsistency in their struggle to deny freedom to those they disagree with, namely gay people. But, any such denial is the most unpatriotic thing a citizen of this wonderful country can advocate.

True freedom is a very precarious thing. It's delicate and quite demanding, requiring an all-or-nothing commitment from societies that dare to enjoy its blessings. When a society claims to be free, yet denies freedom to any segment of its population, everyone's freedom is brought into serious jeopardy. Why? –Because if one person's freedom is denied, how long will it be before someone else's is denied just as easily?

Free societies never stay the same. Power changes hands, social thinking evolves, etc. Therefore, it's always only a matter of

---

[168] *The Bible and Homosexual Practice*, 417.

time before those who enjoyed power eventually must deal with others having that responsibility and privilege. In the United States, political power usually seesaws from Republican to Democrat. The only thing that's guaranteed is that no one group or party stays in power forever.

In order for someone's freedoms to be curtailed, certain legal mechanisms must be put in place—be they the passage of new laws, the setting of new legal precedents by the judiciary, etc. When people are on the "winning" side of such curtailments, they don't perceive a problem in the enactment of such measures. They're so blinded by their dislike of the group being imposed upon that they can't see the danger they've created for their own selves. You see, once the laws and precedents are put into place, what's to prevent the next group from turning those mechanisms against the very people who celebrated their establishment just a few years before?

Conservative Christians celebrate the imposition of their beliefs on society today; but each victory builds a framework upon which their own freedoms can be siphoned away. What happens if Muslims use the same legal arguments used by conservative Christians to allow Muslim judges to place Qur'anic monuments in our courthouses? What happens if White supremacist groups use the same arguments to deny interracial couples the right to marry that mainstream conservative Christians use to deny gays the right to marry? My goodness, go back 50 years and the same conservative Christians were opposing interracial marriage themselves!

Of course, no one wants to believe that these are genuine possibilities. But, that's not the point. When mechanisms are put into place that allow one person's religious beliefs to be imposed on others, the potential exists, whether probable or not, for those mechanisms to be used in the imposition of other beliefs—beliefs that have the potential of being anything but Christian.

So, in opposing gay marriage, conservative Christians not only put their own freedom in jeopardy, but they also oppose the very basis of religious freedom—that the right of the individual supercedes the wishes of the majority in relation to matters of faith. The First Amendment does not offer Christians the freedom to impose their particular views on society.

It's the right of all U.S. citizens to 1) hold to their particular religious beliefs, 2) not hold to other beliefs on whatever basis they personally deem ample, and 3) not have other beliefs imposed upon them. So, how can a country with the freedom of religion prevent gay people from marrying, based overwhelmingly on religious beliefs?

I'll let you in on a little secret. While anti-gay Christians are warning about a gay agenda, they're hiding an agenda of their own. They know they can't offer a religious argument against gay marriage in the courts; so they fabricate social arguments, knowing, as Gagnon admitted, that such arguments don't hold water. But when the social veneer of this agenda is stripped away, the opposition to gay marriage is, indeed, religious in nature.

The fact is that those who oppose gay marriage don't actually support religious freedom. What they support is the freedom of *their* religious expression. They only oppose the restriction of *their* religious beliefs. They have no qualms about curtailing the freedom of others; and that is wholly un-American.

A Christian Nation?

While it's arguable whether or not the United States is really a Christian nation, I don't believe Christians really understand what they're saying when they make this claim. What does it actually mean if the United States *is* a Christian nation?

We already know by virtue of our Constitution that it's not permitted for Congress to pass laws with respect to the establishment of a particular religion. So, even if we *are* a Christian nation, such a designation must mean something other than the imposition of Christian beliefs on society. In other words, being a Christian nation cannot equate to being a theocracy. It cannot mean that Christianity is the national religion. So, *if* the United States is, indeed, a Christian nation, the only thing it can mean is that the standard of freedom (the American hallmark) that biblical Christianity champions is the foundation of American freedom.

This brings up an exceedingly important question. Does biblical Christianity really support the notion of religious freedom, or does it require a belief in Jesus Christ, and submission to Christianity?

Is The Freedom of Religion A Christian Virtue?

We can discuss Constitutional freedom until the proverbial cows come home; but in the end, as Christians, we live by every word that proceeds out of the mouth of God (Matt. 4:4). It's His word that sustains us, and that should motivate us in the activism we engage in, be it social or political. So, the question we must answer is whether or not Christianity supports the notion of religious freedom.

Most conservative Christians would, undoubtedly, answer in the negative—that Jesus is the only way to Heaven and eternal life, and that without faith in Him, there is no salvation; therefore, how can Christianity advocate religious freedom when such freedom comes with the potential for people to go to Hell? Now, I agree wholeheartedly that there is no hope of eternal life aside from Jesus. It's impossible for me to believe the biblical witness concerning human sinfulness and the nature and necessity of Christ's sacrifice, yet believe that other religions offer an alternative path to God. Alternative? Certainly. Path to God? No, sir!

The problem is that that's not what I asked. The question of religious freedom has nothing to do with religious rightness. The question isn't if Islam, Buddhism, Hinduism, Taoism, or other faiths offer valid paths to God. The question is whether it's consistent with the Christian faith to advocate religious freedom—a person's right to believe what they choose to believe. Does Christianity support attempts by Christians to impose their religious values on others?

Some may turn to the pages of the Old Testament kingdoms of Israel and Judah to justify the imposition of Christian values on society. It's true that when these kingdoms ceased to follow the way of the Lord, He was displeased, and ultimately judged them by allowing their kingdoms to fall. But, there are a few problems with justifying religious imposition on this basis. First, Israel and Judah were established by God and subjected by that establishment to the Mosaic Law. In general, Christians may have founded the United States, but Christ did not establish it. It is not a theocracy, governed by Christian institutions. It's a constitutional republic—governed by a secular document drafted by a body not acting in a clerical capacity. Rather than being appointed by God's prophets, its leaders are elected by the citizenry. Therefore, no such analogy is appropriate.

But, even aside from socio-political considerations, there are theological reasons that Christianity does not condone the imposition of Christian virtues on society. Christianity is not simply a religion. It is not a system of rituals and observances that an individual can follow in order to find or please God. Christianity is God's purpose to reconcile mankind to Himself, and have a personal relationship with us. It is nothing if not a matter of the heart. Requiring anything of anyone is absolutely worthless in terms of his/her standing with God; and quite to the contrary, it does a substantial degree of harm.

We've spent a considerable amount of time dealing with the fact that it is essential that the application of God's word take into account the cultural context within which it's applied. In fact, the application of any particular passage or principle in one context may contradict the application of the same in another context. Two great examples are the role of women in the church, and the toleration of slavery. The application of the relevant texts changes because God's primary concern is that people in those societies have the best chance of being open and receptive to the gospel. Always remember—the reconciliation of every person is His highest priority!

Now, if God is interested in saving souls, what good does it do to antagonize unbelievers by imposing our beliefs upon them? Conservative Christians are guilty of turning countless people off to the gospel of Jesus Christ before they've even heard it. Their attempts to force people to live within the framework of their own religious beliefs has resulted in absolutely no actual spiritual fruit, and has ultimately precluded salvation to a great many people.

It's not our responsibility to make our community or nation holy through legislation. That is wrong on so many levels! What good is served by preventing Bill and Joe from getting married if they're still going to have sex? What good does it do to try to prevent Bill and Joe from having sex if they still desire to? You can't legislate what's in the heart, and it's in the *heart* that sin is conceived (James 1:14-15). Jesus said that if a man lusts in his heart, he's already committed sexual immorality (Matt. 5:28). So, conservative Christians can arrest Bill and Joe, and can even castrate them; but they can't change their hearts. At best, they can create an external *form* of godliness; but God is *so* not interested in that (1Sa. 16:7; 2Ti. 3:5). Only the indwelling presence of the Holy Spirit can bring the *power* of godliness—a heart that is committed to the pursuit of holiness. And how does one receive the indwelling presence of the Holy Spirit—by hearing the gospel, believing it, and receiving Jesus as Lord (Ro. 1:16; 10:9; Eph. 1:13). The moral of the story is that it's salvation through the gospel that is the agent of transformation, not legislation. I have no doubt that Jesus is offended by people imposing their system of values on others in His name.

But surely, we should be concerned about how people live, even if they're unbelievers, right? Wrong! Even the most noble of us are stained with sin and destined for Hell if we stand in our own righteousness. So what good does it do for someone to live a moral life, yet remain without the grace that only comes by salvation through faith in the atoning power of the blood of Jesus? Living a moral life is good, and can help people live without a substantial degree of the strife that ungodly living can bring; but it does absolutely nothing in terms of one's eternal destiny—and *that*, as we have seen, is God's primary concern. As Jesus put it, "What does it profit a man to gain the whole world, and lose his soul?" (Mark 8:36)

Telling unbelievers how to live can only ensure that they will never want to hear anything Christians have to tell them about Jesus. All the Jesus they'll care to know is what we've shown them, and it will have been anything but palatable! And to think, we're supposed to be the *salt* of the earth (Matt. 5:13), giving the world flavor. Instead, we're making it dry and tasteless, dull and boring, heavy and cumbersome. So much for Jesus' yoke being easy, and His burden light (Matt. 11:28-30).

Now, although it may seem so on the surface, this is not subjective, liberal religious philosophy. Scripture validates everything I'm saying. In fact, God *demands* that we not concern ourselves with how unbelievers live.

> *"I wrote you in my letter not to associate with immoral*
> *people; [10] I did not at all mean with the immoral people*
> *of this world, or with the covetous and swindlers, or with*

idolaters, for then you would have to go out of the world.
[11] But actually, I wrote to you not to associate with any
so-called brother if he is an immoral person, or covetous, or
an idolater, or a reviler, or a drunkard, or a swindler--not
even to eat with such a one. [12] For what have I to do with
judging outsiders? Do you not judge those who are within the
church? [13] But those who are outside, God judges.
REMOVE THE WICKED MAN FROM
AMONG YOURSELVES."
1Corinthians 5:9-13 [emphasis in original]

Paul makes this point as plainly as it can be made. Unbelievers are the province of God. We're not to concern ourselves with how they live, or judge them, or dissociate ourselves from them. They're doing what they're *supposed* to do—sin. Why would we bother them for excelling at their profession? We're only to concern ourselves with how those who call themselves Christians are living; and since we can't pass laws in the United States that only apply to Christians, we should take a step back and let people live their lives. We should preach Christian morality to those who have submitted themselves to the lordship of Christ, and let the gospel be the only thing we preach to unbelievers.

Unfortunately, I don't think that this message will ever fly with social conservatives. They don't seem to be able to wrap their minds around the idea that how people live is none of their business, and that making it their business is not only unchristian, it directly violates God's word.

Consequently, their approach to social change places them on opposite sides of the issue than Jesus Himself. Even if we were to assume that homosexuality *is* a sin—a horrible abomination—it could never be demonstrated that Jesus supports their efforts to legislate morality.

> "If same-sex intercourse is indeed sin, then an appeal to tolerance is largely misplaced."[169]

> "If the eternal destiny of unrepentant, practicing homosexuals is at stake, or even a full relationship

---

[169] *The Bible and Homosexual Practice*, 28.

with God in the present life, then it would be a
'cruel abuse of religious power' to give false
assurance that these texts do not condemn
homosexual behavior. It can be as much a cruel
abuse of religious power not to say what Scripture
says, however unpleasant it is to hear, as to say
what it says in a cold and callous manner."[170]

"True love 'does not rejoice over unrighteousness
but rejoices with the truth.' (1 Cor 13:6)... If one
fails to reprove another who is engaged in self-
destructive or community–destructive behavior, or
any conduct deemed unacceptable by God, one can
hardly claim to have acted in love either to the
perpetrator or to others affected by the
perpetrator's actions."[171]

This type of reasoning seems so sensible on the surface.
Indeed, how can we neglect to tell someone that the life they're
living is sinful if their eternal destiny is at stake? How can we
"tolerate" their sin if it's going to wind up sending them to Hell? Is
that real love? Is it compassionate and merciful to just let them
continue sinning, oblivious to the consequences of their sin?

The problem with this approach to dealing with the sin in
the lives of others is that Scripture doesn't support it. As we saw in
1Co. 5:9-13, the traditionalist view is born of warped priorities and
does not align with God's. Jesus asked what good it does for a
person to gain everything in this life and still go to Hell. While
traditionalists want to change how people are living, what good
does that do if they only antagonize them and make them enemies
of the cross? What good does it do to make people perceive
Christianity as a religion of hypocritical totalitarians who always
have their noses in other people's private affairs? How does that
further our Great Commission?

Contrary to Gagnon's claim, then, tolerance of sin is not
misplaced. It's a biblical principle—nay, a biblical *command*—in
which God instructs us to align our priorities with His; to tolerate

---

[170] *The Bible and Homosexual Practice*, 331.
[171] Ibid., 34.

the sins of unbelievers; to eat dinner with them as Jesus did; to form friendships with them as Jesus did; to be so kind and such good company that they invite us to their social gatherings, as they did with Jesus.

When was the last time Dobson was invited to an out gay person's birthday party? When was the last time Gagnon was invited to a gay Christian's home for dinner, not to discuss theology, but just to hang out? It tells us something about Jesus' character that sinners actually wanted Him around! His welcoming kindness was an avenue through which He led people to the Father. Traditionalist cruelty, on the other hand, is an avenue through which they push people *away* from Him. If that's not tragic, I don't know what is.

Traditionalists commonly inject the word "love" into their rhetoric, but what they engage in is anything but loving. It's selfish to try to force others to live as you want them to live, especially when they aren't even Christian. Gagnon says that it's not loving to ignore someone's sin. I say it's not loving to turn people off to the gospel through your self-righteousness. How is it loving to make life for your own self better since you won't have to *see* homosexuality displayed in your world, even though it cost the eternal souls of countless people?

Don't misunderstand me here. Love does, indeed, play a role. It's simply not the role traditionalists claim. Love requires us to obey Paul's counsel, whether homosexuality is a sin or not. Love requires us to live and let live as far as unbelievers are concerned, and to only deal with the "sin" in people's lives if they are believers. Love says to preach your understanding of morality in the church house, not in the state House, or street corners. We have to stop trying to clean the fish *before* we catch them!

So, voting against a gay marriage bill, picketing outside of a city hall or court building, and doing anything else to limit the freedoms of gay people in our society is absolutely unbiblical. The question before us is: Do anti-gay traditionalists care? Experience leads me to believe that a great many of them don't, which only proves that morality is not really what they're after (even though what they *should* be after is evangelism, *not* morality). What they're after is the imposition of their worldview on society—to sit in the seat of power and exert their will on others.

But, what about Gagnon's point that love does not rejoice over unrighteousness, but with the truth? The love chapter (1Co. 13) does, in fact, say that. So, how does that come into play?

Although Gagnon's quotation is accurate, his use of it is not. No one is asking Christians to rejoice over activity that they believe is immoral. Although we disagree on the sinfulness of homosexuality, I could respect their beliefs if they but walked them out properly. I'm not telling them to throw a celebration if gay marriage passed in the United States. My point is that they shouldn't oppose it in the public square. They should let people live their lives, while praying for their salvation and deliverance. They have every right to preach their values in their local churches, but they should not attempt to impose—or celebrate the imposition of—their religious views on others.

For a split second, I thought Dallas actually understood this principle; but before his statement ended, he'd proven my optimism a waste of positive energy. Actually, I think he does *understand* it; he simply doesn't care enough.

> "And though it's important to take a moral stand even in this fallen world, it's more important to remember the priority issue—if people are without Christ, they are *dead*; their immorality is secondary. A public stand against their sins should include an invitation to grace and a recognition that their behavior is symptomatic of a larger problem."[172]

I try to give people the benefit of the doubt in this debate. Rather than perceiving them as an enemy, I think of them as people who are where I once was—trapped in a sea of bad theology. My hope has been that once they're exposed to the truth, they'll have the integrity to objectively consider it. Unfortunately, one thing both Dallas and Gagnon have shown me is that many anti-gay Christians know full well where the weaknesses of their arguments lie. They simply don't care. They present the affirming counter-argument so as to get it out in the open, but then gloss over it without giving it due consideration. As someone who wants

---

[172] *The Gay Gospel?*, 220.

to follow the evidence wherever it leads (even if it means that I must cease being affirming), it's frustrating when people ignore biblical fact in preference of their personal ideology and agenda.

This is precisely what Dallas has done here. As he stated that it's more important to lead people to Christ than to take a stand for moral issues, my heart began to warm. In that moment, I'd forgotten about all the other foolish statements he'd made to that point, and thought to myself, *There may be hope for him yet*. But, as quickly as my hope had come, it faded. He then said, "Their immorality is secondary." In other words, we still need to concern ourselves with how unbelievers live. But, this is absolutely not what we learn from Paul's teaching in 1Co. 5.

He went on to frustrate my hopes even more, saying that a public stand against people's sin should "include an invitation to grace." *Seriously?* What planet is he living on? Who is going to want to hear any such invitation when they're being publicly attacked and having their rights opposed? If you believe homosexuality is a sin, fine. That's your right. But preach it to your own congregation. Preach it to people who have already chosen to make Jesus Lord. Why destroy evangelistic potential by tainting its sole intention of reconciliation with your view of what holy living should look like? Can we get people saved before we start telling them how to live?

So no, contrary to Dallas' contention, the immorality of unbelievers is *not* secondary. It's irrelevant! Christians should not take public stands against the immorality of unbelievers. We should simply love them and invite them to Christ. Why hold people to the moral code of someone they never called Lord, especially when, as Dallas admitted, they'll wind up in Hell anyway?

That he was so close to the truth really bugs me. As it is with so many anti-gay Christians, he just can't find it within himself to see past what people are or do. The self-righteous hostility that he holds for gay people won't allow him to see past their sexual orientation, not even long enough to lead them to Christ. If that's not the sickest perversion of the gospel, I don't know what is. It may be a Pharisee's dream come true—kill two birds with one stone: fulfill the Great Commission, and accuse and attack people in the process—but I want nothing to do with that version of Christianity (or rather, with that *perversion*).

Appendices

A
Miscellaneous Arguments Rebutted

B
Personal Reflections

C
Helpful Resources

A

Miscellaneous Arguments Rebutted

Right Back At'Cha!

> "To confront the pro-gay theology, then, is to confront a deception of our time—the tendency to subjugate objective truth to subjective experience."[173]

> "The pro-homosexual, revisionist literature hardly presents a single coherent whole when it comes to its methods of 'exegesis' and the conclusions it comes to."[174]

I could easily lob these arguments right back at traditionalists. As I'm an affirming Christian, I have every reason to say that it's anti-gay theology, rather than affirming theology, that is the deception of our time, a consequence of the tendency to subjugate objective biblical truth to subjective worldviews.

I could also say that anti-gay, traditionalist literature is all over the place in how they apply their interpretation of Scripture. White and Niell went as far as to advocate modern day capital punishment for gay people, while *none* of the other authors were so

---

[173] *The Gay Gospel?*, 108.
[174] *The Same Sex Controversy*, 124.

irresponsibly legalistic. Furthermore, some acknowledged that we are no longer under the Law, while others jumped through all sorts of theological hoops to force certain provisions (particularly, those that appear to condemn homosexuality) to apply, thereby contradicting the notion that we are no longer under the Law—a biblical fact they reject in their fanatical effort to condemn homosexuals.

Ultimately, no two theologians have a carbon-copy view of Scripture, be they affirming or non-affirming. That's the nature of the beast, not an indication that the overall point made by this side or that is right or wrong.

> "The burden of proof is decidedly on anyone who would want to argue that Jesus or any New Testament writer would have been open to same-sex intercourse."[175]

It's easy for Gagnon to contend that the burden of proof is on someone who disagrees with his view; however, in reality, the burden of proof always rests with the person asserting something. As a person who believes homosexuality is morally acceptable, the burden of proof is not on me, for one cannot prove a positive. The burden is on whoever would assert the negative—that homosexuality is *not* morally acceptable.

Let's remember that Scripture has already proven the positive, considering that our new covenant in Christ is a law of liberty (Gal. 5:1; James 1:25; 2:12), and that "all things are lawful" (1Co. 6:12; 10:23). The burden of proof, then, is decidedly on anyone who would want to argue that homosexuality (or any other act) is wrong within our modern context.

Gagnon's point regarding the view of the biblical writers is completely fallacious. I don't have to prove that *any* biblical writer would have been open to same-sex intercourse. Personally, I don't believe that they were. But, then again, they never condemned slavery, so does that mean we should bend to their worldview on *that* issue, as well? Why didn't Jesus have female disciples in His inner circle of 12—those who, with the exception of Judas, became

---

[175] *The Bible and Homosexual Practice*, 437.

the first apostles? Paul enforced a markedly patriarchal worldview, even appealing to creation in doing so (1Ti. 2:13). Should we apply that view to the modern context, as well?

Ultimately, I don't have to prove that *any* biblical individual would have been gay-affirming. I simply have to demonstrate *why* they probably weren't, and how they *would* be if they lived in the modern Western world! This case is made, in part, in Chapter 4, as well as in Section 2 (chapters 4-6) of my book, *Homosexianity*.

I say this with the knowledge that some affirming Christians believe Jesus *was* affirming during His time among us. Personally, I disagree. Although certainly a revolutionary, He was, in some ways, a product of the world He lived in (as we all are). That's why the 12 disciples were all men, and why He never condemned slavery. I'm not saying that He would have owned a slave, but He dealt with people where they were. He even used examples of slavery in His parables, all the while never condemning its existence. This isn't a rebuke of Jesus at all. It's simply an acknowledgement that He lived in a world that was radically different than our own, and that fact cannot be ignored when attempting to understand the type of man He was, and what His view on certain social issues would have been.

> "However, on this issue, as on any other, if a clear, unequivocal, and pervasive stance in the Bible can be shown to exist—across the Testaments and accepted for nearly two millennia of the church's existence—then the burden of proof lies with those in the church who take a radically different approach to the issue."[176]

Gagnon's contention that Scripture presents unequivocal and pervasive support for the anti-gay position is utterly meaningless. It assumes that his interpretation is correct, and then tries to make a case based solely on that assumption. Further, I don't support the view that 2000 years of theology adds anything substantive to the debate. For upwards of 1,000+ years, theology has also supported the papacy, penances and the sale of

---

[176] *The Bible and Homosexual Practice*, 29.

indulgences (when all we must do to be forgiven is ask—1Jn. 1:9), the reverence and deification of Mary (the supposed "Queen of Heaven"), praying to the dead (when Christ alone is our mediator and advocate—1Ti. 2:5, 1Jn. 2:1; and despite the dead knowing nothing—Eccl. 9:5), etc.

Ultimately, none of these quotes raise a point that cannot be easily lobbed right back at traditionalists. Consequently, they don't move the discussion along in any substantive way, and are really just diversions from the theological side of the discussion.

You're Not Getting Off *That* Easily

> "He [Paul] consistently treats the matter as something his readers no doubt recognized as being wrong—as a 'given'—so he spends no time arguing the point."[177]

This is an especially weak argument. Dallas attempts to explain away the near-complete absence of biblical references to homosexuality by saying that it was simply *understood* that homosexuality was wrong. I might be able to buy this, albeit hesitantly, if the New Testament was written only to Jews. Unfortunately for Dallas, it wasn't. Heck, it wasn't even written to people who were under the Mosaic Law. It was written to Christians, comprised of both Jews *and* Gentiles—people who had no knowledge of the Law. Consequently, a single condemnation of male-male sex (three at best, if you include the vice lists) among hundreds of other teachings wouldn't have been something his readers recognized as a given—especially considering that the culture they lived in was fairly friendly toward homosexuality.

So, I'm not buying the argument. It seems a desperate attempt to explain why a matter that occupied a substantial role in both the Greco-Roman and modern cultures occupied such an unsubstantial role in the biblical writings. It's certainly incongruent with the primacy with which many modern conservative ministries engage the issue. Talk about majoring on the minors!

---

[177] *The Gay Gospel?*, 201.

But, does the fact that something was "minored" on in Scripture mean that it wasn't really sinful, or was, at best, a fairly insignificant sin? When I was young and my mom told me to do something, if I didn't do it right away, she'd say, "Don't make me tell you again!" The point was that she should only have to tell me something once for me to obey. If her authority was sufficient to make such a claim, surely God's is, right? Why should He have to condemn homosexuality 50 times in order for us to obey?

This is a legitimate question; however, we have to remember that Scripture was not written to a single individual living within a single environment. It was written over the course of 1,000+ years, and to a large number of people spanning different cultures. That there was, at best, only one condemnation of both male and female same-sex acts is, therefore, a relevant consideration. Why wasn't the warning given to the Roman Christians also given to the Galatians, or to the Ephesians, or to the Philippians, etc. It's not as though these churches had access to Paul's epistle to the Romans until much later. It's also not as though Paul didn't repeat many of the same warnings and other teachings in multiple epistles, not including homosexuality.

It only makes sense that Paul told each community what they needed to know, given what was taking place within their particular area. Now, are we to believe that homosexuality wasn't taking place within any of these other regions? I don't think so! With a population comprised of between 5-10% of gay people, a city would only need 20 residents to have at least one gay person present. With populations in the tens of thousands, there's no reason to believe that homosexuality wasn't a common element within every city in the ancient world, especially considering the fact that the Greco-Roman culture dominant in the region was fairly ambivalent toward homosexuality.

Keep in mind that Paul's epistle to the Corinthians and to his spiritual son, Timothy, only dealt with pederasty, an exploitative sexual arrangement that cannot be considered a condemnation of homosexuality in general. Consequently, the fact that Paul only addressed the matter once is more than relevant. It indicates that there was something especially *Roman* in the nature of the activity he condemned that required him to address the acts taking place there. As we discovered in Chapter 7, he was undoubtedly referring to Roman Bacchanalia—acts that were engaged in within a context directly related to idolatry. Both the historical and textual contexts prove this beyond all doubt. This explains why he didn't address the acts when writing to other cities, where homosexuality took place, but not necessarily Bacchanalian rituals.

Please Stop Comparing Us To These People

"Still, I'm convinced that the acceptance of homosexuality will pave the way for the acceptance of pedophilia. This is so, not because homosexuals desire sex with children, but because the approval of one previously taboo practice makes room for approval of the next, more serious taboo."[178]

"Most people (we hope) would say that this practice is not acceptable; however, we must ask, where is the Bible verse that prohibits this practice of child intimacy? If it doesn't exist, then what is to prevent this horrid practice?[179]

"In the case of the law regarding bestiality, which is in closer proximity to the law regarding homosexual intercourse than is the law concerning intercourse with a menstruating woman and which bears a stronger resemblance, the paramount violation is the merger of two different kinds of creatures that should never be merged."[180]

Traditionalists invariably compare homosexuality to bestiality and pedophilia. As a gay Christian, I'm tired of being in any way compared to a sexual predator, who would prey on the innocence and weakness of children... or even to someone who would have sex with animals. I know people think we're disgusting perverts, but give me a break. Reasonable people should see a huge difference between two consenting adults choosing to enter into a

---

[178] *The Gay Gospel?*, 48.
[179] *The Same Sex Controversy*, 79.
[180] *The Bible and Homosexual Practice*, 135.

romantic relationship and pedophilia or bestiality. Those who don't are obviously not wired correctly, and prove that any attempt to reason with them will be a complete waste of time. But, I have hope that the vast majority of people—including non-affirming ones—will be reasonable enough to see such comparisons as unfair.

Now, on to the arguments themselves... Dallas advocates the manipulation of Scripture for fear that a failure to do so will lead to the acceptance of undesirable things, like pedophilia. He apparently believes that fear is a legitimate method of interpretation, and justifies the twisting of Scripture in order to produce "suitable" doctrine.

The slippery slope argument is inextricably tied to fear. It's not theological, but instead usurps biblical authority and imposes wayward beliefs on the basis of fearing what *may* come down the road.

Scripture doesn't tell us to interpret from a place of fear. It does, however, tell us to do so from a place of love. Jesus said that God's word hinges on the command to love (Matt. 22:37-40). So, instead of allowing fear to steer the course of their interpretation, traditionalists should apply Scripture's antidote—love (1Jn. 4:18).

Most affirming Christians believe that since Scripture doesn't condemn homosexuality in a way that is applicable today, neither can we. White and Niell contend that this is a dangerous way to approach Scripture, as it opens a door to the acceptance of pedophilia, since it, too, isn't condemned in Scripture. But, they fail to consider another biblical rule affirming Christians believe in—that everything must be tested by the standard of love.

Holding pedophilia to this standard removes any possibility that it could be accepted. Love is kind (1Co. 13:4). The sexual exploitation of children is cruel. Love is selfless (does not seek its own way; 1Co. 13:5). The abuse of children for the pleasure of an adult is, on the other hand, selfish. The standard of love, as described in Scripture, is sufficient for preventing any act that traditionalists fear the so-called slippery slope will lead to, including pedophilia. Their fears are, therefore, completely baseless.

Finally, Gagnon contends that because the condemnation of male-male sex in Lev. 18:22 appears closer in proximity to bestiality than to sex with menstruating women, the two must

241

resemble one another. But, does this mean that male-male sex also resembles child sacrifice, which is condemned in the previous verse (v. 21)—precisely the same proximity as the condemnation of bestiality, which comes a verse later (v. 23)? Does it also mean that sex with a menstruating woman resembles marrying two sisters, or having sex with a neighbor's wife (considering that these condemnations are a single verse in proximity to the condemnation of sex with a menstruating woman)?

Further, in chapter 20, the immediate context surrounding the verse condemning male-male sex condemns a man having sex with his daughter-in-law or marrying his mother-in-law (Lev. 20:12-14). Does this proximity make these sins analogous to homosexuality? Surely, Gagnon doesn't subscribe to any of these consequences of his logic, proving that the only reason he used a proximity argument was that it supported his unassailable desire to connect homosexuality with bestiality in the minds of his readers. What a despicable, manipulative tactic.

Are You Gonna Pay For That?

> "When the biblical authors rejected homosexual cult prostitutes—and surely not just because they were connected to Asherah, as the epithet 'dogs' indicates—they were in effect rejecting the whole phenomenon of homosexual practice. They were repudiating a form of homosexual intercourse that was the most palatable in their cultural context. If they rejected that particular form of homosexual practice, how much more all other forms?"[181]

Gagnon basically asserts that the condemnation of any form of a thing is a condemnation of every form of it. But, I doubt he really believes this, except in the case of homosexuality. Consider that if he's right, heterosexuality is also sinful based upon the condemnations of heterosexual prostitution, incest, adultery, or other *forms* condemned in Scripture. Indeed, more forms of

---

[181] *The Bible and Homosexual Practice*, 109.

heterosexuality were condemned than of homosexuality. To use Gagnon's own words, "If they rejected those particular forms of *hetero*sexuality, how much more all other forms?"

Personally, I believe it's more theologically responsible to allow Scripture to speak for itself. If it condemns a thing, so should we. If it only condemns a *form* of a thing, it's best for us not to stretch that condemnation out of its context.

Listen, God is not a toddler, still discovering how to convey his thoughts in word. He knows exactly how to say what He wants to say. All we need to occupy ourselves with is understanding *why* He says what He says, so that we can apply His words to a range of different circumstances in a manner that's consistent with their original intent. This is how we demonstrate reverence for God's word, not in that we force it to mean what we want it to mean, but that we commit ourselves to discerning its meaning so that we can faithfully preserve that meaning in how we live out the word in our daily lives.

> "Given that Philo regarded the seventh commandment against adultery (LXX: sixth) as a rubric embracing the 'special laws' against incest, pederasty, bestiality, prostitution, and other matters pertaining to sexual intercourse (*Spec. Laws* 3.1-82), it is probable that implicit in Jesus' embrace of the seventh commandment against adultery was a rejection of all same-sex intercourse."[182]

> "The collective evidence from Philo and 1 Cor 6:9-11 puts to rest the qualifications imposed on the term *malakoi* by [authors Dale] Martin and [Robin] Scroggs... Although some of the 'effeminate men' may exchange homosexual sex for money, the term is by no means restricted to homosexual prostitution. The 'soft' stimulate outrage from Philo primarily for their attempts at removing all signs of masculinity given by nature, not for selling their services (the latter reason Philo does not even mention)."[183]

---

[182] *The Bible and Homosexual Practice*, 192.
[183] Ibid., 309-310.

"...To adopt the position of [author Martti] Nissinen and others, we would have to ignore the viewpoints on same-sex intercourse of two prominent first-century Jews, Josephus and Philo, undoubtedly representative of first-century Jews generally."[184]

Although my quotations from Gagnon don't reflect this, he referenced Philo and Josephus (Philo, in particular) on countless occasions in his book. I almost got the impression that they were Christian—rather than Jewish— historians.

According to Gagnon, we should assume that Jesus and the other biblical authors viewed the world through the same lens as these particular Jews, simply because they were all Jewish. Not only would such an assumption be irresponsible, but it's also rather narrow-minded—the idea that people of the same race or religion think alike.

In effect, Gagnon *supposes* a *probable implication* based on an *assumption*. *Supposedly*, because Philo believed that the seventh commandment against adultery *probably implies* a condemnation of same-sex sexual activity, Jesus *assumedly* believed it, too. Supposition, probability, implication, and assumption. *Really???*

He seems oblivious to the fact that the commentary offered by these historians comes from a distinctively Jewish perspective, and certainly doesn't represent a Christian view of the time. Is he not aware that Jesus was considered a radical by the Jews of His day? He hardly shared their worldview on a myriad of issues! Yet, Gagnon appealed to them as though he were quoting from the gospels.

If the primary means he has in establishing an interpretation of *Christian* texts is the consideration of extrabiblical, non-Christian historians, Gagnon obviously has trouble proving his case. Just because Philo and Josephus were Jews does not mean that Jewish Christians under the inspiration of the Holy Spirit would not view things through different eyes. It certainly can't be proven that their view of same-sex sexual acts is representative of Paul's view, in relation to his use of the term *malakoi*.

---

[184] *The Bible and Homosexual Practice*, 326.

Ultimately, Gagnon's view requires too many dots to connect for it to be considered a legitimate argument—a theme I found quite recurring in many of the claims he put forward. First of all, one must believe that Philo and Josephus did, in fact, represent Jewish thought for the time period. Second, one must believe that Paul shared their socio-religious worldview. His conversion to Christianity and consequent opposition to traditional Jewish thought challenges this belief. Nevertheless, while it's reasonable to conclude that Paul's view on *every* issue did not change with his conversion, we cannot assume that the particular beliefs that persisted beyond his conversion and the shaping of his new theological framework are or are not related to same-sex sexual activity.

Ultimately, Gagnon desperately wants to believe that Paul's references to *malakoi*, *arsenokoitai(s)*, and *pornois* reflect a condemnation of same-sex sexual activity in general. To get there, he leapfrogs over the biblical context and appeals, instead, to the writings of Jewish historians. This indicates the lack of a credible hermeneutic that supports Gagnon's required conclusion. As demonstrated in Chapter 8, pederastic prostitution was the target of Paul's condemnation, not homosexuality in general.

An Order of Bigot With Extra Baloney, Please!

> "The moment a man takes another male to bed he distorts and diminishes the other male's sexual identity as created and ordained by God, regardless of whether the relationship is fully consensual and non-commercial."[185]

I'm sure that female traditionalists exist, but I can't imagine them being content with how traditionalism necessarily views them. The equality of the sexes simply cannot exist in the traditionalist paradigm because they are required to view women through the prism of the text on the pages of their Bibles—one informed by the social climate of ancient civilizations. This is evidenced by Gagnon's caveman-like claim that same-sex

---

[185] *The Bible and Homosexual Practice*, 311.

intercourse "distorts and diminishes the other male's sexual identity" ("other" referring to the one taking the passive role—in his mind, the *woman's* role).

To Gagnon, then, sex is but one manifestation of the dominion of male over female. Rather than two equal partners coming together sexually into one flesh, one is made to submit to the other. He sees women as being less than men (hence the word "diminishes"), and this fuels much of his disdain for homosexuals. *Surely, a man, ordained by God as the head, should not "diminish" himself by taking a woman's lowly place in the sexual bed*—so appears Gagnon's thought process.

I strongly disagree with this misogynistic view. The passive role doesn't diminish those occupying it, be they male or female. True lovemaking respects each person as an equal partner, which is how sex was originally intended. We must remember that Adam and Eve were told to be fruitful and multiply *before* the Fall, yet God didn't pronounce the woman subordinate to the man until *after* the Fall. This means that the two were equal even though Eve would take a passive sexual role—a fact that utterly destroys the traditionalist view of women and the passive role. Since Christ died for our sins, ending the curse (Ro. 8:2), shouldn't we return to the pre-Fall ideal, allowing the application of Scripture to reflect women's evolved social status? Shouldn't we make every effort to catch up to where God has been all along: "there is neither male nor female"?

In other news, Gagnon also leaked a very bigoted view of gay people in relation to HIV/AIDS.

> "The fact that over a third of the allegedly heterosexual males died of AIDS raises suspicions that they were not heterosexual after all."[186]

> "…Microbes are transmitted in other ways, such as the sharing of needles by intravenous drug users from the homosexual population to the heterosexual one, and vice versa."[187]

---

[186] *The Bible and Homosexual Practice*, 397.
[187] Ibid., 479.

In 1991, Simon LeVay conducted a study in which it was concluded that the hypothalamus of the brains of homosexual males was, on average, closer in size to the hypothalamus of heterosexual females than that of heterosexual males. In his attempt to refute this study, Gagnon concluded that since a number of the heterosexual cadavers used in the study had died of AIDS, they probably weren't heterosexual to begin with. When I first read that statement, I literally had to read it again. I was sure I'd missed a vital word or two; but upon review, I found that I didn't misread his words after all.

What an idiot, I thought to myself. I know... Not the best thing to think about a Christian brother; but I was just so stunned by the ignorance he displayed. First of all, no one dies of AIDS. Thirty years of social education concerning HIV/AIDS and he still got that one wrong. One dies from illnesses contracted because the immune system has been substantially weakened as a result of AIDS (or, more specifically, by the HIV virus). But, AIDS itself doesn't kill.

Second—and this is *sure* to shock the socks off of Gagnon and his ilk—straight people also contract and die from AIDS-related complications! Gagnon, like so many ignorant traditionalists, is apparently still stuck in the 80's, believing that AIDS is a gay disease.

He also apparently believes that HIV is transmitted between the gay and straight communities, rather than simply from person to person. It's as though he said that Asians infected Hispanics, and vice versa—a statement that would be considered incendiary. Gagnon obviously has an us-versus-them mentality. You can't help but admire the traditionalist version of love. Unbelievers have a better revelation!

Nice Try, But No Dice

"The depth of Paul's visceral feelings toward same-sex intercourse finds parallels not only in the level of disgust toward same-sex intercourse exhibited by other Jewish writers of the period but also in the responses to homosexual behavior in Paul's scripture: the narratives of homosexual rape (Ham,

the men of Sodom, and the Benjamites at Gibeah)
as examples of the zenith of detestable behavior;
the intense revulsion against homosexual cult
prostitutes manifested in Deuteronomic and
Deuteronomistic texts; the special attachment of
the label 'abomination' to all male homosexual
intercourse in the Levitical prohibitions; and
possibly the unmentionable character of same-sex
intercourse in Ezekiel, who refers to such behavior
only by the metonym 'abomination.'"[188]

First of all, *none* of the supposed parallels in "Paul's
scripture" actually refer to homosexual behavior. Although
Gagnon spent considerable time attempting to prove otherwise,
Ham did not rape his father. He ridiculed Noah's nakedness, taking
advantage of his drunken stupor; but there's no legitimate evidence
that he raped him. I was quite surprised that someone as
credentialed as Gagnon would so rigorously (and unsuccessfully)
attempt to prove otherwise.

Further, the men of Sodom were not homosexuals. They
attempted bestial rape of angels. The destruction narrative bears
this out, and other references to Sodom harmonize completely
with this interpretation (e.g. Jude 7).

The "sodomites" (*qedeshim*) of Deut. and 1/2Kings were
temple prostitutes, not citizens of Sodom or homosexuals. The
very fact that "sodomite" appears in the text as a translation of
qadesh only demonstrates that while mistranslation can lead to
misinterpretation, the opposite is equally true. Misinterpretation
can, and sometimes does, lead to mistranslation.

So, did the *qedeshim*, who were condemned in Scripture,
engage in same-sex intercourse? The males certainly did. Still, their
condemnation can no more be seen as a general condemnation of
homosexuality than the condemnation of their female counterparts
(*qedeshah*), who also had sex with men, can legitimately be
considered a general condemnation of *hetero*sexuality. What's being
condemned is the *purpose* behind the activity, irrespective of the
biological sex of those engaging in it. Logic simply doesn't permit
the leaps of desperation our authors continue to take.

---

[188] *The Bible and Homosexual Practice*, 269.

Now, while it's true that male-male sex was referred to as an abomination in the Levitical code, the term was used in the same context to describe *all* of the activity condemned in that chapter, not just male-male sex (18:26-30). Gagnon's attempt to demonstrate a particular disgust in the mind of the writer simply on the basis that the term appears specifically in the verses referring to male-male sex is problematic, at best. The fact is that *all* of the acts were called abominations, period.

Finally, Gagnon chooses to interpret the "abominable acts" spoken of by the prophet in Ez. 16:50 as same-sex intercourse; however, 1) female-female sex was never called an abomination, making any reference to homosexuality (in a broad sense) as an abomination inaccurate, and 2) his interpretation is based off of the misinterpretation of the destruction narrative in Gen. 19. Since bestiality was also called an abomination (Lev. 18:23-26), all evidence indicates that *this* was the abomination Ezekiel referred to.

Every example Gagnon used to prove his belief that Paul's supposed feelings toward homosexuality found parallels elsewhere in Scripture proves invalid—every single one! His entire claim, then, rests on how much weight we put on the fact that "Gagnon said so."

In relation to the passage in Ezekiel, Gagnon—as he has a habit of doing—acknowledged the weakness of his own argument. I continue to find it unfortunate that such acknowledgments don't prevent traditionalists from making these arguments in the first place. But, maybe that's just too much to hope for when it comes to an issue that they've shown such irrational disdain over. In any event...

> "Even if, contrary to what we have argued, the texts in Ezekiel and Jude were construed as making no reference to homosexual intercourse, one still would have little basis for inferring that these authors were somehow neutral about homosexual practice."[189]

---

[189] *The Bible and Homosexual Practice*, 90.

Gagnon is ultimately saying, "Even if I'm wrong, that doesn't mean that the people I'm wrong about don't agree with me anyway." Can you believe this guy? In effect, he's acknowledging the weakness of his claim in presenting this unsustainable fallback argument.

Further, he uses the term "construe", which has a negative connotation, in reference to any interpretation that differs from his own, the intention being to give his readers a subconscious aversion to other points of view. This is a despicable tactic given his acknowledgment of the weakness of his argument.

The Sissies of Sodom

> "And why, if these men had innocent intentions, was the entire city destroyed for inhospitality? Whose rudeness was being judged—Lot's, or that of Sodom's citizens?"[190]

Dallas fails to remember that God pronounced judgment against Sodom prior to the entire episode in Gen. 19. Consequently, the incident was symptomatic of their sin, but was not the *cause* of their condemnation.

> "It is possible that Lot is simply buying time, knowing that, in fact, the offer will not be accepted, for these men simply do not have any desire for women. He may feel his daughters are perfectly safe, for those standing before him had shown a firm and unwavering desire for sexual fulfillment with men, not with women."[191]

I found this to be one of the most ridiculous attempts to rationalize an ancient bigotry that I've ever seen. First of all, the text takes great pains to bear out the fact that *all* the men of the city were present in the mob that surrounded Lot's house. In Gen. 19:4, it says, "the men of the city, the men of Sodom, surrounded

---

[190] *The Gay Gospel?*, 175.
[191] *The Same Sex Controversy*, 35.

the house, both young and old, all the people from every quarter." If someone used this much emphasis today, a listener would likely interject, "Okay, I get the point. They were all there. Move on!" Yet, traditionalists *still* missed the point!

What *is* the point? Well, if these men really had "a firm and unwavering desire for sexual fulfillment with men, not with women," how could the city survive past that generation? If literally every man in the town was homosexual (not bi-, but wholly homo-) (which means they've got San Francisco beat by an 85% margin), how did the "young", who were also part of the mob, come to exist, considering that their fathers were so devoid of attraction to women that they rejected Lot's offer of his virgin daughters? It's obvious to anyone with even a smidgeon of objectivity that this incident had nothing whatsoever to do with sexual attraction (vis-à-vis homosexuality).

Furthermore, it makes no sense whatsoever that Lot, knowing the cruelty of his neighbors (2Pe. 2:7), would enrage them further by making a meaningless conciliatory gesture. White and Niell are simply rationalizing an offer by Lot that seems, to modern sensibilities, plain wicked. They fail (or refuse, I'm not sure which) to recognize the relevance of the culture informing Lot's actions. To understand his asinine offer, we must consider the value (or lack thereof) women had within that culture. Objectionable though it may be, it's a historical fact that must inform our interpretation of texts like this one.

We must also consider how essential it was that Lot protect his visitors, especially considering that they were angels—messengers of God (a fact that Lot was well aware of). Notice that one of the concerns he raised to the mob was that the strangers had "come under the shelter of [his] roof" (Gen. 19:8). It was his solemn duty to protect his divine visitors, even if it meant sacrificing the virginity of his property (his own daughters). Yes, it's obscene to us today, but that's irrelevant. We cannot interpret Scripture through a modern lens and expect to rightly divide it.

> "We should note that though these men did not actually accomplish their desires, they are still identified as wicked. The distinction between act

and desire that is so often a part of modern discussions is not to be found in the ancient text."[192]

While it's true that the desire or intent of the men of Sodom was considered wicked despite the fact that they didn't accomplish their goals, that doesn't equate to there being no distinction in Scripture between act and desire. What White and Niell are really attempting to do is justify their condemnation of all homosexuals, whether the same-sex desires are acted on or not. Unfortunately for them, Scripture *does* explicitly make a distinction between desire and act.

> *"But each one is tempted when he is carried away and enticed by his own lust. [15] Then when lust has conceived, it gives birth to sin; and when sin is accomplished, it brings forth death."*
> *James 1:14-15*

The potential for temptation doesn't arise out of thin air. It is born of a pre-existing desire on the part of the one tempted. The purpose of temptation is to cause a desire to turn into a craving that compels someone to take action. It is that craving that, if left unchecked, *gives birth to* sin. But the desire is only the start of this process. It isn't, in itself, temptation. It isn't, in itself, sin. So, the distinction White and Niell believe non-existent actually *does* exist.

Of course, the men of Sodom went beyond mere desire and actually pursued their quarry. Unfortunately for White and Niell, the "wicked" intent was not homosexuality, but was, instead, the rape of visitors—angelic visitors, at that.

Moses Would Be *So* Proud, But Jesus Wouldn't

"...Bestiality is condemned in Leviticus 18:23, just one verse after the first Leviticus prohibition of homosexuality, and yet *nowhere else outside of the Law of Moses* is bestiality mentioned (Exodus 22:19; Leviticus 20:15; Deuteronomy 27:21)."[193]

---

[192] *The Same Sex Controversy*, 37.
[193] Ibid., 76.

White and Niell's argument is that since bestiality is not condemned outside of Leviticus, it demonstrates a need for Leviticus to stand as an applicable moral code, else no basis would exist for condemning bestiality. However, their fear is unfounded, as Jude 7 condemns bestiality in its criticism of the Sodomites' attempt to have sex with non-human beings—going after "strange flesh".

But, let's ignore this fact. Let's act as though White and Niell's claim is actually accurate. Does their argument hold water? Must anything not explicitly condemned in the New Testament be considered permissible; and if so, does that mean that it's safer to extend the applicability of Old Testament laws into the Christian era? Absolutely not! First of all, we can't allow our fear of the implications to force us into an interpretive paradigm that contradicts Scripture (which tells us in multiple places that the Law is no longer applicable).

Second, the chief law—love—is more than capable of addressing specific issues that may not be explicitly mentioned within the pages of our new covenant. As it relates to something like bestiality, we must simply ask whether or not such acts violate the tenants of love as laid out in 1Co. 13 (or elsewhere in Scripture). Is it kind and selfless to have sex with an animal, which is incapable of offering informed consent? Of course not. It's a form of abuse, whether the animal appears to desire or enjoy it or not. No such violation exists with two consenting adults entering into a romantic and sexual union based upon—rather than contrary to—love.

> "The same God who gave the laws of the Mosaic dispensation continues to regulate conduct through the Spirit in believers. A substantial case must be made for affirming conduct that was regarded with such revulsion."[194]

Gagnon is convinced that if God hated same-sex intercourse so much—a point he believes is evidenced by the application of the term, abomination—one must make a case for

---

[194] *The Bible and Homosexual Practice*, 121.

affirming it regardless of whether or not the Mosaic Law is still applicable or not. I, on the other hand, believe that no such case is warranted if the passages proscribing the conduct are no longer applicable.

Gagnon doesn't really buy this argument either. Sex with a menstruating woman was condemned in both Lev. 18:19 and 20:18, yet Gagnon made no case whatsoever in affirming the conduct. He simply stated that the prohibition no longer has "universal validity."[195]

He picks and chooses which proscriptions to consider lasting, and which to render obsolete. The only consistency in traditionalist theology is its *in*consistency!

> "All the laws in Lev 18:6-23; 20:2-21 legislate against forms of sexual behavior that disrupt the created order set into motion by the God of Israel. Each of the laws has as its intent the channeling of male sexual impulses into a particular pattern of behavior."[196]

This is not true. The proscription of bestiality includes female behavior apart from male behavior (Lev. 18:23), and the passing of one's seed to Molech (child sacrifice) also doesn't involve male sexual behavior (Lev. 18:21). If Gagnon's beliefs about intent are correct, these examples represent stray thoughts that arbitrarily found their way into the passage. But, since that can't be the case with inspired Scripture, we're forced to look for an alternate intent.

Actually, intent is explicitly stated (and even acknowledged by Gagnon[197]) in the very chapters in which the proscriptions were given—that the activities were associated with the idolatrous cultures of Egypt and Canaan (Lev. 18:1-5; 20:1-8). In effect, Gagnon sees the truth, for he has acknowledged it within his writings; yet, he wants to keep the interpretive door open to make room for his own view… and he truly is *forcing* that interpretation onto the text beyond all sound logic.

---

[195] *The Bible and Homosexual Practice*, 113.
[196] Ibid., 136.
[197] Ibid., 121.

But why—what's the point of ascribing this view of male sexual impulses to the text, when it's clear that wasn't the intent? The reason is that Gagnon desperately wants to find a reason to extend the application of the proscriptions against male-male sex to modern day, even if it requires him to violate every hermeneutical principle in existence in order to do it. This is called an "agenda", and it's definitely not a gay one!

> "...According to Leviticus 18:27, all the abominations practiced and prohibited in this chapter (adultery, homosexuality, incest, and bestiality) defiled the land when they were committed by the land's inhabitants. God also stated He "abhorred" the people who inhabited the land before Israel did because they practiced these behaviors (Leviticus 20:23). Clearly, these practices offended God no matter who practiced them, or in what context."[198]

> "To limit the Levitical prohibitions against homosexuality to Israel alone, or to a particular period, or a particular geographical location, assumes a view of God and His law that Paul surely did not embrace."[199]

Never forget my warning about the use of words like "obviously", "clearly", etc. It should always raise a red flag; and in this case, it would be a flag well raised. Dallas assumes that the *reason* the acts offended God was that they were inherently immoral. If you actually read Lev. 18, however, you'll notice that he conveniently overlooked the proscription against sex with a menstruating woman (v. 19) when listing the specific prohibitions contained in the chapter. He only listed the acts his readers would most likely agree with, so that his ultimate conclusion would go unchallenged. Personally, I don't know anyone who believes that sex with a menstruating woman is inherently sinful or immoral. Some may consider it gross; but sinful or immoral? I doubt it. The

---

[198] *The Gay Gospel?*, 185.
[199] *The Same Sex Controversy*, 132.

idea that God is offended whenever someone practices the sins proscribed in these two chapters is, then, not as clear as Dallas would like us to believe.

In making the same overall point, White and Niell claim that we cannot isolate the application of the Levitical proscriptions to the Israelites. They contend that such an approach "assumes a view of God and His law that Paul surely did not embrace." Here we go again with colorful language that's supposed to make us lower our guard. According to Paul, nothing is "sure", save Christ and Him crucified (1Co. 2:2). But even beyond that, Paul is the strongest advocate of not living under any of the provisions of the Mosaic Law. His language is as piercing and direct as it can be.

> *"Now we know that whatever the Law says, it speaks to those who are under the Law, so that every mouth may be closed and all the world may become accountable to God... [6:14b] for you are not under law but under grace."*
> *Romans 3:19, 6:14b*

> *"Or do you not know, brethren (for I am speaking to those who know the law), that the law has jurisdiction over a person as long as he lives? [2] For the married woman is bound by law to her husband while he is living; but if her husband dies, she is released from the law concerning the husband. [3] So then, if while her husband is living she is joined to another man, she shall be called an adulteress; but if her husband dies, she is free from the law, so that she is not an adulteress though she is joined to another man. [4] Therefore, my brethren, you also were made to die to the Law through the body of Christ, so that you might be joined to another, to Him who was raised from the dead, in order that we might bear fruit for God."*
> *Romans 7:1-4*

> *"Stand fast therefore in the liberty wherewith Christ hath made us free, and be not entangled again with the yoke of bondage [the Mosaic Law]. [2] Behold I, Paul, say to you that if you receive circumcision, Christ will be of no benefit to you. [3] And I testify again to every man who receives circumcision, that he is under obligation to keep the whole*

Law. [4] You have been severed from Christ, you who are
seeking to be justified by law; you have fallen from grace."
Galatians 5:1-4

It's amazing to me that people use the phrase "fallen from grace" to describe those who they believe have committed egregious sins, like homosexuality; however, the only time the phrase is actually used in Scripture, it describes people who have yielded to even *one* provision of the Law. Circumcision is just an example of the problem of attempting to serve God through the keeping of the Law, rather than through an acceptance of the freedom of God's grace, which was achieved through the victorious death and resurrection of Jesus.

It's apparent to me that Paul absolutely and unequivocally embraced the idea of leaving the Law in its rightful place—history. A substantial degree of his epistles is dedicated to this very point (including much of Romans, most of Galatians, and much of Hebrews; although it's uncertain if Paul authored Hebrews). Still, traditionalists find a way to ignore or twist this fact. Their blinding revulsion, almost reprobate in its ferocity, compels them to engage in any degree of theological gymnastics to condemn homosexuality. It should sicken any student of Scripture, whether affirming or not.

Fact-Check Anyone?

"Because union is the remedy of incompleteness ('for this reason,' Gen. 2:24), humans possess a drive to "leave and cleave" in marriage."[200]

For people who routinely accuse gay-affirming Christians of twisting Scripture, traditionalists have an incredible penchant for getting their facts wrong. Nowhere in Scripture is the idea that union is the remedy of incompleteness supported. This is an example of the consequence of injecting one's own view (e.g. complementarity) into their reading of Scripture.

---

[200] *Straight and Narrow?*, 44.

Let's get the story straight. God pronounced Adam's state "not good" *before* taking his rib. So, when He first set out to remedy Adam's problem, incompleteness wasn't it, for Adam still had his rib at the time!

Union is the remedy of loneliness, not of incompleteness. There is no sex/gender-based requirement that relates to remedying loneliness. What *is* a requirement, according to the Bible, is that the answer is suitable for any particular individual. "I will make him a companion suitable *for him*," God said. *That* is what compels humans to leave and cleave in marriage—a need to remedy the need for intimacy that most humans possess. Thank you, Schmidt, for making a sound and effective case for gay marriage. I had to smooth out a few rough edges, but at least you laid the groundwork!

> "They [male and female] are specifically designed to 'fit' together, both physically and emotionally, and neither is entirely comfortable without the other. There are exceptions, of course, but this is the norm."[201]

Dobson either proves his ignorance or his ignore-ance of the fact that male and male, as well as female and female fit together just as easily as male and female. Indeed, if we're going to examine the biological evidence, the prostate and clitoris glands demonstrate a divine, creative intent to facilitate same-sex intercourse for both sexes. The fact that opposite-sex parts "fit" does not preclude same-sex parts from fitting, as well. Consequently, human simply *fits* with human, regardless of sex. The supposed smoking gun of biology, then, in no way precludes homosexuality as a perfectly natural variation of human sexuality.

Evil Is As Evil Does

> "The most that can be said for divorce is that in certain cases it may be the lesser of two evils."[202]

---

[201] *Marriage Under Fire*, 10.
[202] *The Bible and Homosexual Practice*, 442.

In his attempt to mitigate the danger to legalism posed by various non-ideal accommodations in Scripture, like divorce, Gagnon attempts to justify its toleration as the lesser of two evils. For example, it may be less evil to divorce than to remain married to an unfaithful spouse. Neither circumstance is *good*, but divorce is less bad than the bondage wrought in being married to someone who is unfaithful. Scripture is, indeed, crystal clear on the fact that marriage is intended to be a lifelong union, and that God hates divorce (Matt. 19:8; Mal. 2:16). So, that divorce is permitted under *any* circumstances demonstrates that in a fallen world, in which some situations simply cannot become ideal, a lesser evil is preferable to a worse one. On this point, Gagnon and I agree.

The problem for Gagnon is that his line of reasoning refutes his opposition to homosexuality. Now, I don't consider same-sex intercourse or marriage evil at all. However, for the sake of argument, let's grant that point. What Gagnon ultimately contends is that divorce can be, under certain circumstances, a tolerable lesser of two evils, whereas same-sex marriage, which fulfills marriage's necessary function of providing sexual fulfillment for gay people, can never be, under any circumstances! Now isn't *that* amazing?

Those who support such a contention have a serious problem of logic. In the perfect utopia of Eden, the single thing that was *not* good was that Adam lacked *suitable* companionship. So serious was this need that God was willing to share Adam with another—and that's saying a lot for a God who is, quite deservingly, a jealous God. Apparently, loneliness is so bad that it exceeds the bad of God not having us all to Himself. It is a *greater* of two evils. Now, if loneliness is *that* "not good", how can Gagnon conclude that homosexuality, even if considered sinful, is not a lesser of two evils when compared to the *greater* evil of loneliness?

What is it that's so bad about same-sex marriage? Why would a relationship built on love be worse than the "greater evil" of loneliness? It doesn't make sense, unless one enters their deliberations with the bias that there's nothing worse than homosexuality—a belief based in no small part on people's total lack of understanding in relation to what the word "abomination" means. Most people think it means the worst type of sin; however,

259

that's simply not true. It refers to something God hates because of its association with idolatrous culture, custom, or ritual. Any such designation becomes obsolete the moment the object is no longer associated with idolatry within a given socio-religious context, just as eating pork or engaging in same-sex intercourse (Ro. 1:26-276) no longer are.

There is, therefore, no justification for considering loneliness the lesser of two evils, especially given how bad a state God considers it. In the words of the apostle Paul, "It's *better* to marry than to burn in lust!" It seems to me that Paul and I are in agreement.

Logic proves that even if homosexuality was sinful, it would prove a lesser of two evils compared to the alternatives—loneliness or marriage to an unsuitable companion. Now, if slavery, the subjugation of women, and divorce were biblical accommodations made as the lesser of two evils, *surely* there's room for a few gay couples!

The fact that homosexuality is *not* a sin bolsters the case for same-sex marriage. How can it be a moral *lesser*, when there's nothing in Scripture that indicates it's evil to begin with?

Tell Me He's Just Kidding

> "Most of the Jewish authors proscribing male homosexual behavior speak of a "male/man" having sex with another "male/man," thus reflecting the terms used in Lev 18:22; 20:13."[203]

Is he serious? Wouldn't *anyone* discussing gay male sex speak of men having sex with other men? How is that a reflection of the Levitical proscriptions, rather than a simple description of the activity being discussed? If I go to a Buddhist shrine and ask them to describe homosexuality, they'd likely refer to men having sex with men. I'd hardly think they were reflecting the terms of Leviticus in doing so, seeing as they quite possibly have never even read it!

---

[203] *The Bible and Homosexual Practice*, 163.

I affirm gay sex, provided that it's engaged in within a marital covenant; yet, I would also describe it as a man having sex with a man. I really don't know any other way to describe it (unless you're talking about lesbian sex, in which case the gender nouns would change). But, as a gay-affirming Christian, I *certainly* wouldn't be reflecting back to Leviticus in my choice of language. Gagnon's argument is spurious at best, plain stupid at worst.

If I sneeze in this instant, I have no doubt that Gagnon will find a way to make it relevant to his interpretation of Scripture. "Gay people sneeze; therefore, God is pronouncing judgment on the fact that they are gay, for sneezing is not a manifestation of the health that God would have us walk in as believers." The man is a master of seeing signs where others simply see plain facts.

> "Jesus' rescue of the woman from a fate stipulated by the Mosaic law itself (Deut. 22:23-24; cf. Lev 20:10) constitutes an extraordinary gesture of mercy, obviously designed to stimulate gratitude and obedience in the woman."[204]

> "Jesus forgave sexual sins, like all other sins, in the expectation of transformed behavior."[205]

> "In many different ways besides the explicit sayings given above, Jesus' teachings make clear that repentance, transformation, and obedience to the will of God are essential for salvation; without them, judgment and destruction ensue."[206]

This interpretation of God's grace is highly problematic. It advocates a works-based salvation, in which our status as children of God is contingent upon transformation and obedience. While it may seem weird for me, as a pastor, to say that this isn't true, the fact is that it's not, and that it's antithetical to the work of the cross to claim so. Now, salvation certainly frees us from bondage to sin so that we *can* be empowered to live holy lives; but the idea that

---

[204] *The Bible and Homosexual Practice*, 216.
[205] Ibid., 217.
[206] Ibid., 220.

our salvation is contingent upon that proper end is wrong. Indeed, if it *were* contingent on such a thing, it would no longer be a work of grace.

> "...who [being God] has saved us and called us with a holy
> calling, not according to our works, but according to His
> own purpose and grace which was granted us in Christ Jesus
> from all eternity."
>
> 2Timothy 1:9

> "He saved us, not on the basis of deeds which we have done
> in righteousness, but according to His mercy, by the washing
> of regeneration and renewing by the Holy Spirit."
>
> Titus 3:5

Does God desire and expect that we walk uprightly before Him, in large part as a result of His love and grace? Absolutely. But, there's a difference between an expectation and a prerequisite. Forgiveness is not hinged upon transformation, but upon the grace of God, prompted solely by acknowledging our sin to Him, thereby recognizing His standard, and the heart-wrenching fact that we didn't live up to it. (1Jn. 1:9)

> "For we know that the Law is spiritual, but I am of flesh,
> sold into bondage to sin. [15] For what I am doing, I do
> not understand; for I am not practicing what I would like to
> do, but I am doing the very thing I hate. [16] But if I do the
> very thing I do not want to do, I agree with the Law,
> confessing that the Law is good. [17] So now, no longer am
> I the one doing it, but sin which dwells in me. [18] For I
> know that nothing good dwells in me, that is, in my flesh;
> for the willing is present in me, but the doing of the good is
> not. [19] For the good that I want, I do not do, but I
> practice the very evil that I do not want. [20] But if I am
> doing the very thing I do not want, I am no longer the one
> doing it, but sin which dwells in me. [21] I find then the
> principle that evil is present in me, the one who wants to do
> good. [22] For I joyfully concur with the law of God in the
> inner man, [23] but I see a different law in the members of
> my body, waging war against the law of my mind and
> making me a prisoner of the law of sin which is in my

> *members. [24] Wretched man that I am! Who will set me*
> *free from the body of this death? [25] Thanks be to God*
> *through Jesus Christ our Lord! So then, on the one hand I*
> *myself with my mind am serving the law of God, but on the*
> *other, with my flesh the law of sin."*
>
> Romans 7:14-25

This is one of the most profound passages in Scripture. In it, Paul, in an instance of praiseworthy transparency, reveals an ongoing struggle he has with at least one area of sin in his life. He doesn't identify this sin—and for good reason, considering how judgmental Christians are when they know the specifics—but his point applies to all believers no matter what areas they struggle in. And what was the point? –That even when patterns of behavior have not changed, God's grace is still present and active in our lives. Whereas Gagnon's logic concludes that such persons are not truly saved because of a lack of transformed behavior—an essential component of salvation, in his view—God continues to affirm us, as He did Paul, even when we find ourselves losing to whatever area of sin we struggle with.

Now, take care to understand that this is not an attempt to justify sin. Believers who claim to love God should *never* have a nonchalant view of the sin in their lives. Jesus said that if we love Him, it should be manifested in our obedience. (Jn. 14:15)

So, the point of Paul's teaching was clearly not that it's okay to sin. As he asked in the previous chapter (6:1-2), should we continue in sin since grace abounds? Absolutely not! Our intention should always be to serve God as obedient children. That said, we must still deal with the continuing reality of sin in our lives—Gagnon's sin included. This is an essential part of accomplishing our goal of holiness; otherwise, we'd likely give up trying, finding the distance of our goal much too far to ever hope achieving. We must remember that even when we sin—even if habitually (indicating a lack of transformed behavior)—we are *not* condemned precisely because we are in Christ. (Ro. 8:1)

I'm exceedingly disappointed that Gagnon advocates this works-based view of salvation because it runs contrary to the essence of biblical Christianity. One of the first things we come to understand is that our standing with God is based wholly on the unmerited grace of God, activated by our faith alone. We do not earn it by way of moral conduct, and we certainly do not lose it by lack of the same. I lack the words to adequately describe the offense I take at seeing the glorious gospel of Jesus Christ reduced to the legalistic futility of a works-based salvation akin to the Mosaic Law (Ro. 8:3). If I could pen spit into the pages of this book, this is the spot where I'd do it, for a works-based theology is worthy of no higher regard.

> "With the help of fellowship, counseling, prayer, and the Holy Spirit, God may even restore the homosexual to a fulfilling sexual life in a lifelong union with a member of the opposite sex. If that does not happen, the church must inwardly groan together with all the sexually broken and offer support."[207]

How incredibly compassionate. We may be consigned to a life of "not good" solitude, but at least the church groans with us. Somebody give me a big hug!

Give me a break! Thankfully, Scripture is more pragmatic than the cold, unrelenting legalism of traditionalists. Gagnon portrays a kindhearted tenderness with his choice of language, but it's really anything but. Those who do not affirm homosexuality, thereby consigning gay people to a lifelong state that God considered "not good", would do well to heed Jesus' warning.

> *"One of the [teachers of the Law] said to Him in reply,*
> *'Teacher, when You say this, You insult us too.' [46] But*
> *He said, 'Woe to you [teachers of the Law] as well! For you*
> *weigh men down with burdens hard to bear, while you*
> *yourselves will not even touch the burdens with one of your*
> *fingers... [52] Woe to you [teachers of the Law]! For you*
> *have taken away the key of knowledge; you yourselves did*
> *not enter, and you hindered those who were entering."*
> *Luke 11:45-46, 52*

---

[207] *The Bible and Homosexual Practice*, 451-452.

B

Personal Reflections

No Trespassing. Existing Doctrine Only.

I am deeply troubled when I see otherwise reasonable and sincere Christians oppose every semblance of logic and sound biblical hermeneutics in their effort to cling to their traditional anti-gay beliefs. In fact, since I became affirming and began advocating inclusive and affirming theology, I've found myself in this troubled frame of heart on countless occasions.

These periods prompt in me times of quiet reflection, as I consider why it is that so many Christians can't bring themselves to cross the theological threshold into affirming truth, despite the utter failure of their arguments on every single pertinent point. I'd like to take this moment and share some of the things I've concluded about this travesty during these times of reflection.

Impetus #1: Fear

Although most people would never admit it, plain and simple fear is, without a doubt, the biggest factor that keeps them from seriously considering affirming theology. It's really sad when you think about it. People have literally become captive to their particular version of Christianity—to their understanding of God and the Bible. The prospect of something so seemingly simple and primal as sexuality being so drastically misunderstood is just too hard a pill to swallow.

But the problem runs deeper than that. It runs to the very core of their Christian experience. Certainty gives people confidence. Theological certainty assures them that when it comes to this thing that is most important in their lives, and to this thing that holds the key to their afterlife, they don't have to wonder or worry. They live in a state of peace, knowing that they know what they know.

Then, up pops someone telling them that something that appears so theologically obvious is absolutely wrong. And not only is their personal view wrong, but so, too, is the view of a substantial majority of the Christian community. *Well*, they think to themselves, *if so many could be wrong about this, what else could we possibly be wrong about? Can we trust what we read in the Bible? How do we know that Jesus really is God at all?*

Homosexuality becomes a slippery slope into an abyss of theological uncertainty. It gives cause to question *everything* about God, faith, Scripture… the whole shebang. For most Christians, it's much easier to just refuse the possibility of being wrong, thereby returning their certainty to its place of comfort and peace.

I strive to see the world, and Christianity, beyond perception. Just because I believe something and it gives me peace and comfort doesn't necessarily make what I believe right. I'd much rather be in conflict in my quest for truth than to confidently and comfortably believe a lie! I only wish more Christians felt this way—that their desire for truth permitted these conflicts, ultimately producing a faith that can withstand the challenging winds of circumstance.

The uncertainty that is so feared by Christians should actually be embraced. Uncertainty keeps us seeking more and more revelation. We should never be so certain of anything that we end inquiry. I love to reflect on Paul's point that he was determined to *know* nothing, save Christ and Him crucified. I agree. The only thing I'm absolutely certain of is that Jesus Christ truly is God in the flesh, and that He truly died for our sins and rose again from the dead in bodily form. When it comes to anything else, let's sit down and have a rigorous, Bible-based discussion. May we all adopt this view.

Impetus #2: Religiosity

From the day we are introduced to God, our religious box begins to form. What we come to understand about Him continues to shape that box, most often making it smaller and more tailored to our own socio-religious context. Without realizing it, our infinite God becomes reduced to a set of simple notions and ideas enclosed within our theological boundaries. And because our box can never be larger than our ability to perceive and understand, God is never bigger than our small minds can wrap themselves around.

This all-too-natural process of encapsulating God is the epitome of religion. It quietly creates a systematic approach to our faith that makes things familiar, comfortable and unchallenging. But contrary to the serene, protected environment this religiosity veneers, it's a plague to true and growing faith—a cancer that eats away at our ability to perceive a God who is infinitely greater than the box we've fashioned for Him.

Unfortunately for religion, God is not as comfortable with boxes as many of His people are. In His grand ambition to simply be who He is and not who we would have Him be, He finds a way to disturb the religious order—be it through situational adversity, personal tragedy, or yes, even challenges to our doctrine and theology.

But we don't respond kindly to this assault on our emotional and spiritual stronghold. We rebel in what is often called a crisis of faith—when our understanding of God, the Bible, and Christianity is radically shaken, resulting in either the total loss of our faith or a deeper faith than we previously fathomed. Either way, God steps out of the box, and we're forever changed. One might wonder why I'd call such a terrible crisis a form of rebellion, but that's precisely what it is—a rebellion against our constant need to expand our minds and perceptions of God. If such expansions came easily, this challenge wouldn't be considered a crisis. But, our resistance makes it such a chaotic experience.

So what do we do? Rather than get the point, and engage our minds to ever-expand our understanding and perception of God, we simply enlarge the size of our box just enough so that this newfound revelation of God can fit snugly inside. Instead of tearing down the walls and letting God exist in our hearts and minds as He is in reality, we only make the box a wee bit bigger. We then audaciously pat ourselves on the back and testify about our triumph of faith!

Why are we such faithful preservers of the religious order? Because it's natural. Because it takes a conscious effort to engage an expanded mind, and most people prefer to coast through their Christian experience. But the only way to coast through is by way of religion. Since most people still haven't found a way to separate God from religion—or even realized there's a need to—they blindly ally themselves with the element most familiar to them. It's what they see and interact with on a regular basis… what they're most familiar with… what makes their world seem right. Unfortunately, it's not God. It's religion.

God is, without a doubt, the only stable thing in our lives. But unfortunately, many of us equate stability with stagnancy. It never occurred to us that God operates by progressive revelation, only showing bits and pieces of Himself at a time, so as not to overwhelm us with the exceeding greatness of His majesty.

So, as He shows us more, we have a difficult time fathoming it. We fight to hold to our present perceptions. Without realizing it, we literally tell Him that the God we know is all the God we *want* to know—that we just can't handle any more. We wind up shutting ourselves down to the very possibility that God is different than we perceive Him to be—than we *allow* Him to be. In the end, we're the only ones that suffer, for we turn religion into an idol.

Impetus #3: Culture

We greatly underestimate the power that the cultural environment has on our way of thinking. We'd like to believe that we're immune to the influences of our surroundings, but I don't think that fully applies to a single human being. We are, unavoidably, though certainly not absolutely, products of our environment.

We have a need to be affirmed by those around us. A series of poor experiences has given many people—especially gays—a degree of immunity to such needs, but they're still a part of the human condition. The whole notion of peer pressure wouldn't exist if not for people's need to have the support of those around them.

268

I've found that when it comes to homosexuality, many people are not as convinced of their position as they'd like others to believe. But, they're too dependent on other people to actually consider the possibility that they're wrong.

This is an especially serious consideration for pastors, who are often under pressure from their congregations and/or denominations to toe the line on issues as controversial as this. Even if they *were* affirming in their personal view—or at least questioning the legitimacy of the non-affirming position—they could never let it be known publicly, else they'd lose their pastorate. And this isn't some theoretical concern. It has already happened on a number of occasions, even when the pastor is him/herself heterosexual.

So yes, there are definitely practical cultural considerations that influence people's willingness to 1) bother engaging in discourse on this issue, 2) thoughtfully consider what affirming Christians have to say, and 3) actually admit that their view is wrong. It's hard to criticize people for allowing such factors to impact their approach to what amounts to a theological issue with very serious sociological and personal implications; but I really have no choice but to do so. While I understand such pressures, I also know that there are things that matter more than the affirmation of those around us. Love is one of those things. Truth is one of those things. Justice is one of those things. And these are the things that we sacrifice on the altar of social acceptance. It must end.

The Result: Theological Incapacity

This is a consequence of the aforementioned impetuses. What I mean by theological incapacity is a real inability on the part of some people to digest and objectively consider the evidence based solely on the fact that it's presented in favor of a belief that is incompatible with their existing socio-religious worldview. In other words, some people literally cannot engage in critical thought on homosexuality because the perceived implications are too much for them to handle. In effect, they just don't want to hear it, and there's little you can do to change their minds.

In the vast majority of cases, I'm sure that such people don't even realize what they're doing; but it happens, regardless.

Arguments are completely ignored, glossed over in a wholly inadequate manner, or responded to with accusation, ad hominem attacks, straw man arguments, slick diversions, or the oft-used exit strategy: "I need to study this further." On multiple occasions, people have gone so far as to acknowledge the insufficiency of their arguments, but still retain their beliefs on the basis that they aren't adequately studied on the subject to mount a defense. This is despite the fact that 1) they somehow still know they're right, regardless of not being able to prove it (1Pe. 3:15), and 2) they don't feel so inadequate that it stops them from engaging in an hour of discussion before the spontaneous revelation that they're not studied up on the issue.

What these people possibly *don't* realize is that they used practically every argument that exists; so while it made them feel better to blame their own supposed theological insufficiencies, the true culprit was the position itself.

Can you see how dangerous this is? It's impossible for a person's position to change when they approach theological matters with this unreasonable level of blind dedication. Rather than simply holding to the truth as they see it, they've literally made of their doctrines an idol—a stand-in for the true God of gods who is, alone, unadulterated truth. Bad theology is not an idol until it's clung to despite all evidence to the contrary; and this is an all-too-common occurrence amongst anti-gay Christians.

Although I haven't, to date, engaged in a discussion or debate with him, author and scholar, Robert Gagnon, is one of the best examples of this phenomenon. As I read *The Bible and Homosexual Practice*, I was amazed at how many times he acknowledged the biblical truth of counterarguments that destroyed his position, yet held onto his position nonetheless, on the basis that his interpretation "may be" or "possibly is" still relevant.

Although on occasion, I hope against hope that a person will have a spontaneous manifestation of intellectual honesty and integrity and simply admit that they're wrong, I've learned that when people demonstrate a theological incapacity, there's not much use in further discussion. I have to just consider it a seed sown and move on.

A *Selah* Moment

The world is filled with debates covering a huge range of issues. From politics to sociology, from the past to the future, from race to religion, people are always engulfed in the exchange of ideas. Sometimes those exchanges are cordial, sometimes they're heated; but what's invariably true is that there's never a shortage of beliefs, and never a shortage of people willing to share them.

In this great philosophical milieu, it's easy to put ourselves on autopilot. We're so sure that we can't be wrong that we cease to really engage ourselves in what the other side is actually saying. We've heard it all before, so there's no sense in really paying attention. In fact, we already have our rebuttals ready before their argument has finished being made.

I imagine it's always been like this; but still, I can't help but think that there *had* to be a time when the search for the truth was more valuable to people than simply being right in one's existing beliefs. Was there ever a time when we aspired to better ourselves—to shed the limitations of our own fallibility and think wiser, know fuller, and simply *be* better human beings?

Surely, we could never reach such a goal alone. It seems it would necessarily require an ever-evolving exchange of ideas, so that we could refine our beliefs, getting rid of the impurities in our thinking, and ending up with an unadulterated product in the end.

Think about the Tower of Babel. Sure, it was a time when God judged the world for its arrogance; but resident within that narrative is also the key to our greatness. When we simply *communicate*, there's no limit to what we can accomplish as a people. Our collective potential is inextricably linked to our ability to share. We may not all think alike, but it is in our diversity that we can ensure that no stone is left unturned, and that we reach every height we set our minds to. The thought of our untapped potential overwhelms the imagination!

It saddens me to think that all of this potential is squandered in our pride. We're so bent on *being* right that we've forgotten about the journey to *becoming* right. What good does it do to know I'm right if, in fact, I'm not? How can I improve myself as an individual if I don't find anything about me that stands improving?

Debates are no longer about rigorously comparing notes and both sides learning more in the end. They're now simply about winning. In that, we've lost our ability to grow—to smooth out the rough edges in our own conclusions, and to know *better* and *more fully* on the other side of discourse.

While our need to listen is dire on a myriad of issues, I'm especially concerned about our ability to listen on this contentious subject of homosexuality. Because it surrounds a matter of faith that also impacts a core element of a person's life (their sexuality), the potential for drawing lines in the sand that we won't allow our minds to cross is enormous. And listen, people on all sides of this issue are guilty of creating such boundaries, and we simply *must* do better.

At some point, we have to stop talking and listen. We have to thoughtfully, critically consider what the other side is saying—not simply so that we can formulate better rebuttals, but so that we can actually learn something. Whether homosexuality is a sin or not, all sides of this issue can learn something from other sides. No point of view or perspective has a monopoly on revelation, and we would do well to allow that sense of humility to direct how we move forward.

Let me just put it out on the table right now... Yes, I believe I'm right. I wouldn't have written this book had I thought otherwise. But, even in my certainty, I must remain open to the possibility that I'm wrong—wrong on my whole position, wrong on this point or that one... Whatever the case may be, I'm subject to error, and the best way to discover where those errors lie is to listen—to listen to my allies, as well as my adversaries!

There was a time not too many years ago when affirming Christians were my theological adversaries. Where would I be today if I failed to listen? I was sure there was no way homosexuality could be correct, but I listened. Granted, I was quite dismissive with what I heard, and only put stock in what Scripture itself was saying; but at least I heard enough to look again. And here I am today, having dedicated my life to cleansing the Church of anti-gay theology.

We could learn a lot from a single, simple word King David spoke in a number of his psalms. From time to time, he would encourage people to stop reading/singing—to take a time out and consider what he just said. That wonderful word—*selah*—means to "pause and think about that."

I hope that as we continue to engage in this great debate, we are not so wholly given to winning that we fail to actually consider what the other side has said. I pray that we have the theological and intellectual integrity to actually *think* about what we're hearing.

May we take a cue from David and take time out from time to time to contemplate what those around us are saying. May we learn… May we grow… May we be better Christians and better human beings on the other side.

Selah.

Take My Yoke Upon You, and *Unlearn* of Me

I've been in the Church almost all of my life, and have been saved since my early teen years. During that time, I've been involved in many aspects of church life. I've sat in the pews, holding no title or role. I've served on the usher board, as an officer of the church's local chapter of our youth association, as a choir member, as the pianist, and as the choir teacher and director. I've served on the church finance committee, as a pulpit minister, a church elder, and I now hold the pastorate.

It goes without saying that I've seen quite a bit of church life. I know its ins and outs—its politics, its doctrines, its protocols, its very culture. I simply know *church*. But in all that I've experienced, I can say without an inkling of exaggeration that I've never seen a more ironic—or better, oxymoronic—expression of passionate faith than the misguided belief that the manner in which traditionalist Christians handle the homosexual issue actually serves godly ends.

In fact, the spirit in which the church deals with—or in many cases, *refuses* to deal with—this issue is so far from any semblance of true Christian virtue that one might assume such an approach was never the intent. However, experience compels me to disagree with that assumption. I've found that many Christians are sincere in the belief that their uncompassionate, dogmatic

273

approach to this issue is what God desires. That's not only scary; it's also heartbreaking. They perceive themselves as faithfully holding high the banner of truth in the face of a concerted effort to deny the lordship of Jesus Christ, the authority of Scripture, and the integrity of the Christian faith.

Because of this misguided view, theology alone is insufficient to get the Church where it needs to go. It's not enough that we change course at this point in the journey and start heading in the right direction. Too many issues have been impacted by our lack of understanding. Our approach to spiritual matters has become too warped. Consequently, we have to put ourselves in theological reverse, wipe away the stain of all the bad theology we've received over the years, and rebuild our theological house around the truth. We especially need to revisit the person of Jesus Christ, and allow His character of love and compassion to overwhelm the legalism that has guided so much of our Christian experience.

I don't speak this accusatorily, but from experience. When my uber-conservative mind was first challenged with affirming theology, believe me when I say that I didn't want to have anything to do with it. On multiple levels, I opposed it with all the strength and vigor I could muster. At the time, I believed that the best way to approach Scripture was face value—read what it says, believe what it says, live what it says. It's precisely why I did not believe that same-sex sexual activity could, under any circumstances, be godly. It's also why I believed that women should not occupy ministry offices that required them to exercise authority over men (including the offices of apostle, pastor, bishop, and elder).

So, when my eyes began to open and I started to let go of my face-value approach to Scripture—and I thank God I did—it impacted a lot more than simply my view on homosexuality. It also changed my view of women, allowing me to finally reconcile in my mind something that I was never able to adequately address: how a God who is no respecter of persons, and in whom there is neither male nor female, could restrict people in such a way and on such a seemingly inconsequential basis. I always knew that a penis didn't especially position me for leadership, but that logical conclusion was powerless to overcome the *theological* belief I had, which was based on my face value readings of Scripture.

So, I had to reevaluate my approach to God's word, and allow that shift to impact a number of issues that I simply missed the mark on. I had to tear down some theological houses and rebuild them, not completely from scratch, but certainly from a new perspective.

I don't pretend that any such effort is easily undertaken; but I know from experience that the world looks so much brighter on the other side. Accepting affirming theology may cause you to have to shift your thinking on more than just this issue. But, I encourage you to do it. *Unlearn* some of the bad things you've been led to believe, and let yourself become a better Christian and a better servant of God as a result.

The End of the Ice Age

The Christian Church is, in my view, the greatest institution ever to exist on the face of the earth. With all the good it's done in its roughly 2,000-year history, the highest heights of its potential are yet to be realized. But, I believe we're living in the generation that shall see that potential manifest to the full.

The problem is that a huge stumbling block exists, preventing the Church from pressing into this radiant phase. It's an inexcusable failing on the part of the Church because Jesus' life, recorded in the gospels, should have precluded any such obstacle from existing.

I speak of the Church's almost reflexive tendency toward sanctimony, self-righteousness, and judgment. These characteristics so resemble the Pharisees of Jesus' day that it should be impossible for us to fall prey to these spiritual vices. Still, they are in great abundance amongst Christians of every denomination.

Jesus prophesied that as we approached the end, many would wax cold. I think it's difficult for anyone, despite their theological belief, to objectively consider the Church's handling of homosexuality and conclude that it's not filled with a type of cold contempt. We don't need to consider the fringe groups—like Fred Phelps and his Westboro fanatics—in order to see that people have said and done things that have *not* represented the heart of Christ. Jimmy Swaggart joked about killing a gay man should he

275

ever *look* at him "that way," and his audience erupted in applause and amens. This is just one example of how many Christians are oblivious to the fact that such cruelty is never justified, whether directed at "sinners" or not.

Did Jesus laughingly threaten to "kill the slut" if she tried to have sex with him? No. He lovingly lifted her from her despairing state and forgave her. And when it came to those accusing her, He challenged them to get their own houses in order before daring to cast judgment against this woman, plain though her guilt may have been.

How is it that we have strayed so far from Jesus' example? How have we turned into the very cold-hearted Pharisees that Jesus opposed on so many levels during His ministry? I'll tell you how. Human nature loves exaltation. To some, the idea of being better than others, for whatever reason, makes life worth living. We see this manifested in regard to sex, race, economic status, etc. It's no wonder it easily manifests when it comes to sexual orientation. By accusing and attacking gays, people feel better about their own Christianity. It makes them feel vindicated, believing that, at the very least, their sins aren't as bad as homosexuality.

We completely ignore passages that tell us to judge not, to not impose our views on unbelievers, or that mercy is much better than religiosity. We relinquish any responsibility to exude the more tender virtues of compassion, tenderness, and lovingkindness in preference of qualities that make us superior to others. It's a harsh rebuke of how perfectly we've turned into the very adversaries of Christ that we read about in the gospels.

Upon first reading this accusation, one may assume that I'm criticizing the anti-gay, traditionalist wing of the Church. Undoubtedly, they're among those targeted by my criticism; however, the fact is that no particular group is wholly exempt from this charge. Traditionalists are certainly coldhearted in their anti-gay theology; but the sad fact is that some affirming Christians reciprocate their callousness.

Some affirming Christians—gay people especially—have been on the receiving end of vitriol and cruel treatment for so long that we've become somewhat antagonistic toward all who don't affirm homosexuality. Our hearts have become embittered, and we've grown angry with those who don't accept us for who we are. Understandable as this may be, it's no less wrong.

We have to remember that beliefs, opinions, and perceptions don't exist in a vacuum. People's views are formed as a result of many factors, only one of which may be personal bigotry. Some people are simply the victim of their own theological ignorance, others of a form of brainwashing that results from hearing the same poisonous filth being spewed about homosexuals from the pulpits of their local churches over and over again. Others were raised from a young age with this aversion to homosexuals being pounded into their heads from parents and other family members. Everyone has a story, and few are simply, at their core, bigoted—even though what manifests on the surface can oftentimes be called nothing but.

Ultimately, we *all* have some repenting to do. It's easy to point the finger at those we perceive to be the enemy; but when it's all said and done, there aren't many of us with clean hands as far as this is concerned. We have to find it in ourselves to start treating people with love, compassion, and grace, whether they treat us with like kindness or not. Was it not Jesus who, having his hands and feet driven through with nails, pleaded with God to forgive those who were causing Him unspeakable pain in their effort to take his very life? Can we not learn from His example of prodigious grace that we should not only be merciful toward those who deserve it, but toward all people, as a result of God's boundless love for us all?

Is this a tall order—a lot to be asking of someone whose life has been ruined by hypocritical bigots who seem bent on ruling the world? Absolutely; but don't think that Jesus didn't recognize this when He commanded us to "love [our] enemies, bless those who curse [us], do good to those who hate [us], and pray for those who despitefully use [us], and persecute [us]."

We can all stand to have the cold contempt we have for the other side melted away—warmed by God's consuming fire of love. Wherever our hearts have turned to stone, let's pray that God turns them to flesh—that He gives us a great abundance of kindness, humility, and the other virtues that characterize love. Only then will we be worthy of the designation we often take for granted—Christian!

An encouraging thought is that the time of self-righteousness, judgment, hurt, and bitterness is coming to an end relatively soon. I strongly believe that we're living in the latter part of the end times, and that Jesus is returning soon. It is, then, only a matter of time before the Church experiences theological and cultural upheaval, as it realigns with the character of Christ.

In Ephesians 4:13, Paul prophesies that the body of Christ will grow to the measure of the fullness of the very stature of Christ. Now, since Christ is love, this means that the Church is going to have a major invasion of love as we draw closer to the end.

Furthermore, Ephesians 5:27 says that Christ will present us to Himself as a purified Church, not having spot or wrinkle, holy and blameless. 1Thessalonians 3:12-13 defines this blameless holiness as the end—the destination—of love that we have toward "all people."

It's love that perfects holiness. As we increase and abound in love, we draw closer to perfecting holiness; and as we draw closer to perfecting holiness, we set the scene for the return of the Lord!

So, take heart. The spiritual ice age of the Church, bred from self-righteousness and delusions of spiritual superiority, is coming to an end. The Church is about to be radically transformed! Receive ye the word of the Lord.

"Since you have in obedience to the truth purified your souls for a sincere love of the brethren, fervently love one another from the heart, [23] for you have been born again not of seed which is perishable but imperishable, that is, through the living and enduring word of God."
1Peter 1:22-23

Helpful Resources

(***) Indicates Pastor Weekly's Ministry Resources

Emergency and Phone Support Services
GLBT National Help Center
1-888-THE-GLNH (1-888-843-4564)

The Trevor Project
1-866-4-U-TREVOR (1-866-488-7386)

Books
Homosexianity: Letting Truth Win The Devastating War Between Scripture, Faith, and Sexual Orientation***
by Pastor Romell D. Weekly. Judah First Publishing, 2011.

Gay Christian 101: Spiritual Self-Defense For Gay Christians
by Rick Brentlinger. Salient Press, 2007.

The Children Are Free: Reexamining The Biblical Evidence On Same-Sex Relationships
by Rev. Jeff Miner and John Tyler Connoley. Jesus Metropolitan Community Church, 2002.

Organizations/Websites

The Center For Affirming Theology*
www.AffirmingTheology.com

The Gay Christian Fellowship*
www.GayChristianFellowship.com

The Gay-Friendly Church Directory*
www.GayFriendlyChurches.org

Gay Christian 101
www.GayChristian101.com

The Gay Christian Network
www.GayChristian.net

Beyond Ex-Gay
www.BeyondExGay.com

Pastor Weekly is available for conferences and workshops related to the Bible and human sexuality, as well as other topics of theological concern.
www.JudahFirst.org

Were you aware? Pastor Weekly has also written two other life-changing books, both available through Judah First Ministries, or Amazon.com.

- ✓ Homosexianity: Letting Truth Win The Devastating War Between Scripture, Faith, & Sexual Orientation

- ✓ Financial Prosperity Unveiled: Discovering God's *Real* Perspective On Riches & Wealth

You can support Judah First publications by placing book reviews on retail websites like Amazon.com, and by requesting that your local bookstores carry copies in-store. Thank you for your support!

Notes

www.ingramcontent.com/pod-product-compliance
Lightning Source LLC
Chambersburg PA
CBHW060251100426
42742CB00011B/1711